Henry Kissinger:
The Anguish of Power

Books by John G. Stoessinger:

Henry Kissinger: The Anguish of Power
Why Nations Go to War
Nations in Darkness: China, Russia, America
The United Nations and the Superpowers
Power and Order
Financing the United Nations System
The Might of Nations: World Politics in Our Time
The Refugee and the World Community

Henry Kissinger:
The Anguish
of Power

John G. Stoessinger

W · W · NORTON & COMPANY · INC ·

NEW YORK

FIRST EDITION

Library of Congress Cataloging in Publication Data

Stoessinger, John George.
    Henry Kissinger: the anguish of power.

    Includes index.
    1. United States—Foreign relations—1969–1974.
2. United States—Foreign relations—1974–
3. Kissinger, Henry Alfred. I. Title.
E855.S76 1976   327'.2'0924   76–22585
ISBN 0–393–05589–2

    2 3 4 5 6 7 8 9 0

For

HANS J. MORGENTHAU

Who Always Spoke
Truth to Power

With Deep Affection

Contents

Preface   ix

1. Prologue: Harvard 1950   1

PART I THE SCHOLAR

2. Of History and Destiny   7
3. Of Stability and Peace   11
4. Of Inspiration and Organization   15
5. Of Force and Power   21
6. Of Tragedy and Survival   31
7. Of Theory and Action   39

PART II THE STATESMAN

8. The Indochina Tragedy   49
9. Détente with Russia: Beyond the Cold War   79
10. China: Toward Reality   113
11. Europe: The Troubled Partnership   137
12. The Third World: Toward North-South Rapprochement   155
13. The Middle East: The Thirty Years' War   175

PART III THE ANGUISH OF POWER

14. The Anguish of Power   207

Index   229

Preface

There was a time when Henry Kissinger could do no wrong. While men around him crumbled, he went on to even greater heights. Not only did he wield great power; he was also fervently admired. As a negotiator, he was compared to a magician. Next to him, great stars paled into insignificance in the political firmament. He was like a comet blazing brightly in a darkened sky.

But then the comet flickered and the brightness waned. Suddenly, Kissinger was accused of doing nothing right. Critics appeared from everywhere and nowhere. Attacks were heaped upon him in a rising chorus of ferocity. One looked in vain for a word of kindness, let alone of praise.

I have watched the American public's attitude toward Henry Kissinger with rising consternation. I must confess to an uneasy suspicion that many people who invested Kissinger with magic in his halcyon days, may have made him a symbol of their own hunger for a moment of perfection and of glory. And I suspect that many of those who later attacked him without mercy might have done so out of their own frustration, bitterness, and disappointment. What has been sadly lacking, however, is a sense of reality and balance.

This book is an effort to redress that balance. Henry Kissinger is a man of great intelligence who fashioned a foreign policy that evolved over a quarter century of reflection and experience. I have attempted to portray the human being and the statesman behind the myths of accolade and condemnation. Reality is complex and seldom black and white. One should think about it with a sense of its nuances and colors. Kissinger is no exception.

Finally, this is a book about a man for whom I feel a deep affection. For twenty-five years, Henry Kissinger has been a kind and generous friend. Despite my friendship with him, or perhaps because of it, I have tried to paint a truthful and objective picture. Unlike the myths and legends that have grown around him, I have always found Henry Kissinger to be "human, all too human." And I somehow feel that the American people never really allowed themselves to know him, stripped of fantasy and fiction, in the strengths and weaknesses of his humanity. Hence, this book, I hope, will help to build a bridge of understanding between Henry Kissinger the man and statesman and the country that he chose to serve.

J.G.S.

New York City
May 1976

Henry Kissinger :
The Anguish of Power

1

Prologue:
Harvard 1950

Harvard was a turbulent place that autumn. America was at war again. Five years after the end of the Second World War, young men once again were dying, this time under the bleak skies of Korea.

To the young graduate students embarking on their pursuit of a Ph.D. degree in Harvard's Department of Government, the problem of war and peace was no mere academic abstraction. Most of us were of draft age, and deeply involved, both emotionally and intellectually, in the upheavals that were shaping our lives. We would talk long into the night about these events: The course of the Korean War, China under Communism, Stalin's incursions into Western Europe, or Senator Joseph McCarthy's latest description of Harvard as "The Kremlin on the Charles River."

Our studies reflected these concerns. One of us was engrossed in Stalin's bloody purges; another studied the growing military establishment in the United States; a third was working on modern European politics. All of us believed that the atomic bomb had deeply and irrevocably altered the nature of international relations. Things would never be the same again. As children of the new atomic era we felt that it was only natural that we should immerse ourselves in these new challenges that were affecting our very survival.

Brimming with impatience and eager for action, most of us looked at the study of history with a certain impatience and even suspicion. After all, men seemed to have learned but little from the past. Perhaps, the study of twentieth century history could still pay some dividends. But anyone who delved into the nineteenth century surely wasted his time and ran the risk of being regarded by us as an antiquarian. After all, we had glimpsed the future. Its terror was embodied in the events of Auschwitz and Hiroshima, its hope in the signing of the United Nations Charter. We stood at the gateway of the second half of a century. We had to fashion new concepts, new models. The past could not help us much to unlock the secrets of the future.

There was one anomaly in our midst. We had heard that a senior at Harvard College had submitted a 377-page undergraduate honors thesis, modestly entitled "The Meaning of History." Rumor had it that Professor William Elliott had read the first one hundred pages and awarded the young senior a *summa cum laude.* This aroused our interest and envy for several reasons. In the first place, a *summa cum laude* was extremely rare and exempted the fortunate recipient from the dreaded oral examination for the doctorate; second, we were struck by the contents of the thesis: this undergraduate had dared to take on Spengler, Toynbee, and Kant; and finally, and most incomprehensibly, this Bachelor of Arts had apparently announced his intention to write a doctoral thesis in the Department of Government on the diplomacy of the early nineteenth century. Our curiosity was aroused even further since none of us had met the author of "The Meaning of History." The young man had a reputation for brooding in the stacks of Widener Library while we were discussing the latest events on the world scene. But one day, in early October 1950, he joined us at our luncheon table. That was when I first met Henry Kissinger.

That first meeting is etched indelibly in my mind. Kissinger, who was twenty-seven then and several years older than most of us, seemed lean and intense. Inevitably, the conversation drifted to the subject of his proposed dissertation. He was interested in the problem of peace, he explained, and particularly in the shaping of the peace of Europe after the defeat of Napoleon. The challenges of those distant days struck him as analogous to those of our own time. We were astounded. Had he not heard of the atom bomb, someone asked. What could Metternich and Castlereagh possibly teach us? Someone else at the table suggested that it might be best if Henry transferred to the History Department, a supreme insult to any self-respecting student of international relations in the fall of 1950.

What impressed me most about Henry Kissinger during that luncheon discussion was the power of his mind. He had an uncanny ability to cut through to the essence of a problem. He argued forcefully for the abiding importance of history. Quoting Thucydides, he asserted that the present, while never repeating the past exactly, must inevitably resemble it. Hence, so must the future. Perhaps the diplomats of 1815, in fashioning such a durable peace treaty at the Congress of Vienna, had taken secrets to their graves that we would do well to ponder if we were to escape an atomic holocaust. Hiroshima did not usher in a new epoch. Its occurrence merely proved that we had not properly surveyed the vast laboratory in which the life and death of states could be studied in detail. That laboratory was history. Hence, why not focus on one of the few successful peace treaties of modern times? Why not try to fathom its secrets? To ignore such an historical goldmine would be an act of folly and of *hubris*, Kissinger warned. More than ever, we were told, one should study history in order to see why nations and men succeeded and why they failed.

It did not seem to me, as I listened, that Henry Kissinger was particularly interested in impressing or converting anyone around him. It seemed almost as if he were carrying on a dialogue with himself, rather than with his interlocutors. We did not quite know what to make of him. There was something austere and remote about him. And one also sensed a fierce ambition.

When he had completed his exposition, Kissinger left the table.

The rest of us immediately began to discuss his thesis. Someone asked under which professor Kissinger was planning to work. It turned out that William Elliott had agreed to continue as his mentor. Elliott was one of the two most powerful professors in the Government Department. The other was Carl J. Friedrich. Both men taught political philosophy and were bitter intellectual rivals. Any doctoral student found out soon after his arrival that he had to make a choice between Elliott and Friedrich. It apparently was impossible to be on cordial terms with both. Perhaps the most remarkable thing about Henry Kissinger, most of us thought, was the fact that he had managed to be on excellent terms with both these supreme rivals of the Harvard Government Department. I wonder how he managed that, one of us wondered wistfully, not without envy. No one knew the answer.

Part I

The Scholar

2

Of History
and Destiny

History is the memory of states.

Henry Kissinger
A World Restored

Henry Kissinger has written history as a scholar and made history as a statesman. His diplomacy as secretary of state is deeply rooted in the insights of the young doctoral student at Harvard of a quarter century ago. It is, in fact, a virtual transplant from the world of thought into the world of power. Hence, if we are to understand the secretary of state, we must first understand the historian.

Kissinger's favorite book in those early student days at Harvard was Oswald Spengler's *The Decline of the West.* The deep strain of pessimism that permeated every page of Spengler's classic struck a responsive chord in Kissinger. It was reflected in a concluding passage of his undergraduate honors thesis where he observed that "life involves suffering and transitoriness," and that "the generation of Buchenwald and the Siberian labor-camps [could] not talk with the same optimism as its fathers."

Spengler, however, was no conclusive answer for Kissinger. What offended him about *The Decline of the West* was its utter acceptance of the inevitability of historical events, in short, the author's total submission to historical determinism. Kissinger insisted on the power of the individual to affect his destiny. "Spengler," he wrote in that same concluding passage, had "not grasp[ed] that inevitability [was] a poor guide and no inspiration. Spengler merely described a fact of decline, and not its necessity."

This dualism, this vacillation between hope and despair, between freedom and necessity, best describes the young Kissinger of those distant days. There always was about him a sense of brooding melancholy. I knew, of course, about his youth as a Jew in Nazi Germany and his escape, barely in time, from the ensuing holocaust. He knew my similar history, but we seldom talked about it, partially, I suspect, out of fear not to cause the other anguish with painful memories, but also because one response to metaphysical despair was action in the here and now. "The past is dead," Kissinger wrote in a final answer to Spengler, "but freedom governs the future."

Twenty-five years later, this basic dualism about the human condition still prevailed, virtually unchanged. "As a historian," Kissinger told James Reston in a far-ranging interview in 1974, "one has to live with a sense of the inevitability of tragedy. As a statesman, one has to act on the assumption that problems must be solved."

The past always hovered over him. Despite his enormous intellect, I soon began to sense in him an equally enormous personal insecurity. Much later, speaking from a safer distance and from a position of great power, he bore out this early impression when he observed that "living as a Jew under the Nazis, then as a refugee in America, and then as a private in the army was not exactly an experience that built confidence." In a sense, he felt then that the *only* thing he had was his intellect, and hence he often perceived a criticism of his ideas as an attack upon his person. Only much later did there appear that wry and often brilliant sense of humor, but the intense vulnerability of his youth remained.

There are two fundamental ways in which a man can deal with tragic experience: he can get stuck in the past and do battle with its ghosts, or he can come to terms with it—and try to fashion it into a strength. I believe that young Kissinger took the latter course. He tried to accomplish this by developing a theory of peace in the relations among states in an anarchic world.

Kissinger regarded history as the memory of states. As the knowledge of a person's past gives us some clues about his future, history provides us with clues about a nation's future. It never repeats itself exactly. If it can teach us anything at all, it teaches through analogy, not through identity. Like the Oracle at Delphi, a particular historical event may be open to several interpretations. The supreme challenge of the statesman is to make the correct analogy. In this undertaking, he may be given only a single opportunity, for he is his own subject. In effect, he performs the experiment upon himself and his own nation. He may not have a second chance.

Kissinger's choice of a subject for his doctoral dissertation was deeply influenced by these considerations. He stated those reasons in his preface with perfect clarity:

> The success of physical science depends on the selection of one crucial experiment; that of political science in the field of international affairs, on the selection of the crucial period. I have chosen for my topic the period between 1812 and 1822, partly, I am frank to say, because its problems seem to me analogous to those of our own day.

Thus, Kissinger's interest in the diplomacy of the early nineteenth century was not academic in the usual sense. He wanted to know how these statesmen in the distant past had managed to erect such a durable structure of peace; and he wanted to find out whether their insights could be transplanted into the modern world. For most students pursuing a Ph.D. degree, the dissertation is viewed as a gateway into the academic world. This was only partially true of Henry Kissinger. He hoped that the knowledge he would derive from his research would prepare him for action on a larger stage.

3

Of Stability
and Peace

Those ages which in retrospect seem most
peaceful were least in search of peace.

Henry Kissinger
A World Restored

When Henry Kissinger began to immerse himself in the era of
Metternich and Castlereagh in his quest for the secret of peace
among states, he discovered very rapidly that neither of these statesmen had made peace the main objective of his policy. This was so
because of the presence of Napoleon who harbored an ambition for
global conquest. Had Prince Metternich of Austria and Britain's
Foreign Secretary Viscount Castlereagh openly made peace their
primary objective, they would have placed their nations at the mercy
of the French Emperor. It would then have been clear to Napoleon
that even his most ruthless demand would be met in order to preserve
the peace. Thus, in the eyes of Metternich and Castlereagh, Napoleon had to be removed if Austria and England were to survive. This
was accomplished through a policy of cunning, manipulation and,
ultimately, force, when France's strength had ebbed sufficiently.
Only after Napoleon's defeat did peace become a possibility since, in
the post-Napoleonic era, all European leaders shared a common vi-

sion: the recognition that no one's survival must be challenged. This consensus about a stable international order made possible the accommodation of conflict through diplomacy rather than through war. Diplomacy, then, brought about a balance of power among Europe's leading nations. France was brought back into the system through a settlement that emphasized stability rather than punishment. The end result of these policies was a European continent without a general war for an entire century.

The impact of these discoveries on Kissinger was profound and permanent. Stability, it seemed, was a necessary precondition of peace, and the willingness to use force made effective diplomacy possible. These two insights led Kissinger to a crucial distinction that he never abandoned: that between a "legitimate" and a "revolutionary" state. A legitimate state pursued limited objectives, generally through diplomacy, and accepted as axiomatic the survival of an adversary. Austria under Metternich and England under Castlereagh fell into this category. A revolutionary state based its policies on ideological assumptions, pursued unlimited objectives, welcomed war, and threatened the survival of other states within the system. France under Napoleon was a good example. Germany under Adolf Hitler was another. The attainment of a stable international order thus depended on the creation of a system of legitimate states and on the elimination from such a system of the revolutionary state. Peace became a kind of bonus that history awarded to those statesmen who were able to create a stable international equilibrium of states that recognized each other's right to permanent existence.

Kissinger admired Metternich for three fundamental reasons. First, the Austrian statesman had correctly recognized Napoleon as a revolutionary aggressor whose ambition would never be satisfied until he had succeeded in the total conquest of his adversaries. No compromise, no concession, no accommodation would satiate Napoleon's lust for power. Thus, Metternich had to plot Napoleon's destruction in order to ensure Austria's survival. The achievement of that virtually impossible goal through the artful and cunning use of alliances and counteralliances elicited Kissinger's respect. What impressed him even more were Metternich's intricate maneuvers that gradually weakened Napoleon until the French Emperor was virtually isolated. And during all this time, Napoleon never even recognized these maneuvers for what they actually were. But most admirable of all, in Kissinger's view, was Metternich's wisdom in resisting the temptation of a punitive peace after the final defeat of Napoleon had been accomplished. As he wrote, Metternich aimed for "equilibrium, and not retribution, legitimacy, and not punishment." In this quest he was joined by Castlereagh, who insisted on a policy of moderation while most of England was clamoring for vengeance. For this, Kissinger singled out the British statesman for special praise. He also noted that the two leading statesmen at Vienna were generous even toward Napoleon: "The early nineteenth century," Kissinger concluded wistfully, "was not yet a period which measured the extent of its triumph by the degree of personal retribution exacted."

What lessons, then, did the young doctoral student learn from his excursion into the world of the early nineteenth century? First, the wise statesman recognizes a revolutionary situation and will not delude himself about it. This insight is a fundamental precondition of superior statesmanship.

Second, as the conservative statesman maps his strategy against the revolutionary, he should not be inhibited by too many moral scruples, for he must remember that the attainment of a stable world order is a prerequisite for peace and thus a higher good. The key question the wise statesman must pose for himself, as he casts around for allies against the revolutionary, is not the question of morality, "Who is right and who is wrong?" but the question of power, "Who is weak and who is strong?" Finally, however, and most important, once the revolutionary leader is brought down, a peace treaty of moderation, not of vengeance, should be agreed upon with the defeated state. As soon as possible, that state should be brought back into the legitimate order. No victor should be completely satisfied because that would mean that the vanquished would be completely dissatisfied and thus prepare to start another war. A treaty in which no one's objective is completely fulfilled, and in which everyone is only partially happy would probably be durable, since the relative insecurity of each state would then guarantee the relative security of all. This is how, in Kissinger's view, Metternich and Castlereagh fashioned the Vienna settlement of 1815 and ushered in a century without a global war. Peace thus became the necessary by-product of a stable world order.

I remember that I found Kissinger's vision of peace through stability both compelling and disturbing. My own doctoral dissertation, on which I was working at the time, was a kind of mirror image of Kissinger's. It dealt with the world refugee problem, the human flotsam that had been abandoned by the world's system of sovereign states, rejects that had to live in its interstices. Hence, my own view of a stable world order was somewhat colored by my research into the fate of people who had neither states nor homes to call their own. On one occasion, I questioned Henry Kissinger about his concept of stability. What, I asked, would be his view if the leader of a legitimate state pursued unjust ends while the revolutionary had justice on his side? Then, the statesman must choose, Kissinger replied without hesitation. How, I wondered. Kissinger replied with a quotation from Goethe: "If I had to choose between justice and disorder, on the one hand," he said, "and injustice and order, on the other, I would always choose the latter."

There was no harshness in his answer, nor did I feel an indifference to the dilemmas of morality and justice. But I did sense the melancholy of a man who had seen some of the bleakest aspects of the human landscape, one who knew that, in a tragic world, choices seldom could be made between right and wrong, but much more often had to be made between one wrong and a greater wrong. His answer was a painful one, and conveyed a painful message: that the political act may be inevitably evil, and that to expect otherwise might lead a statesman to paralysis.

4

Of Inspiration
and Organization

Men become myths, not by what they know, or
even by what they achieve, but by the tasks
they set for themselves.

Henry Kissinger
A World Restored

States, to Henry Kissinger, were living entities. Like people, they
could also die. The life and death of states depended, above all, upon
the quality of the men who led them. Like Hegel, Kissinger believed
that certain statesmen, by virtue of their inspiration, stood at history's
fateful junctions and through an act of vision and of courage earned
their right to immortality. The inspiration of the statesman, however,
was almost always challenged by the restraints imposed upon him by
organization: the need for securing domestic support for his policies.
To conceive was not enough. A statesman was more than a philosopher. He had to implement his vision and execute his policies. And
in order to achieve these ends, he had to come to terms with the
restraints imposed upon him by his nation.

Kissinger never made a secret of his preference for inspiration over
organization, for policy-making over administration. Emotionally, he
has always been attracted to the creative solitary figure. But intellectually, he recognized the need for a dependable bureaucracy and for

solid domestic support, though a profound contempt for mediocrity sometimes made him underestimate their power. A poignant paragraph from his thesis is quite revealing on his attitude:

> It is the inextricable element of history, this conflict between inspiration and organization. . . . Inspiration is a call for greatness; organization a recognition that mediocrity is the usual pattern of leadership. . . .

If Kissinger had a hero among the statesmen of the early nineteenth century—and I doubt very much that he did—it was not Metternich, but Castlereagh. He applauded Castlereagh for having understood that a peace of retribution over France would never serve the interests of Britain. After Napoleon's escape from Elba, although all of Britain was clamoring for vengeance, Castlereagh refused to contemplate a victor's peace. The fact that France did not become a permanently dissatisfied power was attributed by Kissinger primarily to the vision of the British statesman. In the end, however, Castlereagh's vision outdistanced the experience of his people. When he attempted, a few years after the Vienna Congress, to take Britain into a European alliance system, he was unable to gain parliamentary support. By now, he stood alone. When confronted with a decisive rejection of his policy, he committed suicide.

Metternich's great achievements were the formation of the alliance that brought down Napoleon, and his successful pursuit, together with his British fellow statesman, of a peace of reconciliation. But what did Metternich do for Austria after his victory? Here Kissinger's judgment becomes harsh. Metternich employed his considerable diplomatic talents in the service of the status quo, until the Austrian empire became virtually petrified. He remained so close to the domestic structure that his policies left Austria's fundamental problems unresolved. No effort whatsoever was made to adapt the monarchy to the changing demands of a revolutionary epoch. Finally, Metternich's policies made Austria into an anachronism. Thus, brilliant though he was in his diplomacy, in Kissinger's view, his triumph was one of manipulation, not of creative vision. Ultimately, it was his sterile policy that hastened Austria's decline and self-destruction.

Kissinger's own vision of statesmanship is clearly derived from his studies of Metternich and Castlereagh, and his observation that the strength of one was the weakness of the other. He made his judgment very succinctly:

> A statesman who too far outruns the experience of his people will fail in achieving a domestic consensus, however wise his policies; witness Castlereagh. A statesman who limits his policy to the experience of his people will doom himself to sterility; witness Metternich.

Can a statesman meet both the challenges of inspiration and of organization? Kissinger was not optimistic. "It is for this reason," he wrote at the end of his thesis, "that statesmen often share the fate of prophets, that they are without honor in their own country, that they always have a difficult task in legitimizing their programs domestically, and their greatness is usually apparent only in retrospect when their intuition has become experience. The statesman must therefore be an educator; he must bridge the gap between a people's experience and his wisdom, between a nation's tradition and its future."

Kissinger believed that the conciliation between inspiration and organization would always be uneasy and precarious, if it were possible at all. Once, in our student days, we spoke about the outbreak of the First World War. Kissinger complained about the overwhelming mediocrity of the personalities involved and observed that most of the leaders, diplomats, and generals were badly flawed by arrogance, stupidity, carelessness, or weakness. There was little insight and no vision whatsover. And yet, he wondered, could a man of vision have stemmed the drift to war? Could a determined leader have prevented the outbreak of a conflict that his people were experiencing as a liberating explosion? He did not think so.

There are two further themes that permeate Kissinger's writings about the nature of statesmanship. The statesman who does not wish to come a cropper must accept uncertainty and tragedy as integral elements of his existence.

Kissinger knew and emphasized the role of accident in history. Who could have predicted, for example, that Castlereagh would take his own life? Metternich was totally unprepared for this event and suffered terribly because of the loss of his one reliable friend among the diplomats of Europe. Any quest for certainty, any technical approach to the solution of a diplomatic problem always offended Kissinger. The application of mathematical or engineering models to international relations infuriated him. He had no sympathy for those who were engaged in the search for simple formulas in their efforts to improve the human condition. "Genius," he once said, "cannot be quantified; nor can catastrophe or tragedy." "Americans," he would write later, in his book *The Troubled Partnership*, "live in an environment uniquely suited to a technological approach to policy-making. As a result, American society has been characterized by a conviction that any problem will yield if subjected to a sufficient dose of expertise. . . . But Europeans live on a continent covered with ruins testifying to the fallibility of human foresight." Any statesman, in other words, must realize that his grand design may collapse in a heap of rubble.

If Kissinger believed in the inevitability of anything, it was in the inevitability of tragedy as an integral part of the human condition. "No longing is completely fulfilled," he wrote in his undergraduate thesis at the age of twenty-six. "Nothing is more difficult for Americans to understand than the possibility of tragedy," he stated twenty-five years later. Nothing was more alien to him than the kind of optimism that assumed all problems to be soluble, if only the right formula was found. But, equally, nothing was more alien to him than a blind submission to the tragic element in history. In this recognition of the limits of the statesman, but also in the simultaneous affirmation of his possibilities, we find the core of Kissinger's belief. He studied Metternich and Castlereagh in order to discover both their strengths and weaknesses. He was generous with praise to each, but in the end found both men wanting.

Kissinger always harbored a romantic preference for the unfettered creative spirit. He felt that "an obsession with safety and predictability would produce an attitude fearful of risk, striving to reduce everything, including man himself, to manipulable quantities." It was this deeply felt romanticism that, more than any other quality, became responsible for his personal style, his difficulties in delegating responsibility, and his later emergence as a solo performer. In a revealing interview with Oriana Fallaci in 1972, this quality came through with extraordinary clarity:

> I have always acted alone. Americans admire that enormously. Americans admire the cowboy leading the caravan astride his horse. . . . This romantic surprising character suits me, because being alone has always been part of my style. . . . And finally, conviction. I am always convinced of the necessity of whatever I am doing. . . . In a sense, however, I am a fatalist. I believe in fate.

There is little doubt that this small vignette of Hegel's *Zeitgeist* in a wild west town captures one aspect of Kissinger's complex personality. But, again, only part of it. "No, I won't tell you what I am," he said at the end of that interview. "I'll never tell anyone."

5

Of Force and Power

Our generation has succeeded in stealing the
fire of the gods and it is doomed to live
with the horror of its achievement.

Henry Kissinger
Nuclear Weapons and Foreign Policy

In 1950, when Henry Kissinger began his research on the diplomacy
of Metternich and Castlereagh, international relations was still a
young discipline in most American universities. The man who, more
than any other single scholar, had placed it on the academic map, was
another Jewish refugee from Germany to whom all of us who labored
in the field owed an enormous intellectual debt. This man was Hans
J. Morgenthau whose *Politics Among Nations*, first published in
1948, was destined to become a classic.

Like Kissinger, Morgenthau had escaped the Nazi holocaust and
arrived in the United States in 1937. Not surprisingly, the older
scholar's vision of the world was a tragic one which rejected the
Wilsonian belief in the progress of civilization and in the rationality
of man. Morgenthau advanced a "realist theory" of international
relations which made power the main signpost on the landscape of
world politics. "Statesmen think and act in terms of interest defined

as power, and the evidence of history bears that assumption out," he wrote. He went on to say that "the threat of physical violence is an intrinsic element of politics." A statesman must be willing to resort to war if his policy is to be credible. Since power depends on what an adversary thinks it is, this psychological element of threat becomes decisive. But power must be based on capabilities. If diplomacy fails and war breaks out, the physical relation between two bodies replaces the psychological relation between two minds. Power, in short, prevails in times of peace, while force predominates in war.

Morgenthau's work appealed to Kissinger. After all, his thesis on nineteenth century diplomacy was leading him to similar conclusions. He had observed that when a statesman had made peace the main objective of his policy, he was at the mercy of the most ruthless member of the international community. Hence, it was true, as Morgenthau had written, that diplomacy, to be successful, had to risk resort to war. Power, in effect, made diplomacy possible.

The problem that occupied Kissinger after he had completed his doctoral thesis was that of power in the nuclear age. In the Napoleonic era, diplomacy had always been linked to the threat of war. This threat had been an inducement to negotiations. But in the nuclear era, could a statesman really resort to such a threat? If he meant it, the result might be a world holocaust; if he bluffed, the threat would not be credible and the global order would then be at the mercy of its most ruthless member. It was this dilemma of nuclear destruction versus total paralysis that now became Kissinger's main concern.

Just around that time, in the winter of 1954–55, an unusual opportunity arose. The senior officers of the Council on Foreign Relations in New York City, on the recommendations of Professors Elliott and Arthur Schlesinger Jr. at Harvard, offered Kissinger the position of *rapporteur* of a special study group on nuclear weapons that was meeting regularly under the Council's auspices. Kissinger, who was ready to leave Cambridge anyway, at least temporarily, and taste the real world, accepted with alacrity, stating that "not only [was] the study group directed in the main line of my own thought, but also the Council seems to furnish a human environment I find attractive."

The study group consisted of nineteen extremely high-powered individuals, most of whom had had extensive government experience at the highest levels. Kissinger was invited to use the group as a sounding board and then to produce a book of his own, without any obligation to heed the advice of his interlocutors. Henry Kissinger accepted this appointment and made his entrée into a new circle of people, whom otherwise he might never have met, with total ease and intellectual self-confidence. The study group ended its deliberations one year later with a generous gesture: "Good luck, Dr. Kissinger," said Gordon Dean, its chairman. "If you can make anything out of the efforts of this panel, we will be eternally grateful." The result was Kissinger's highly controversial second book, published almost simultaneously with his doctoral thesis. The title of this book was *Nuclear Weapons and Foreign Policy.*

The book appeared at a crucial juncture in the evolution of American strategic doctrine vis-à-vis the Soviet Union. Official policy in the mid-1950s was still the Dulles doctrine of the Great Deterrent, or of "massive retaliation." Its essence was the assumption that a Soviet military attack upon any member of the North Atlantic Treaty states might be countered with a crippling atomic attack. This American commitment would spread a kind of "atomic shield" over America's NATO allies and thus place them under virtually invulnerable protection.

At the time Kissinger's study group was engaged in its deliberations, haunting doubts had begun to torment both American and European strategists in NATO. It seemed that the massive retaliation policy was highly inflexible and tended to commit the United States to a kind of "all or nothing" posture. The Great Deterrent seemed an efficient instrument in case of an all-out Soviet attack, but what if the Soviet Union should choose to provoke some more local conflict? Or if it should limit itself to aggression through infiltration? In such cases, the Great Deterrent seemed to be a disproportionate application of military force. This in turn raised the question of credibility. If a threat was to be effective, it must be believed or at least considered within the realm of the possible. Would the Soviet Union believe that the United States would unleash massive retaliation with atomic weapons in case of an East German attack on West Berlin, or of a Soviet attack on West Germany? Or would this strategy be invoked only in case of a Soviet attack on the United States itself? Might not the Soviet Union assume that, in a showdown, the United States would not be able to bring itself actually to use the Great Deterrent?

In other words, the Dulles doctrine was beginning to appear like a gigantic bluff.

The shortcomings of massive retaliation were already apparent while Kissinger was still at Harvard. In 1953, Secretary Dulles had announced that the policy of "containing" Communism was no longer sufficient. In order to win the struggle against Communism, the Secretary declared, the United States would embrace a policy of "liberation" toward the Eastern European nations under Communist rule. Whether "liberation" meant military or political or merely moral support by the United States was never clearly spelled out. The first test of the new policy occurred in June 1953 when, in a spontaneous revolutionary outbreak, East German workers and students rose against their Communist regime. When West German Chancellor Konrad Adenauer asked the United States government whether it planned to intervene on the basis of the liberation policy, the answer was negative. The second test took place during the Poznan uprising of June 1956 in Poland. In this instance, even while the Soviet Union was weighing alternatives, Secretary Dulles announced that, in case of Soviet military intervention, the United States would take no action. The most dramatic test of the liberation formula, of course, was the Hungarian revolution of October 1956. In this case, when Soviet tanks entered Budapest and crushed the uprising, the United

States' attitude proved to be one of complete paralysis, with the liberation policy petering out in a lame American recommendation in the United Nations to "study suitable moves." These three events amply demonstrated that since the liberation policy, coupled with the strategy of massive retaliation, could too easily lead to World War III, it was in fact felt to be too risky to be actually invoked.

The apparent bankruptcy of the Great Deterrent left many NATO allies almost as fearful of American protection as of Soviet aggression. Their thinking began to run something like this: "If the Americans mean what they say and unleash the Great Deterrent, we shall become an atomic rubble heap; but if they do not mean what they say and are bluffing, the Red Army will take over Western Europe without a shot. Either way, we are the losers." As a result, most of America's allies began to raise their voices for "no annihilation without representation." By the time Kissinger's *Nuclear Weapons and Foreign Policy* was published in 1957, there was almost unanimous agreement in the United States that the concept of massive retaliation had become obsolete. The timing could not have been more propitious for a new strategic doctrine to emerge.

What Kissinger in effect proposed was a strategic doctrine based on limited nuclear war. He presented his thesis by submitting the following assumption:

> If the Soviet bloc can present its challenges in less than all-out form, it may gain a crucial advantage. Every move on its part will then pose the appalling dilemma of whether we are willing to commit suicide to prevent encroachments, which do not, each in itself, seem to threaten our existence directly, but which may be steps on the road to our ultimate destruction. . . .

Massive retaliation, he continued, had created a "psychological gap," since the NATO allies had become convinced that they had nothing to gain from it—and the Soviet leaders had begun to feel that they had nothing to fear from the threat of it. Thus, "the dilemma of the nuclear age reside[d] in the impossibility of combining maximum horror with maximum certainty."

It was from this type of thinking that Kissinger's new strategic concept of "graduated deterrence" through limited nuclear war emerged. The concept was based on the simple assumption that to make the threat *less* horrible would render it *more* credible. The United States would not have to place itself in a position of risking its national substance every time a stand had to be taken against aggression. Instead, each aggressive act would be punished in proportion to its seriousness. The United States would not say to the Soviet Union: "If you march into West Berlin, we *may* do something terrible to you, even use massive retaliation." It would warn, rather: "If you march, we *shall* make you pay a price that will exceed the prize gained from your act; tactical nuclear war will then be one of the options we shall consider to achieve our ends."

Kissinger's argument was that his new strategic concept would combine a minimum threat with a maximum of credibility. It would enable the American ship of state to avoid the Scylla of paralysis as well as the Charybdis of all-out nuclear destruction. The concept reflected Morgenthau's emphasis on the psychology of power in world politics, but added to it a distinctive thrust that was completely Kissinger's own.

> As a nation, we have used power almost shame-facedly, as if it were inherently wicked. We have wanted to be liked for our own sakes, and we have wished to succeed because of the persuasiveness of our principles rather than through our strength. Our feeling of guilt with regard to power has caused us to transform all wars into crusades, and then to apply our power in the most absolute terms. We have rarely found intermediary ways to use our power and in those cases we have done so reluctantly.

Nuclear Weapons and Foreign Policy immediately became a best seller and almost completely obscured the simultaneous appearance of *A World Restored.* President Eisenhower and Vice-President Nixon were reported to have read the book and to have been favorably impressed. Nelson Rockefeller thought highly of the book and formed a lasting friendship with its author. All of a sudden, Henry Kissinger had been catapulted into national prominence as one of the most original thinkers on American strategic policy.

The book, however, was not received without criticism. It was pointed out that Kissinger's doctrine of limited nuclear war rested on the dubious assumption that action of the opposing side would always be governed by rationality. Critics admitted that massive retaliation had purchased deterrence at an exorbitant risk, but expressed serious doubts as to whether a limited war in the atomic age—especially one fought with nuclear weapons—would *remain* limited. Kissinger's premise was based on a kind of nineteenth century chivalry: that the two superpowers would not unleash the ultimate weapon against each other. But how would an American president know what "the other side" would do, and whether it would always react rationally? Even if its rationality could be counted on, would it believe an American "guarantee" to make the punishment fit the crime? And most important, would not the use of "tactical" nuclear weapons by the United States result in the use of similar or more powerful "tactical" weapons by the other side, until one of the two antagonists would decide to use "strategic" atomic weapons from which it would only be a short step to massive retaliation? In other words, the critics of the Kissinger doctrine felt that a war in the nuclear age could *begin* as a limited war, but was likely to *end* as an all-out war, if atomic weapons were introduced at all.

The fatal weakness of Kissinger's doctrine lay in his belief that nineteenth century diplomacy, with its common ground rules of limited objectives, could be applied to nuclear diplomacy. Kissinger ignored his own crucial distinction between "legitimate" and "revolutionary" states and assumed that conflict in a revolutionary era could be contained by the same rational rules of conduct that had evolved in the Age of the Enlightenment. Thus, his doctrine involved a dreadful paradox: in order to keep a limited war limited, the Soviet Union must be presumed to have the *same* understanding of force and power as did the United States; yet it was precisely because such an understanding was lacking on Russia's part, that the United States would have gone to war in the first place.

The contemporary critics who portrayed Kissinger as a neurotic "Dr. Strangelove who loved the bomb" could not have been more wrong. Kissinger had little interest in nuclear technology and even less in technical solutions to problems of diplomacy. His error was precisely the opposite: an anachronistic faith drawn from an earlier and far less savage era when the victors were two magnanimous aristocrats who believed that a basic rationality governed the relations among contending states. For a man who warned Americans that "states could die", this assumption of a nineteenth century sense of chivalry almost seemed naive.

Numerous critics were harsh and even vituperative in their attacks. Kissinger, whose intellect was so strongly tied to his inner self esteem, reacted to them in an intensely personal way, and suffered greatly in the process. But he grew remarkably during that period of self-doubt. Ultimately, he changed his mind almost completely as a direct result of an intensive re-evaluation. In 1960, he published *The Necessity for Choice* in which he retracted virtually all of his earlier beliefs about tactical nuclear war. But the *succès d'occasion* of his earlier work had established him as a formidable thinker to be reckoned with. The fact that most arms specialists in the academic community now regarded him with a measure of suspicion made little difference. When he returned to Harvard in 1957, he had attained a power base that was no longer limited to Cambridge, and when the university, two years after his return, offered him a professorship with tenure, Kissinger was not surprised. The years of apprenticeship were over. In his quest for intellectual independence, he had made a serious misjudgment. But he had survived and grown, both as a person and as a scholar. For the first time in his life he now enjoyed a measure of security and power.

6

Of Tragedy
and Survival

I believe in the tragic element in history.

Henry Kissinger
Harvard, 1950.

Henry Kissinger has always denied that his tragic experience as a young Jew in Nazi Germany had anything to do with the shaping of his later life. "That part of my childhood is *not* a key to anything," he insisted. "I was not consciously unhappy. I was not so acutely aware of what was going on. For children, those things are not that serious. It is fashionable now to explain everything psychoanalytically, but let me tell you, the political persecutions of my childhood are not what control my life."

On one level, no doubt, this statement is quite true. It would be patently absurd to try to draw direct analogies between Kissinger's early life and his later policies, or to make simple causal connections between early emotional experiences and later intellectual choices. Yet, it seems that Kissinger learned to perceive the world darkly, through the glass of a survivor of early tragedy and chaos, and that this experience may have infused his later life with a particular intensity.

The reason why these early shattering events did not stunt his personal and intellectual development may have been due to his great good fortune in having had a stable home and parents who, despite the torments and indignities imposed upon them by the Nazis, protected their two sons emotionally against the constant humiliations to which they were exposed. The older Kissinger lost his job as a teacher in the local high school, but comforted his son when he was beaten up by Nazi bully boys and was forced to attend an all-Jewish school. "My father," Kissinger once said, "was a truly good man in a world in which goodness had lost all meaning." The immediate reason why the Kissingers left Fürth in 1938 was their concern that their sons could no longer obtain a good education in their native Germany. Thus, it seems that his parents' protectiveness and strength gave young Kissinger the capacity to survive the trauma of his early life intact and later to transmute it into philosophy and action. Yet this early tragedy may have affected the coloration of his world outlook and echoed down into his later life in his adopted country.

It was probably no accident that Kissinger was so attracted in his youth to Oswald Spengler's melancholy classic, *The Decline of the West.* An ingrained fatalism in his thinking, a deep apprehension of tragic possibilities and a survivor's rejection of all certitude in human life may have placed him on Spengler's wavelength years before he ever heard of the great German pessimist. The things young Kissinger had seen as a Jew in Nazi Germany had made him quite prepared to accept the possibility that Western civilization might indeed be doomed. Tragedy was not just a possibility for him. He had experienced it as an everyday reality in the formative years of his existence. But he had managed to survive. His parents took him out of Germany before it was too late. In 1945, at the age of twenty-two, he returned to gaze at Germany in ruins as a sergeant in the U.S. Army; it was a sight not easily forgotten.

Kissinger's philosophy of history became an issue of some importance during the 1976 presidential campaign. Critics accused him of excessive pessimism and suggested that he was prepared to accept the decline of the United States to a second-class power vis-à-vis the Soviet Union.

These charges do not stand up under careful scrutiny. It is true that Kissinger, the historian, accepted the transitoriness of all historical periods. Neither the *Pax Romana* nor the *Pax Britannica* lasted forever. Why should the *Pax Americana* be chosen by history to be less vulnerable to transience? On the other hand, Kissinger devoted much of his academic life to an effort to understand the nature of "revolutionary" disruptions of the international order. In other words, how did the Hitlers and the Stalins of the world manage to become so dangerous and how could they be stopped without catastrophe? Kissinger's work is dominated by the theme of the opposition between the forces of chaos and the forces of order. The corollary of Kissinger's sense of the tragic is his passion for stability and balance. But none of this ever led him to accept capitulation in the face of an expansionist aggressor. Rather, the essence of Kissinger's statecraft became the use of diplomacy, backed by force, to achieve a stable equilibrium. Hence, while Kissinger, the historian, tended to be a pessimist, Kissinger, the statesman, was a fighter to whom struggle was the very essence of the human condition.

One characteristic of the survivor is the need to struggle ceaselessly in order to maintain his internal sense of equilibrium. He must work more relentlessly and strive more tirelessly than ordinary men. Achievement matters little, only the process of achieving does. The narrow beachhead of security known to the survivor must be conquered again and again, because even the smallest experience of failure rekindles the memory of chaos and catastrophe. Perhaps this explains the fierce tenacity, the almost driven quality of Kissinger's approach to work. I remember him as happy only when he was engaged in struggle. But I also recall the deep and terrible disappointment that he felt when Harvard failed to offer him a professorship in 1954 because some of his colleagues doubted his commitment to university life. It is true that he was ready for a larger arena, but he wanted to leave Cambridge on his own terms, not on terms imposed upon him by outside circumstances.

Many of Kissinger's writings make reference to tragic figures in Greek mythology, such as Prometheus or Nemesis. But it is Camus' myth of Sisyphus that comes to mind when I think of Henry Kissinger. Sisyphus, according to Homeric legend, had been condemned to exert his entire being to roll a rock to the top of a mountain only to see it fall back each time into the depths. The legend does not tell us whether Sisyphus knew that the rock was destined each time to roll back down again. For Kissinger, each assault upon his rock seemed to generate new energy. He, too, did not know the outcome of the struggle, but he loved to be involved in the encounter, possessed great physical stamina, and was most comfortable with himself when straining steadily against his rock. If one can accept Camus' paradox of Sisyphus as happy *because* he was engaged in struggle, one gets a glimpse of Henry Kissinger.

This unremitting struggle against chaos and ceaseless striving for a sense of order may have become the fuel that powered Kissinger's vital energies. So completely did this passion seem to rule him that, in a moment of self-revelation in his thesis, he judged Prince Metternich severely for not possessing it:

> Lacking in Metternich [was] the attribute which has enabled the spirit to transcend an impasse at so many crises of history: the ability to contemplate an abyss, not with the detachment of a scientist, but as a challenge to overcome—or to perish in the process.

Here, perhaps, may be a reason why Kissinger became an advocate of order and stability. A survivor frequently rejects the revolutionary who threatens him with chaos. The imperfections of a stable order can be tragic, but they are more tolerable than the risks of revolutionary transformation. Thus, it was probably no accident that Kissinger chose the early nineteenth century as a theme for his research. After all, its *leitmotif* was the battle between the spirit of revolution and the forces of conservatism. Needless to say, Kissinger cast his lot with Metternich and Castlereagh, the apostles of stability and order, rather than with Napoleon, the great destroyer of the *status quo*.

It has frequently been pointed out that Kissinger found patrons at crucial turning points in his meteoric rise to power: Fritz Kraemer, William Elliott, Nelson Rockefeller, and Richard Nixon. But what is much more interesting is the fact that these four men all shared one deeply held conviction: that the use of force was justified and necessary to preserve the established order against the threat of revolution.

Kissinger met Kraemer in 1943 when the older man spoke eloquently to 1,200 G.I.s about the moral necessity of fighting Nazi Germany. Kraemer was a German intellectual who had left his country voluntarily when the Nazis came to power. He described the war against the Nazis as a struggle for the survival of civilization. Kissinger was so impressed that he wrote Kraemer a fan letter. "Dear Pvt. Kraemer," the letter read, "I heard you speak yesterday. This is how it should be done. Can I help you somehow? Pvt. Kissinger." Professor Elliott's nickname at Harvard in 1950 was "Wild Bill." Kissinger's academic mentor had been a driving force in the Office of War Mobilization during World War II and later had a reputation as a passionate cold warrior. He was also an ardent defender of America's special moral calling in a hostile world. Kissinger greatly admired Elliott even though he was somewhat of a bore and probably his intellectual inferior. Rockefeller represented the quintessence of the American establishment and its determination to defend itself by force if necessary. In 1968, Kissinger spent most of his energies in helping Rockefeller in his bid for the Republican nomination for the presidency. And what attracted him to Richard Nixon one year later was not only access to enormous power, but also Nixon's determination not to yield on the issue of Vietnam. Moreover, Nixon, too, was a political survivor, a man who had come back from numerous defeats and one who felt most comfortable in the relentless struggle of the political arena.

Kissinger had known a world "without goodness." He had felt in his bones the danger of calamity and of unhappy endings. He was therefore deeply drawn to men who recognized how force and power could be used to avert catastrophe. And to him, catastrophe was synonymous with the destruction of a stable global order through anarchy and revolution. "A man," Fritz Kraemer once said in an interview about Henry Kissinger, "does not know the world until he has been out alone on the docks of Marseilles, hungry and with only one suit, being stalked by another man who wants that suit. Then being reasonable or good doesn't matter. Then a man has to stand up for himself or die." Little wonder, then, that Kissinger justified the use of force against the "revolutionary" in order to assure the survival of the "legitimate" order. Nothing is more frightening to the survivor of a world in chaos than the risk—once more—of chaos.

I recall how every convulsion that we witnessed as students at Harvard in that turbulent year of 1950 was experienced by Kissinger almost as a personal threat. To him, the evidence was obvious: Against the Nazis, the Kissingers of Europe had no power, so death destroyed six million defenseless Jews. Against the Russians, the East Europeans had no power, so totalitarian rule displaced their freedom. The list of tragedies was long enough to justify his deep conviction that power was the elemental force in history.

Finally, there is that ultimate loneliness, that sense of metaphysical despair, that special sense of guilt that marks the survivor of great tragedy. "Why is it that I am alive at all?" he asks. "Toward which end have I been spared?" This question imposes a sense of special responsibility and calling. Such a man can never be a seeker after power for the sake of power without purpose. Power must always be employed in the service of that calling. In his moments of despair,

Kissinger has been drawn to kindred spirits. His relationship with Hans Morgenthau is quite illuminating when considered in that light. The older scholar often criticized Kissinger quite severely for his later policies, particularly on Vietnam and in the Middle East. Yet Kissinger never responded to these charges with his usual vulnerable self. On the contrary, a genuine sympathy and friendship continued to unite the two men over the years despite profound intellectual and policy divergencies. Morgenthau once said to me that he felt emotionally toward Kissinger as if he were a brother. Their common background as well as their common experience of tragedy provided a strong and lasting bond.

Integral to Henry Kissinger's complex personality is the insecurity that is part of a survivor's heritage. His great emotional strength and enormous intellect enabled him to transcend his personal anguish and cast it into a larger vision of stability and order. Yet, the insecurity remained. His tragic vision of the world, and of the contingent nature of all human planning testify to this. "I believe in the tragic element in history," Henry Kissinger once said to me. "I believe there is the tragedy of a man who works very hard and never gets what he wants. And then, I believe there is the even more bitter tragedy of a man who finally gets what he wants and finds out that he does not want it."

Kissinger, the survivor, must remain as a hypothesis that I can never prove. What *can* be proved, however, is that the intellectual convictions that Kissinger developed a quarter of a century ago survived almost unchanged and were applied by him in a conscious and deliberate effort to pursue his vision of a stable world order. We are witness here to a unique experiment in the application of scholarship to statesmanship, of history to statecraft. The pages that follow will attempt to make that process clear, before we attempt to make a judgment on its successes and its failures.

7

Of Theory
and Action

In the years ahead, the most profound challenge to
American policy will be philosophical . . .

Henry Kissinger
American Foreign Policy, 1968

When in July 1959, Henry Kissinger received his appointment as a tenured associate professor at Harvard University, he was thirty-six years old. Despite his relative youth, his reputation as a scholar of originality and scope was solidly established. Harvard had welcomed his return from New York City and now was ready to retain him on its faculty for life.

While Kissinger appreciated the atmosphere of intellectual independence that prevailed at Harvard, he was by no means totally committed to the academic life and the strictures it imposed. In his view, professors in universities struggled too hard for prizes that were often pitiful. As he put it to me once when he was still a graduate student: "The fights among academics are so dirty because the stakes are so low." The power struggles of his colleagues often impressed him as tragicomical in the narrowness of their pursuits.

Kissinger had never limited his ambition to a professorship at Harvard. While still a student under William Elliott, he laid plans in 1951 for an international seminar which provided the opportunity for young men and women who had achieved a certain prominence in their respective countries, to visit Cambridge for eight weeks each year as guests of Harvard University. Kissinger selected the members of the seminar, and every summer, over a period of fifteen years, he served as its guiding spirit and instructor. The result was that an entire generation of prospective leaders from all over the world came to the United States as students of Henry Kissinger. This network of contacts later was to prove invaluable.

Again with Elliott's encouragement, Kissinger founded and became the editor of a journal entitled *Confluence* in 1952. This venture, too, was a success, serving as a vehicle for the opinions of intellectuals throughout the world. Thus, even with his thesis only half completed, Kissinger had started to reach out to the world beyond Harvard.

The publication of Kissinger's third book, *The Necessity for Choice*, coincided with the election of John F. Kennedy to the presidency of the United States. While the book had a good reception in academic circles, Kissinger had little hope of becoming part of the group of Harvard professors who were asked to come to Washington to join the New Frontier. He did not know the new president and if he was identified with any political figure at all, it was Nelson Rockefeller, a Republican. Nevertheless, he was asked to serve as a consultant to the president and, in that capacity, made frequent trips to Washington. But essentially, Kissinger continued to teach, to write, and to reflect in Cambridge about American foreign policy.

The works he published in those years were sharply critical, though never partisan. His *Nuclear Weapons and Foreign Policy* and his *Necessity for Choice* were not conceived as attacks on Eisenhower or on Dulles but as critiques of the American approach to foreign policy regardless of label or of party. His *Troubled Partnership*, a study of the problem areas in NATO, which appeared during the Johnson years, again was not conceived as an assault upon the President. All of these books were intended as critical reflections on the shortcomings of the United States as a nation among nations, regardless of the party in control. It was during that decade of reflection that Kissinger labored to express his thoughts in a coherent doctrine of American foreign policy. He found that doctrine in the pursuit of a stable international order, based on a realistic appraisal of both the limits and the possibilities of statesmanship. The main lines of his thought during those years are well worth examining. They were deeply rooted in the past, but were soon to be translated into a program of action for the future.

Kissinger's point of departure was the need to develop a general *philosophy* of foreign policy. He deplored the American habit of responding pragmatically to crisis situations instead of developing a coherent doctrine *a priori*. As he put it:

> The challenge of our time is whether we can deal consciously and creatively with what in previous centuries was adjusted through a series of more or less violent and frequently catastrophic upheavals. We must construct an international order *before* a crisis imposes it as a necessity.

Yet, he was skeptical. "A philosophical deepening," he wrote, "will not come easily to those brought up in the American tradition of foreign policy."

Kissinger perceived the deepest problem of the international order of the 1960s to be a cleavage between two styles of policy: the "political" as against the "revolutionary" approach to order, or, if reduced to personalities, the distinction between the statesman and the prophet. "The statesman manipulates reality; his first goal is survival," Kissinger declared, while "the prophet, by contrast, is less concerned with manipulating than with creating reality. He believes in total solutions and will risk everything because his nation is the primary reality to him." The "political" approach dominated Europe between the Congress of Vienna and the outbreak of World War I, while the prophetic mode was in the ascendancy during the French and Bolshevik revolutions. Both styles had produced considerable achievements, in Kissinger's view, though the prophetic style was likely to involve the greater dislocations and more suffering. Kissinger clearly preferred the statesman to the prophet.

The distinction, of course, resembled closely Kissinger's earlier dichotomy between "legitimate" and "revolutionary" states, drawn from the nineteenth century. He also reiterated the importance of domestic structure in the context of a successful foreign policy. But then he added two further thoughts that were clearly new. In the first place, he wrote, "power no longer automatically translated into influence." Expressed more crudely, since everybody was somebody, nobody was anybody. In such a world, psychology assumed profound importance, for deterrence occurred, above all, in the minds of men, and a bluff taken seriously might be more effective than a serious threat interpreted as a bluff. These new psychological distinctions between power and force were clearly adapted to the nuclear age. Second, Kissinger addressed himself to the dilemma of conjecture which he described as the statesman's most difficult and tragic problem.

> When the scope for action is greatest, knowledge on which to base such action is small or ambiguous. When knowledge becomes available, the ability to affect events is usually at a minimum. In 1936, no one could know whether Hitler was a misunderstood nationalist, or a maniac. By the time certainty was achieved, it had to be paid for with millions of lives.

While Kissinger was reflecting on philosophy and doctrine, the United States was deepening its involvement in the Vietnam war. Between 1965 and 1969, there was no American foreign policy. With half a million Americans involved in combat, there was only a Vietnam policy. During those years of military escalation, Kissinger wrote

little. He did not wish to take a public stand on the Vietnam controversy, though privately he considered the American involvement a
blunder of the first magnitude and Johnson's military escalation a
disaster. He did not remain silent on Vietnam because he had no
convictions on the subject. He remained silent for two other reasons.
First, he was interested in a global, conceptual approach to foreign
policy of which Vietnam would only be a part; and second, he was
looking for the opportunity to test that plan in action.

Kissinger's first chance to test his theory came in 1968 during
Nelson Rockefeller's short-lived campaign for the Republican nomination for the presidency. All of Rockefeller's statements on foreign
policy were written by Henry Kissinger, who worked with an intensity
as if the success of the campaign depended exclusively on him. He
became the mind behind Rockefeller's voice, his alter ego on America's role in the world arena.

It was thus in the guise of Rockefeller's campaign speeches that
Kissinger's grand design for a stable world order first made its appearance in systematic form. Kissinger anchored that design to one basic
assumption: his belief that the Soviet Union and China had ceased
to be "revolutionary" states. This term had a special connotation in
Kissinger's vocabulary. It was reserved for nations that were irrevocably committed to the destruction of their adversaries. The leaders of
China and the Soviet Union were no longer comparable to Napoleon
or Hitler, in Kissinger's opinion. In the first place, a greater degree
of rationality seemed to govern their behavior; second, a strategic
balance had been struck between the Soviet Union and the United
States which served as a deterrent against wantonly irresponsible
behavior; and finally, a profound split seemed to separate the Soviet
Union from China.

The heart of Kissinger's design appeared in Rockefeller's first major campaign address. The candidate spoke of the need for close
relations with both the Soviet Union and China and concluded by
declaring that

> In a subtle triangle with Communist China and the Soviet Union,
> we can ultimately improve our relations with *each*—as we test the
> will for peace of *both*.

Kissinger believed that the time had come to explore new initiatives
vis-à-vis both China and the Soviet Union. He did not deceive himself into believing that either China or the Soviet Union would
abandon Communism and become a "bourgeois" state, but he did
believe that prudent risks would have to be taken to achieve progress
toward a stable international order.

The gulf that existed between China and the Soviet Union, Kissinger believed, confronted the United States with both dangers
and opportunities. It was essential to persuade the Chinese leaders that any overtures in the direction of the Soviet Union were
not interpreted as anti-Chinese moves; and equally, to convince
the Soviet leadership that rapprochement with China was not a
hostile act against the Soviet Union. By keeping the United
States equidistant from both Moscow and Peking, and uncommit-
ted in the deepening struggle that separated them, the United
States might gain in leverage over each. In short, America might
become the "lady in the triangle," to be courted by two suspicious and jealous suitors.

The Vietnam problem, in Kissinger's opinion, could not be resolved in isolation. He was contemptuous of both "hawks" and
"doves," because of their fixation on a single issue and their inability
to analyze it within a larger global framework. Kissinger believed that
the commitment of half a million men had been a tragic blunder, but
since it *had* been made, American credibility was now at stake. He
believed that the solution of the Vietnam problem lay within the
context of improved relationships with both the Soviet Union and
China. If a relaxation of tensions could be achieved with the two
main centers of communism in the world, the Vietnam impasse, too,
should yield to the common quest for stability and order. Thus, in
the view of Henry Kissinger, improved relations with China and the

Soviet Union would produce dividends in other areas of concern in the United States. This concept of the linkage of problem areas, of the interrelationships among the major issues of the time, was a basic postulate of Kissinger's design. His objective, above all, was to secure a stable international order. All specific policies were subordinated by him to this fundamental quest.

Thus, by the time Rockefeller lost the Republican nomination to Richard Nixon, Kissinger had had the opportunity to articulate a general philosophy of foreign policy. This doctrine was deeply rooted in the insights Kissinger had gained from his research into the diplomacy of the early nineteenth century. Then, as now, the world consisted of sovereign states; then, as now, the system was essentially anarchic; then, as now, if a statesman made peace the direct objective of his policy, he placed himself at the mercy of the most ruthless state. Then, as now, a stable world order would have to be the necessary precondition for a more peaceful world order.

True, the world was also very different now. The European order had passed into the pages of history. The world's leading powers were no longer Austria, Prussia, Russia, England, and France. They now were the United States, the Soviet Union, China, Western Europe, and Japan. But even though the players had changed, the game, essentially, had not. In an anarchic world, peace still remained the bonus that history awarded to the statesmen who balanced the national interests of states most successfully in the common pursuit of a stable global order.

As yet, the vision was incomplete. Kissinger had not thought out the implications of his general philosophy for the war-torn Middle East. Nor had he addressed himself in any systematic manner to the revolution of rising expectations among the new nations of the world. But the outlines of a general doctrine were definitely present by 1968.

Richard Nixon had also pondered the basic problems of American foreign policy and had come to similar conclusions, though at times for different reasons. He has read Kissinger's *Nuclear Weapons and*

Foreign Policy and was impressed with the author's depth and imagination. Nixon, too, believed that new initiatives toward China and the Soviet Union were overdue and knew that his long, unbroken record of anti-Communism would serve him well in this regard with the American voter. Besides, he had written earlier that "lawyers in politics need non-lawyers around them to keep them from being too legalistic, too unimaginative." In Kissinger, Nixon found such a non-lawyer who also had evolved a general philosophy which the new president found congenial to his own. For Kissinger, in turn, the appointment in 1969 to the post of Assistant to the President for National Security Affairs afforded him the chance for the first time in his life to test his theories in the world of power.

Henry Kissinger in 1969 was a man of forty-six with firmly held intellectual convictions. He had developed these convictions over two decades of reflection and experience. But it had never been enough for him to remain an intellectual. The arena of the world of power had always beckoned. Now, by a stroke of singular good fortune, the opportunity to test his general philosophy arose at exactly the time when his thought had reached its full maturity. When Kissinger left Harvard for Washington in 1969, it would not have been easy to find a candidate more qualified to test the proposition of the intellectual in power. A philosopher-historian was about to become a leading practitioner of policy and statecraft. The lessons of the past were about to become a prologue for the future.

Part II

The Statesman

8

The Indochina
Tragedy

> I am uniting Vietnam and both sides are
> screaming at me.
>   Henry Kissinger, 1972

"My nightmare!" was Henry Kissinger's favorite description of the Indochina war. The phrase was apt since Kissinger's basic policy was an effort to spring the United States from a lethal trap in which the country had become ensnared. But the quest for stability and order which was so basic to his grand design made him seek a "peace with honor". In the search for such a peace, the war was widened and the trap tightened even more. Cambodia, a neutral nation, was drawn into the conflict. North Vietnam's harbors were mined and its major cities bombed to rubble. At long last, Kissinger thought, peace seemed to be "at hand". But the Paris cease-fire accords—Kissinger's reward for years of strain and diplomatic effort—too, proved to be illusory. When they broke down, and North Vietnam began to overrun the South, Kissinger's call not to abandon an ally failed to inspire an exhausted nation. America's defeat was a most unhappy ending even for a man who had made tragedy a cornerstone of his philosophy. His nightmare after Saigon's fall was that 56,000 American fighting men might well have died in vain in the Indochina war.

On numerous occasions, during the 1960s, Henry Kissinger expressed his disagreement with official policy. When John F. Kennedy committed 16,000 military advisors to South Vietnam, Kissinger stated that he did not think that the United States could accomplish with 16,000 advisors what France had failed to do with 200,000 combat troops. When Kissinger returned from his first visit to Vietnam in 1965, he believed that the military escalation then underway was not only imprudent but absurd. When the American commitment reached a figure of 500,000 men, Kissinger thought of Indochina as a national disaster.

In view of these earlier dissents, what is the explanation for Kissinger's later policies, once he came to power? The answer is *not* that Nixon's hard-line views prevailed over the more liberal outlook of his new Advisor for National Security Affairs. The explanation, rather, must be found in Kissinger's overall philosophy of foreign policy. For the sake of its global commitments and for the morale of her other allies, America would have to depart from Indochina in such a way that she would not appear to have abandoned an ally to whom she had committed 500,000 troops. American credibility was now at stake. And since a stable equilibrium with Russia would depend upon America's steadfast honoring of her commitments, an abrupt or precipitous withdrawal was no longer possible. A "peace with honor" would now have to be sought, or at the very least, a "decent interval" between America's departure and a victory for communism in Vietnam. Thus, though Kissinger despised the war, his larger conceptual design for a stable world order deepened the entrapment and prevented him from acting on his earlier instincts. His global policy now dictated a harder line on Vietnam, but the harder line on Vietnam made the attainment of his global objectives that much more difficult. This was the paradox of Kissinger's approach to the Indochina war and its tragedy as well. He defined the problem clearly enough in 1968:

The commitment of five hundred thousand Americans has settled the issue of the importance of Vietnam. For what is involved now is confidence in American promises. However fashionable it is to ridicule the terms "credibility" or "prestige," they are not empty phrases; other nations can gear their actions to ours only if they can count on our steadiness.

Kissinger was convinced, when he assumed his new office in 1969, that a correct combination of diplomacy and power would bring about a resolution of the Vietnam war. He was so optimistic that he measured his timetable in months, not years. "Give us six months," he told a group of antiwar activists, "and if we haven't ended the war by then, you can come back and tear down the White House fence." The reason for Kissinger's optimism was a plan which he had worked out a few weeks before he moved into his White House office. The plan was entitled "The Vietnam Negotiations" and appeared in the January 1969, issue of *Foreign Affairs*, published by the Council on Foreign Relations.

The heart of Kissinger's approach was a new procedural formula that quickly came to be known as the "two-track" plan. He proposed that, on one track, the United States and North Vietnam would negotiate a *military* settlement of the war; on the other track, the Saigon regime would negotiate with the Communist National Liberation Front about a *political* solution for South Vietnam. After a settlement was reached on both tracks, an international conference would be convened to work out guarantees and safeguards.

If the formula should fail and the war continue, Kissinger had a contingency plan. A strategy should be adopted whereby the South Vietnamese Army would be strengthened to permit a gradual withdrawal of American combat forces. During the twilight period of "honorable disengagement," the war would gradually be turned over to the Vietnamese. Kissinger's hope was to leave behind an anti-Communist South Vietnam with a friendly government installed in Saigon. He did not say how long such a friendly government would last. But enabling the South Vietnamese to carry their own battle to the enemy would ease the burden of the United States, and thus make it more bearable for the American people.

Kissinger's plan was generally well received. In the climate of frustration which then permeated official Washington, it was welcomed as a realistic retreat from a hopeless pursuit of military victory and as a reasonable compromise. Senator William Fulbright, perhaps the leading critic of the Vietnam War during the Johnson administration, stated that the President and Dr. Kissinger were in accord with his own views about the war. If the war was brought to a speedy conclusion, Fulbright predicted, President Nixon would become a national hero "just as Charles de Gaulle was when he ended France's war in Algeria."

Kissinger's optimism about his plan was based, above all, on his belief that he would be able to persuade the Soviet leaders to help him end the war. This would be achieved through *linkage,* one of the basic conceptual themes of Kissinger's policy. If the Soviets would cooperate, they might receive more attractive trade terms and the United States might acquiesce to an all-European security conference, long an objective of Soviet policy. Nixon agreed that the linkage approach might work and, on March 4, 1969, attempted to convey a signal to the Soviet Union: "I am sure," he declared, "that the Soviet Union is keenly aware of the fact that we would be greatly gratified by anything they can do that would pull some of the support away from the government of North Vietnam." At the time Nixon made this statement, about eighty-five percent of North Vietnam's sophisticated military equipment came from the Soviet Union.

To Kissinger's disappointment, neither the "double track" formula for negotiations nor the linkage initiative with the Soviet Union seemed to work. In Paris, the North Vietnamese negotiatiors insisted on a single-track negotiation, maintaining that the military and political elements of a settlement were inseparable. Moreover, they rejected Kissinger's proposal for mutual withdrawal and insisted on an

American pull-out; and most vexing of all, they insisted that the Saigon regime of President Thieu be dismantled in favor of a coalition government including the National Liberation Front. On the linkage idea, Kissinger had made numerous overtures to Soviet Ambassador Anatoly Dobrynin, but was told that the Soviet Union's influence over North Vietnam's leadership was not great enough to extract the concessions demanded by the United States. Thus Kissinger found himself stalled on both of his initiatives to end the Vietnam war.

It was at this moment that Kissinger began to act on his belief that diplomacy, to be effective, must be backed by force. It had come to his attention that approximately 50,000 North Vietnamese soldiers were massed in staging centers along a ten-mile wide area in Cambodian territory, bordering on South Vietnam. Kissinger believed that a bombing program against these enemy troops would not only prevent them from inflicting heavy casualties on the American forces, but would also make the North Vietnamese more flexible in their negotiations in Paris.

The raids began in March 1969 and were conducted in utmost secrecy for over a year until they were officially acknowledged in May 1970. During that period about 3,000 sorties were flown over Cambodia and more than 100,000 tons of explosives were dropped over the area. A "double-entry" bookkeeping system was devised which made it appear that all the bombs actually dropped on Cambodia were dropped on targets in South Vietnam. The operation was known to the ruler of Cambodia, Prince Sihanouk, who chose not to take a stand; it was known to the leadership of South Vietnam; and, of course, to the North Vietnamese troops on whom the bombs were dropped. The American people found out about the raids in May 1969 as a result of a report by the Pentagon correspondent of the *New York Times*. This apparent leak infuriated Kissinger so much that he cooperated with the FBI in a search for its source. As a result, the FBI in May 1969, placed wiretaps on thirteen government officials including seven members of the National Security Council staff. Some of these taps remained in effect until early 1971.

A few days after the raids on Cambodia had become public knowledge, Nixon delivered a major speech on Vietnam in which he offered his plan for a negotiated settlement and attempted to counteract the unfavorable publicity that had been created by the bombing raids. Kissinger had worked on an early draft of the speech. Its essence was the beginning of the "Vietnamization" program, under which American troops would gradually be withdrawn from South Vietnam. North Vietnamese troops would also withdraw in proportionate numbers until, within a year, the bulk of all non-South Vietnamese troops would have left the South. An international supervisory body would then be established to arrange for fair elections. Finally, all prisoners of war would be exchanged as soon as possible. Kissinger gave an advance copy of the speech to Dobrynin and warned the Soviet ambassador that, if the Soviet Union did not cooperate, the United States would escalate the war. In order to emphasize the sincerity of American intentions, Nixon announced in June 1969, that 25,000 American combat troops would be withdrawn by August. Kissinger hoped that this first tangible American move would help establish an atmosphere of trust and persuade Hanoi to move toward a compromise. He was also eager to establish personal contacts with a North Vietnamese leader, confident that his skill as a negotiator would help to move the Paris talks off dead center.

In August, Kissinger was able to have his first meeting with a high North Vietnamese official, the leader of Hanoi's peace delegation in Paris, Xuan Thuy. The meeting was arranged by a French intermediary, Jean Sainteny, a personal friend of Ho Chi Minh and took place in Sainteny's Paris apartment. Kissinger's hopes for a breakthrough were dashed, however, when Xuan Thuy merely restated North Vietnam's old position.

At the root of the impasse was a problem of different perceptions of the same situation. Kissinger really believed that the beginning of

an American troop withdrawal would move Hanoi toward a negotiated settlement. He perceived the American offer as a reasonable
compromise. Ho Chi Minh, however, had bitter memories of another
international agreement, made in Geneva in 1954. On that occasion,
too, elections had been promised, but the promise was broken two
years later when South Vietnam's new Premier Diem did not permit
these elections to take place. Ho Chi Minh felt that he had been
deprived at the conference tables in Geneva of the gains he had made
on the battlefield against the Western invaders. Now again, fifteen
years later, the Americans were offering a similar deal. Ho Chi Minh
simply did not trust them. As Pham Van Dong, North Vietnam's
premier said, in a statement that must have struck Kissinger with
heavy irony: "Never Munich again, in whatever form." Moreover,
the North Vietnamese leadership probably perceived the American
troop withdrawal as weakness and as the beginning of the end of the
Saigon regime. The Americans, apparently, were finally on the run.

Kissinger was thoroughly disheartened. Neither his new public
initiatives nor his personal diplomacy had led to any significant results. A group of Asian diplomats were visiting Washington at the
time and one of them, according to the Kalb brothers' book on
Kissinger, asked the American negotiator how they could be sure that
he would not repeat the mistakes of the Johnson administration.
"No, we will not repeat those mistakes," Kissinger replied sadly. "We
will not send five hundred thousand men to Vietnam. We will make
our own mistakes, and they will be completely our own."

By this time, the anti-war movement in the United States had
gathered considerable strength. On October 15, 1969, peaceful protest demonstrations took place all over the nation in a moratorium
against the war. Kissinger visited Harvard to solicit advice from his
former colleagues. Almost all of them showed considerable impatience and reminded him not only that the "six months" he had
requested to end the war had long ago run out, but also that there
seemed to be no end in sight. They advocated new concrete peace

initiatives and a timetable for American troop withdrawals.

Kissinger did not take the advice that was offered to him at Harvard. He agreed with Nixon that peace would come more rapidly by taking a hard line. "If the North Vietnamese want a reasonable compromise," he said, "we will meet them halfway. If they insist on American humiliation, we will resist."

In early November, Nixon, in a nationwide address, asked the American people for their support and patience. The speech gained time for Kissinger to engage in several meetings in Paris with Le Duc Tho, North Vietnam's chief negotiator. Despite four trips to Paris between February and April 1970, however, the deadlock remained unbroken. Then, in the spring of 1970, a series of events overtook Cambodia that were to have fateful consequences for Kissinger and the course of the Indochina war.

In March 1970, Cambodia's neutralist ruler, Prince Sihanouk, was overthrown by Lon Nol, a right-wing officer who promptly turned Cambodia's neutrality into anti–Communism. His poorly trained forces began to engage the North Vietnamese in battle, with disastrous results. By mid-April, Cambodian Communists, supported by the Hanoi regime, threatened to cut off Phnom Penh, the capital. Lon Nol, in desperation, appealed for American military assistance to prevent his country from falling to the Communists. The Saigon regime echoed Lon Nol's appeal for help.

On April 20, Nixon had announced that 150,000 American troops would leave Vietnam by May 1971. He was now concerned that a Communist victory in Cambodia would give the North Vietnamese a new power base which would threaten the Vietnamization program and thus slow down the American troop withdrawal. Besides, the President worried about his credibility in the Communist world, especially in Moscow and Peking. He leaned very strongly toward some kind of military intervention in Cambodia. The question which was debated in the White House during the next ten days was not whether there should be an intervention, but whether the basic thrust of a military move should be led by South Vietnamese or by American forces.

The main participants in the deliberations were the President, Henry Kissinger, CIA Director Richard Helms, Secretary of State William Rogers, Secretary of Defense Melvin Laird, and the Joint Chiefs of Staff. Kissinger, in a crucial briefing before this group, argued that the new Communist sanctuaries in Cambodia would give Hanoi the capability of inflicting heavy casualties on American forces in South Vietnam, threatening both Vietnamization there and American troop withdrawals.

Rogers and Laird favored a South Vietnamese intervention, fearing that an American attack would further inflame anti-war sentiment in Congress and throughout the nation. Nixon and Helms favored the use of American troops. Kissinger, who had little confidence in the South Vietnamese army, agreed with the President. He argued that, if an intervention was to take place to deny Cambodia to the Communists, then it was vital that the operation succeed. Failure would be disastrous. Since the South Vietnamese army was a dubious bet, only the United States could be counted upon to carry out the mission successfully.

Kissinger also discussed Cambodia with five members of his National Security Council staff. Four out of five spoke out strongly against an American invasion. Anthony Lake, who later resigned over the matter, stated that an invasion would extend the war and that the cost in domestic upheaval simply was not worth it. He warned that there might be blood in American streets if the United States went into Cambodia.

On April 30, President Nixon announced the American "incursion" into Cambodia in a nationwide television address. He declared that "if, when the chips are down, the world's most powerful nation acts like a pitiful, helpless giant, the forces of totalitarianism and anarchy will threaten free nations and free institutions throughout the world." The speech had Kissinger's full support. Both men believed that by wiping out the Communist sanctuaries in Cambodia and thus keeping Vietnamization and American troop withdrawals from South Vietnam on schedule, the incursion would shorten the war.

By May 4, Anthony Lake's prediction had come true. Hundreds of university campuses were in upheaval. At Kent State University in Ohio, four students were killed in a clash with National Guardsmen who had opened fire. Kissinger, even though he fully supported the President's policy, was near despair. As he followed reports from the battlefront, he also maintained close contact with numerous former academic colleagues, most of whom now attacked him without mercy and some of whom asked him to resign. "If I resign," Kissinger responded in a lame attempt at humor, "Nixon will have a heart attack and Agnew will be President." "I am dead," he is reported to have said later and more seriously to a former Harvard colleague. "Every war has its casualties. I am a casualty of this one."

Nevertheless, Kissinger held to his fundamental credo that an effective diplomacy must be backed by force. His loyalty to the President during those weeks of despair was unwavering. He insisted that steadfastness of purpose would afford a new opportunity to negotiate an honorable settlement of the war with the North Vietnamese. To him, American Indochina policy appeared as a bastion of the forces of order against anarchy and revolution.

Kissinger's faith in the use of American power in Cambodia proved to be mistaken. Far from shortening the war, the American invasion widened it. Nor was its goal ever attained, not even in the short run. By the time the more than thirty thousand American troops who participated in the invasion had left in July 1970, half the country was in Communist hands. The bombing of Cambodia was stopped only in August 1973 by Congressional action after half a million tons of bombs had been dropped on that unhappy country. Far from saving Cambodia from Communism, the American invasion had dragged the country into the war and brought it closer to a Communist takeover.

In July 1970, after American troops had left Cambodia, Kissinger recommended that another concession be made to North Vietnam. He urged the President to propose a "cease fire in place" in South Vietnam. This proposal would allow the North Vietnamese to remain in the areas that they had captured in the South. It signified a retreat from the earlier proposal for a "mutual withdrawal." In effect, Kissinger was prepared to offer an American withdrawal from the South while the North Vietnamese would be permitted to remain. Nixon made the offer, but once again, North Vietnam rejected it; the Hanoi leadership continued to insist on a complete political victory in the South. And this meant nothing less than the total removal of the Thieu regime in Saigon.

This new frustration led to yet another military escalation. In early 1971, Nixon, with Kissinger's backing, allowed the South Vietnamese army to cross the border into Laos in order to cut the network of Ho Chi Minh trails that led into South Vietnam. After the Cambodian experience, neither Kissinger nor Nixon was prepared to employ American troops for such an operation. They did decide, however, to give air support to a force of 20,000 South Vietnamese troops who entered Laos in February. Less than two months later, despite this air support, the South Vietnamese were beaten back by Communist forces from the North. The Laotian military action ended as a total failure.

After the collapse of the Laos operation, Kissinger again took the diplomatic initiative. He persuaded the President to offer yet two further concessions to the North Vietnamese in the hope of breaking the deadlock. The first was a pledge to withdraw all remaining Americans within six months after the signing of the agreement; the second, a promise that President Thieu would resign one month before elections were held in South Vietnam. Six times during 1971, Kissinger went to Paris to try to reach agreement with Le Duc Tho. Six times, North Vietnam's negotiator rejected a compromise and continued to insist on Thieu's immediate removal and a date for total American withdrawal.

It was only in the fall of 1971, three years after he had become actively involved in the Indochina war, that Kissinger realized that Hanoi would not compromise. It finally became clear to him that North Vietnam expected the United States to join it in removing Thieu. Only then would the United States be allowed to depart "with honor". Kissinger had believed that his new concessions were a genuine compromise that Hanoi could accept. Hanoi, however, interpreted these concessions as a prelude for American cooperation in the displacement of the Thieu regime. When Le Duc Tho, in turn, recognized that this was not Kissinger's position, but that the American sought a genuine compromise, he broke off the negotiations. But this time, North Vietnam, rather than the United States, would move from diplomacy to military escalation.

In early April 1972, the North Vietnamese army launched a full-scale invasion of South Vietnam, comparable in ferocity to the Tet offensive of 1968. Almost the entire military force of North Vietnam was thrown into the battle. Heavy Soviet tanks and Soviet long-range artillery accompanied the invading forces. The South Vietnamese defenders reeled under the attack and within days had fallen back to defense positions only sixty miles away from Saigon.

It was clear to Kissinger that the invasion could not have taken place on such a massive scale without Soviet tanks and long-range artillery. He was dismayed and puzzled since a summit meeting between the President and Secretary Brezhnev was scheduled to be held in Moscow in late May. Kissinger hoped that an historic agreement on the limitation of strategic arms (SALT) would be signed on that occasion. He did not wish to see the summit jeopardized, yet, on the other hand, such a massive Soviet-backed offensive simply could not be ignored.

The President and his top advisers debated the resumption of bombing raids against the North. The last such raids had taken place in March 1968. Nixon now considered the possibility of bombing North Vietnam's capital, Hanoi, along with its major port, Haiphong.

Laird and Rogers advised against such raids. They feared renewed Congressional opposition to the war and believed that American attacks on North Vietnam's two major cities would destroy the Moscow summit. Kissinger, however, advised the President to authorize the strikes. In his opinion, this would force Hanoi to abandon its offensive and would signal the Soviets that America was determined to stem the Communist offensive even at the risk of endangering the summit. Kissinger believed that the risk had to be taken to demonstrate the American commitment to an ally fighting for his life.

Nixon made his decision on April 15. Hanoi and Haiphong were to be bombed, with the oil depots in the two cities as the main targets. Four days later, Kissinger left for Moscow in order to confer with Brezhnev about the forthcoming summit. He asked the Soviet leader to reduce arms deliveries to North Vietnam in the interest of détente. Brezhnev stated, in response, that he was committed to help a "fraternal ally." Kissinger, in turn, declared that the United States would not accept a Communist military victory in South Vietnam. Both men realized that the escalation of the Vietnam war had begun to jeopardize the summit.

In the meantime, the North Vietnamese offensive continued to advance. The bombing of the oil depots was not achieving its objective. On May 1, the Soviet-built tanks of North Vietnam entered Quangtri City, the northern provincial capital of South Vietnam. The Saigon régime became frantic with anxiety and Kissinger now concluded that the entire Vietnamization program was in serious peril.

Kissinger persuaded the President to offer Le Duc Tho yet another concession. If Hanoi would agree to a cease-fire in place and the return of American prisoners of war, the United States would withdraw its remaining troops from Indochina within four months. Another journey by Kissinger to Paris led to yet another frustration. Le Duc Tho flatly rejected even this latest concession and continued to insist on the ouster of the Thieu regime. He was simply unwilling to compromise, especially after the spectacular Communist victory in Quangtri. The meeting was a fiasco.

Upon his return to Washington, Kissinger went over the military options with the President. The bombing had made little difference. The reintroduction of American ground troops was rejected as politically unfeasible. Both men also rejected the use of nuclear weapons. This left another option—the mining of the port of Haiphong, a course that had been rejected by Lyndon Johnson as too dangerous. Nixon, once again, called in Rogers, Laird, Helms, and also, his Secretary of the Treasury John Connally, to ask for advice. All four men supported a blockade of Haiphong on the grounds that the resulting shortage of war matériel would cripple the North Vietnamese offensive.

Kissinger, however, did not go along with the others. While he agreed that the Soviet Union had supplied the weapons for the offensive, he felt that a blockade of Haiphong would surely kill the Moscow summit. SALT, in his opinion, was too important to be abandoned in favor of the uncertain benefits of a blockade. He recommended a more intensive bombing campaign as an alternative to the mining of Haiphong.

Nixon decided to go against Kissinger's advice and to gamble. However, he stopped just short of an actual blockade of Haiphong. He did not prevent ships from entering the port, he merely warned them that the port was mined. In that sense, the Haiphong action did not go so far as the quarantine of Cuba that had been announced by President Kennedy ten years earlier. On that occasion, Soviet vessels on their way to Cuba were actually stopped by the American Navy. Nixon wanted to give the Soviet Union a chance to avoid a confrontation. In short, he gambled on getting away with the Haiphong mining and yet retain the Moscow summit.

Kissinger expected that the Soviets would probably cancel the summit, though, in a briefing, he expressed the hope that "the Russians would not sacrifice everything we have gained between us for the sake of Vietnam." When a reporter asked him why "he had taken action that had jeopardized everything," Kissinger replied that "the President felt that the mining [had been] necessary."

This was the first time that Kissinger dissociated himself from the President. On all previous occasions, he had announced decisions in a way that made Nixon's policies indistinguishable from his own, as they probably were. But on the mining of Haiphong, he made an exception to this long-standing rule. While he continued to be loyal to the President, he was apparently less willing than Nixon to risk the summit.

As it turned out, Nixon won his gamble. The Soviets contented themselves with verbal attacks and never even hinted that the summit meeting was in doubt. Brezhnev, too, needed détente with the United States. He had staked his reputation on it, and did not want a two-front cold war, with the United States on one side of the Soviet Union and China on the other. Moreover, he needed technology and trade to strengthen Russia's economy. SALT, too, was high on his agenda. Hanoi was not worth all this. Thus, Brezhnev looked the other way and prepared to welcome Nixon and Kissinger in Moscow.

As it turned out, the mining also broke the North Vietnamese offensive. Hanoi abandoned a planned attack on the provincial capital of Hué, and Saigon found time to regroup its battered armies. Kissinger admitted that the President's gamble had worked. He now described the Haiphong mining as a "knockout punch." When he left with Nixon for Moscow two weeks later, his despair about Vietnam had given way to renewed hope. Perhaps the mixture of diplomacy and military force would finally yield the coveted reward: a negotiated settlement of the Indochina war.

In Moscow, Brezhnev came closer than ever before to Kissinger's view that Vietnam should not be permitted to threaten the evolving pattern of détente between Russia and the United States. That Hanoi launched a major offensive before a Soviet-American summit, but did nothing to disrupt a Chinese-American summit three months earlier, had infuriated the Soviet leader. Being more fearful of China than of the United States, Brezhnev resented Hanoi's action more than Nixon's counteraction. Moreover, the dividends he was deriving from détente far outweighed the importance of Vietnam. Finally, the Soviet leader reasoned, once the Americans had withdrawn, Hanoi could be counted upon to win the struggle over South Vietnam, after a "decent interval" at any rate.

It was this logic that persuaded Brezhnev to lend the United States a helping hand in its effort to extricate itself from the Indochina war without a total loss of face. Brezhnev promised to reduce arms deliveries to North Vietnam and on June 15, President Nikolai Podgorny of the USSR flew to Hanoi and told the North Vietnamese leaders that the time had come for serious negotiations with the United States. After all, the Americans had now agreed that North Vietnamese troops could remain "in place" in South Vietnam and this concession would ensure the North's ultimate victory. Four days later, Kissinger appeared in Peking and urged the Chinese leaders to help him negotiate a settlement with Hanoi. Chou En-lai, fearful of the growing American détente with Russia, promised to cooperate.

Kissinger's shrewd exploitation of the Sino-Soviet split during the summer of 1972 marked a crucial turning point in the Vietnam negotiations. Hanoi suddenly felt very much alone. Its two major allies were now more interested in improving relations with the United States than in aiding a "fraternal ally." As a result, in late June the leadership of North Vietnam hastily convened a special meeting, including its top negotiators, in order to consider its deteriorating diplomatic situation.

Kissinger's hopes for a breakthrough were justified. In his meetings with Le Duc Tho near Paris during August, he noticed a softening in Hanoi's posture. For the first time since the negotiations had begun, Le Duc Tho no longer insisted on the resignation of President Thieu as a precondition for a settlement. Instead, he now spoke of "three political groupings" in South Vietnam: the Thieu régime, the

National Liberation Front, and a "middle group" which was left undefined. In the meantime, Kissinger had read in Hanoi's official newspaper, to his delight, that the North Vietnamese government had chastised *both* Russia and China for "throwing a lifesaver to a drowning pirate and bogging down on the dark, muddy road of compromise." He was further encouraged by the news that both China and the Soviet Union had cut back their military support of North Vietnam.

The time had come, Kissinger now thought, to travel to Saigon. Thieu was probably as suspicious of Kissinger as Hanoi was of Brezhnev. Kissinger saw Thieu and tried to allay the South Vietnamese leader's fears by telling him that he would remain in power in Saigon. Then Kissinger returned to the United States. It was now late August and the Republican convention was in progress. The elections were only weeks away. If Kissinger wanted a pre-election settlement, he would have to hurry.

Kissinger, convinced that the Soviet linkage to Vietnam provided the best hope for an early Vietnam compromise, flew to Moscow in September. The timing was auspicious. The Soviet grain harvest was a disaster and Russia faced a serious shortage of bread and other staple foods unless the United States would extend easy credit terms for Soviet grain purchases in America. Kissinger and Nixon, eager for more Soviet assistance on Vietnam, agreed to a trade pact with the Russians whereby they could purchase a sizeable amount of American grain in order to offset their crop failures. When food prices soared in the United States as a result, Kissinger argued that the price was well worth a Vietnam settlement. The linkage policy seemed the most promising avenue to achieve a settlement before November.

In late September, Le Duc Tho made two further concessions. He now proposed a "National Council of Reconciliation and Concord" for South Vietnam, to be composed of three equal segments. The Council would lack governmental responsibility and would operate on the principle of unanimity. Kissinger was pleased with this new proposal since a "council" was clearly not a coalition government. He knew that Thieu had adamantly refused to accept a coalition. Second, the unanimity principle clearly implied that Thieu would have a veto over all decisions of the council. A number of ambiguities remained, however. It was not clear, for example, who the "third segment" in the council would be and whether the cease-fire "in place" would extend to all of Indochina or only to South Vietnam. But Kissinger was sure that these obstacles could be surmounted. He counted on his triangular policy with China and the Soviet Union. The Soviet crop failure and China's fear of the Soviet Union, he reasoned, made for a favorable constellation to extricate the United States from the Indochina war with a shred of dignity.

At a meeting on October 8, Le Duc Tho and Kissinger further narrowed their differences. The North Vietnamese negotiator now clearly accepted Kissinger's two track policy and was ready to separate the military from the political aspects of the war. Hanoi and the United States would end the war by compromise. There would be a cease-fire, an American troop withdrawal and a prompt return of American prisoners of war. And there would be a compromise among South Vietnam's political factions with Thieu continuing in power.

Suddenly, the pace of the negotiations quickened. Le Duc Tho and Kissinger worked virtually around the clock. Nixon had made clear to Kissinger that he wanted a pre-election settlement, and Hanoi, believing that Nixon would be re-elected in November, thought that the American president would be more flexible before his re-election. In his eagerness to conclude the settlement, however, Kissinger virtually ignored Saigon. Thieu was briefed about the Paris negotiations only in the most general terms. Kissinger, who had more respect for Hanoi than he had for Saigon, was confident that he could convince Thieu to go along with any agreement that did not force his resignation. Besides, the United States would stand behind the settlement. On October 12, after four days of bargaining interrupted only by a few hours of sleep, Kissinger and his North Vietnamese counterpart reached agreement. Kissinger promised to come to Hanoi on October 22 to initial the agreement and both men agreed to return to Paris on October 30 for formal signature. A pre-election settlement was now in sight, if Kissinger could persuade Saigon.

Kissinger arrived in Saigon on October 18. So confident was he of his ability to persuade Thieu that he had allotted only three days for the task. At their first meeting on October 19, Kissinger presented the agreement to the South Vietnamese leader in the most favorable possible light. Not only would Thieu remain in power, but he would have a veto over all decisions of the National Council of Reconciliation and Concord. This Council, Kissinger stressed, was not a coalition government, but merely an administrative structure. Moreover, the agreement would leave Thieu in control of about eighty-five percent of South Vietnam and with an army of more than a million men under his command. The agreement, Kissinger told Thieu, was a good one, worthy of their joint efforts. Thieu made no immediate response. He promised to study the document and to convey his reactions to Kissinger that evening. Kissinger eagerly waited for this meeting which, he hoped, would seal the agreement with Thieu's approval. But that night Thieu was evasive and requested a Vietnamese-language copy of the draft agreement, which Kissinger delivered to him before midnight.

The atmosphere next morning was tense. Thieu began by asking Kissinger why he had not given him an advance copy of the agreement. Kissinger replied that the document was too sensitive to be entrusted to the regular diplomatic channels. He wanted to deliver it in person. Then Thieu moved on to his substantive objections to the document. In the first place, he pointed out, the Vietnamese text revealed that the Communists *did* interpret the National Council as a coalition government, not a mere administrative structure; second, Thieu refused to yield sovereignty over any part of South Vietnam; this, in turn, led to his third objection: there would have to be a North Vietnamese military withdrawal from occupied South Vietnam. Otherwise, the agreement would legitimize conquest through aggression, Thieu maintained. Kissinger was stunned and angry, but was unable to convince the South Vietnamese leader to accept the deal. He suddenly realized that he would not be able to be in Hanoi on schedule for the initialing ceremony. In frustration, he cabled Le Duc Tho in Hanoi, suggesting a few days delay. Le Duc Tho agreed and Kissinger gained a little more time for his efforts to convince the South Vietnam régime to go along with him.

Kissinger's negotiations with Thieu continued in an atmosphere of rising tension. By October 22, the strain had reached a breaking point. Thieu refused to sign the agreement. "If necessary," he exclaimed, "we will fight alone." Kissinger was furious. "I have succeeded in Peking, in Moscow, and in Paris," he was quoted as saying to an aide. "How can I fail here?" According to Oriana Fallaci, Thieu concluded the meeting with the following emotional appeal to Kissinger:

> You are a giant, Dr. Kissinger. So you can probably afford the luxury of being easy in this agreement. I cannot. A bad agreement means nothing to you. What is the loss of South Vietnam if you look at the world's map? Just a speck. The loss of South Vietnam may even be good for you. It may be good to contain China, good for your world strategy. But a little Vietnamese doesn't play with a strategic map of the world. For us, it isn't a question of choosing between Moscow and Peking. It is a question of choosing between life and death.

Kissinger now knew that the price he would have to pay for a pre-election settlement with Hanoi was an open rupture with Saigon. He sent a cable to Nixon requesting new instructions. The President replied that he did not want a separate peace with North Vietnam. He told Kissinger to request another delay from Le Duc Tho and offered, as an incentive, to suspend all bombing north of the twentieth parallel on October 25.

Nixon sensed that the *promise* of an early Vietnam settlement, including all the parties to the conflict, might be better for him on election day than a settlement without Saigon. Thieu was not only aware of this leverage over the United States, but also knew that if the Americans pushed him too hard, the entire Saigon government might collapse. The ensuing disaster would then endanger the withdrawal of the remaining American forces. Thieu's very weakness, therefore, now became a source of power. Kissinger, whose energies had been concentrated largely on Hanoi, suddenly realized that he would have to pay a great deal more attention to Thieu.

On October 26, without any warning, Hanoi revealed its offer of October 12 in a public broadcast and then demanded that the agreement be signed no later than October 31. "Peace is at the end of a pen," the North Vietnamese spokesman declared. "All that remains is for the United States to grasp that pen." Kissinger believed that the North Vietnamese had concluded that the American delay was a sign of bad faith and that their suspicions were now aroused. He urged the President to permit him to reaffirm the American commitment to end the war and to reassure Hanoi that the delay was not some nefarious scheme to double-cross Hanoi. Nixon agreed and Kissinger immediately decided to make a statement that was destined to become historic.

"Peace is at hand," was the fundamental theme of that celebrated briefing of October 26. While "six or seven concrete issues remained to be settled," this could be accomplished in one more negotiating session with Hanoi, Kissinger declared. He warned North Vietnam, however, that the United States would not be stampeded into an agreement until its provisions were acceptable; and he reassured the American electorate that peace was within reach in a matter of weeks or even less.

The reaction to the briefing in the United States was generally favorable. When the question was asked why such a settlement could not have been attained four years earlier, Kissinger replied that the North Vietnamese had consistently refused to separate the political from the military issues until finally they did agree to do so on October 8. As soon as Hanoi had made that concession, a draft agreement was drawn up with all deliberate speed. Kissinger also denied that the timing of the settlement had anything to do with the elections. "The implication that this is all a gigantic maneuver which we will revoke as soon as this period is over is unworthy of what we have gone through," he declared. October 26 was a moment of high hope for Kissinger. He had no reason, that day, to doubt that, indeed, peace was within reach.

Nixon did not quite share Kissinger's optimism. He was very much impressed by what had been achieved, but equally concerned about what still had to be done. Besides, during Kissinger's long absences from Washington, other men, not friendly to Kissinger, had seen more of the President. Laird had warned Nixon that he had intelligence reports that Hanoi was planning a massive lang-grabbing operation in the South immediately after the proclamation of a cease-fire; Rogers thought that the draft agreement prepared by Kissinger was sloppy and full of ambiguities; and Nixon himself was concerned by Thieu's daily denunciations of the document as a "sellout." He was also suspicious of Hanoi's sudden eagerness to sign so quickly. Thus, the President, on November 2, delivered a nation-wide address which, while very hopeful about an early settlement, implied that Kissinger's timetable of "one more negotiating session" might be somewhat optimistic. He also authorized a massive airlift of war matériel to Saigon to demonstrate his loyalty to Thieu and to strengthen the South Vietnamese leader's hand as much as possible before the agreement went into force. He believed that Thieu, thus reassured, would become more tractable when the time came to sign a final settlement.

Nixon's expected landslide re-election on November 7 made his pace even more leisurely. In a conference with Kissinger, he asked him to divide the "six or seven" remaining problem areas into two categories: issues of major importance and minor items. Four items were included in the former category: the President wanted at least a token withdrawal of North Vietnamese troops from the South; he insisted on a cease-fire throughout all of Indochina rather than in South Vietnam alone; he wanted a clearly defined demilitarized zone which would become an inviolate border between the two Vietnams; and he insisted on a strong international peace-keeping force to supervise the agreement and to keep violations to a minimum. The minor category included linguistic differences between the English and Vietnamese language texts and the problem of whether all four parties or only two should sign the final document.

Kissinger now realized that his task was far from over, but still retained his optimism that these final obstacles could be removed without much difficulty. He agreed to meet Le Duc Tho again in Paris on November 20. On November 17, he stated that the agreement was already "ninety percent completed" and that the remaining "ten percent" could be settled quickly if Le Duc Tho showed good will. The President also instructed Kissinger to make a major effort to persuade Thieu to go along, but agreed with Kissinger that Thieu should not be allowed to veto an agreement that was acceptable. The United States, the two men agreed, would sign an accord, with Thieu, if possible, but without him, if necessary.

At his first negotiating session with Le Duc Tho on November 20, Kissinger made an immediate distinction between Nixon's and Thieu's minimum demands. He wanted to make sure that Hanoi understood the difference. He then launched into a presentation of Nixon's major problem areas. The meeting remained inconclusive. While engaged in these difficult negotiations in Paris, Kissinger received unsettling news from Saigon. Apparently, a campaign against him had been launched in the South Vietnamese press depicting him as an ambitious man, eager to become a legend at the expense of South Vietnam. Some of these attacks had anti-semitic overtones. One source quoted Thieu as saying: "The Jew professor comes to Saigon to try to win a Nobel Peace Prize." The report remained unconfirmed, but was enough to anger Kissinger.

To make matters worse, the talks with Le Duc Tho suddenly deteriorated. On November 23, the North Vietnamese negotiator, without warning, revived his earlier demand for the ouster of the Thieu regime. He also ruled out the demilitarized zone (DMZ) as a boundary line and rejected even a token pullout of Communist troops from South Vietnam. Kissinger was stunned. Suddenly the outlook for a settlement seemed almost hopeless and the October break-through a distant memory. Peace was no longer "at hand"; it now appeared more remote than ever.

Kissinger tried to understand the sudden hardening of Le Duc Tho's position. He came to the conclusion that Nixon's massive airlift to Saigon and his new demands had probably aroused Hanoi's suspicion even further. Perhaps Hanoi even suspected Nixon of a grand deception aiming at a lowering of its guard so that its armies in the South could be crushed by Saigon immediately after a cease-fire. Nixon's delays, Kissinger thought, probably added further weight to these suspicions. Kissinger was suddenly exhausted. In a moment of despair, he said to James Reston: "I had the illusion that maybe we could get through these peace negotiations without heartbreak, but that was probably expecting too much. The war has been heartbreaking from the beginning."

Negotiations continued through most of December. There were times when Le Duc Tho came close to his original commitments of October 12 and the differences had narrowed sufficiently for Kissinger's hopes to rise again, but by mid-December he was faced once more with complete stalemate. One reporter wrote that "The mood of the negotiations had oscillated from deepest optimism to soaring pessimism." Kissinger could not get Le Duc Tho to agree to an inviolate DMZ; and he could not persuade him to pull out any troops from South Vietnam. These two concessions would have implied North Vietnam's recognition of Thieu's regime and this was precisely what Hanoi was no longer prepared to do. On December 14, Kissinger reported a "total deadlock" to the President.

Nixon, angered by the stalemate, was ready to resume the bombing. He dispatched a cable to Hanoi warning the North Vietnamese leadership that "serious negotiations" would have to be resumed within seventy-two hours. When no response arrived by December 17, Nixon gave the order for massive and concentrated air attacks by giant bombers against North Vietnam. Kissinger asked Nixon first to warn Hanoi through Moscow or Peking, but was overruled. Once the President had made his decision, Kissinger supported him fully, despite the anguish that it caused him. As he put it later to the Kalb brothers:

> It was an agony for me to think that at the very end—when I knew the end was in sight—that all the things we had tried to do . . . were blowing away again—but that did not mean that I disagreed with the decision. The decision was the most painful, the most difficult, and certainly the most lonely that the President had to make since he has been in office."

Charles Colson, a former member of Nixon's palace guard, has a different recollection. In his book *Born Again,* he maintains that Kissinger had opposed the bombings and that Nixon was so infuriated by this insubordination that he not only issued an order to tap Kissinger's telephone, but began "counting the days until Henry left to return to Harvard." Only his troubles with Watergate finally convinced Nixon that he needed Kissinger.

Nixon's logic was that he was bombing for peace. He was trying to bomb Hanoi back to the negotiating table and trying to convince Saigon, by this show of force, that he was loyal to his ally. Both parts of Vietnam, Nixon reasoned, would be ready to sign with the United States once the shock treatment was over. By this reasoning, much of Hanoi and Haiphong was reduced to rubble.

The "Christmas bombing" resulted in a worldwide outcry of protest. Sweden's premier compared it to Lidice and Treblinka; Brezhnev threatened to delay his scheduled visit to the United States and Chou En-lai declared that China's new relationship with the United States was endangered by the bombings. As the raids gradually increased in ferocity, public opinion in the United States, too, was aroused. "War by tantrum" was Reston's description in the *New York Times* and the *Washington Post* condemned the "terror bombing in the name of peace."

On December 30, North Vietnam finally succumbed and agreed to return to the negotiating table. The Hanoi leadership feared that if it did not give in, the entire country might be totally destroyed. The bombing had done its work.

Kissinger again met Le Duc Tho in Paris on January 8, 1973, for what was to be their final meeting. This time there was another breakthrough. Le Duc Tho agreed to all of Nixon's demands and on the next day, the two men reached agreement. "Happy birthday, Mr. President," Kissinger cabled Nixon. January 9 was Nixon's sixtieth birthday. Thieu's approval, too, was secured without much further difficulty. On January 23, in an anti-climactic ceremony, Kissinger and Le Duc Tho initialed the document that was to bring peace to Indochina. Then Kissinger left for the United States.

On the next day, January 24, Kissinger explained the agreement to the American people at a major news conference. In summing it up, knowingly or not, he quoted virtually word for word from his doctoral dissertation, written twenty years before:

> It was always clear that a lasting peace could come about only if neither side sought to achieve everything it had wanted; indeed, that stability depended on the relative satisfaction and therefore on the relative dissatisfaction of all the parties concerned.

It was true, Kissinger thought, everybody got something, but nobody got everything. Nixon got his peace with honor and the American prisoners of war; Hanoi had succeeded in getting the Americans out; Thieu retained a hold on power in Saigon; and the Vietcong got a measure of political legitimacy in South Vietnam. And once again, as so many times before in history, diplomacy had to be backed up by force. By Kissinger's own later admission, the "Christmas bombing" had made only a marginal difference. He would have been content to settle for the terms agreed on with Hanoi in October, but Nixon had assumed complete control during the last two months. The horror of that terrible finale had cast a pall over the final settlement.

As Kissinger finally turned away from Vietnam to other problem areas of foreign policy, he did so with a feeling of malaise. He did not know how long the "decent interval" would last. The fact that he shared a Nobel Peace Prize with Le Duc Tho soon afterward did little to dispel his doubts.

Two years elapsed and Indochina receded into the background of America's concerns. During that time, cataclysmic events took place that shook the world. Two weeks after Henry Kissinger was confirmed as Secretary of State in the fall of 1973, war broke out in the Middle East. In August 1974, the Nixon presidency was destroyed by Watergate. Kissinger had to form a new relationship with Nixon's successor, Gerald Ford. In early 1975, he was deeply involved in diplomatic initiatives in the Middle East when, without warning, Indochina surfaced once again. The Paris accords of January 1973, it seemed, were near complete collapse.

The war had never really stopped after the American withdrawal. Casualty figures had not decreased, either for Saigon or for North Vietnam. But it had been Nixon's and Kissinger's hope that Saigon would be able to defend itself against the North with military and financial assistance from the United States. For two years, that hope seemed justified, but then the dam broke. In the spring of 1975, the Communist insurgents in Cambodia, the Khmer Rouge, marched upon the capital, Phnom Penh, and forced Marshal Lon Nol, Cambodia's American-supported president, to flee the country. At the same time, the South Vietnamese army lost what remained of its fighting spirit and collapsed entirely. In a matter of weeks, almost all of South Vietnam fell to the Communists. In the United States, a test of wills took place between Ford and Kissinger, both of whom favored continued military assistance to Cambodia and South Vietnam, and the Congress which refused to cooperate. In a last, futile effort to extract close to one billion dollars in military aid for South Vietnam from a reluctant Congress, Kissinger declared on March 26: "The United States cannot pursue a policy of selective reliability. We cannot abandon friends in one part of the world without jeopardizing the security of friends everywhere." But, by then, the American people had simply become tired of the war and had reconciled themselves to a Communist victory in Indochina. Finally, the United States was left with the elementary human responsibility of rescuing terror-stricken refugees fleeing from the advancing North Vietnamese armies. In April, Saigon surrendered to the Communists and was renamed Ho Chi Minh City.

Thus, all of Kissinger's efforts to bring a peace with honor to Indochina had come to naught. He had tried to transplant the lessons of Metternich and Castlereagh to the twentieth century. For one brief moment, in early 1973 at Paris, he hoped that a genuine compromise, patterned after the model of an earlier age, had at long last been attained. He believed that the right admixture of diplomacy and force had finally yielded a negotiated settlement without victory or defeat.

But there was one terrible flaw in Kissinger's approach. North Vietnam had never ceased to be a "revolutionary" state in the sense of Kissinger's own definition of the term. The North Vietnamese would not be deterred even by the threat of death and thus the threat, in the end, lost all its meaning. They even risked the possibility of nuclear bombardment since the fury of the American leadership might have gotten completely out of hand.

It was this "revolutionary" quality that Kissinger had failed to comprehend. He regarded his meetings with Le Duc Tho as negotiations between two "legitimate" states that would ultimately have to strike a bargain. But North Vietnam was never interested in a bargain. It regarded the Americans as invaders who used the Saigon regime as their puppet. Death was not too high a price to pay in order to rid the country of such intruders. Kissinger did not want another Munich; but neither did Hanoi. And its determination to outlast the United States guaranteed its final victory.

I saw Henry Kissinger on that terrible April day when Saigon fell. I could not help but think of the innumerable hours that he had spent in his search for compromise. Flawed though it was, the search had been sincere. He had pushed himself beyond the limits of even his extraordinary physical endurance. All this effort was now crumbling into dust. Total failure stared him in the face. "Vietnam is a Greek tragedy," he said quietly. "We should never have been there at all. But now it's history." For a moment his face was the very essence of despair. Then, after a brief pause, he changed the subject with finality.

9

Détente with Russia: Beyond the Cold War

Détente is rooted in a recognition of differences and based on the prevention of disaster.

Henry Kissinger
Statement to the Senate
Finance Committee, April 1, 1974

Henry Kissinger always had a keen sense for the irony of history. Throughout history, man was faced with a shortage of power, he observed in 1957, until, with the coming of the atomic era, suddenly he had an excess of it, and his very survival depended on "his ability to use that power subtly and with discrimination."

Five years after Kissinger wrote these words, the fate of mankind hung in the balance when the United States and the Soviet Union had their showdown over nuclear missiles in Cuba. President John F. Kennedy, in reviewing the thirteen days of the crisis, estimated that the probability of disaster at the crucial point of the confrontation had been "between one out of three and even." In the light of this estimate, mankind's escape from the nuclear abyss was truly awesome. A slight shift of the pendulum might have doomed more human lives to sudden extinction than ever before in history. Previous calamities, whether man-made or natural, would have been dwarfed by comparison. Fortunately, the two men who held this terrible power in their hands did show the ability to use it "subtly and with discrimination." But it was clear to participants and onlookers alike that mankind might not be so fortunate a second time.

While Kissinger was deeply shaken by the Cuban missile crisis, he also saw in it an element of hope. He had always believed that America, unlike Europe, was rather innocent of tragedy and there-fore incapable of truly understanding that states, like men, could die. Now, at last, America had gazed into the abyss, and seen that nuclear death was indeed possible. The Soviet leader, too, had been chastened by the brush with nuclear catastrophe and had shipped his missiles back to Russia. What heartened Kissinger was that both superpowers apparently had learned a lesson. The narrowness of their escape had left a mark. Both leaders realized, not only in their minds but also in their hearts, that neither could say to the other any longer: "Do as I say or I shall kill you," but were now reduced to saying, "Do as I say or I shall kill us both."

Thus, the Cuban missile crisis of 1962 came to represent a water-shed in Soviet-American relations. Slowly, the frozen hostility of the cold war thawed and gave way to a less abrasive relationship, marked by a greater degree of realism and a measure of ideological decontami-nation. The first concrete result was the partial nuclear test-ban treaty, concluded in Moscow in 1963, less than a year after the missile crisis. During the remainder of the decade, despite the rapid escala-tion of the Indochina war, Soviet-American relations gradually im-proved. Agreements were hammered out to prevent the spread of nuclear weapons and insulate outer space from the atomic arms race. With a wary eye on China, the Soviet leadership slowly started to cooperate with its great capitalist adversary. A sense of détente—a relaxation of tensions—had begun to form between the world's two most powerful nations.

Henry Kissinger's perception of the Soviet Union was deeply al-tered by these events. Before the Cuban missile crisis, he had viewed the Soviet Union as the world's leading "revolutionary" power, insatiably bent on global conquest. By the time he joined the government in 1969, Kissinger had changed his mind. A realistic hope now existed, in his view, to create a community of interests between the Soviet Union and the United States, based upon their common need to avoid a nuclear catastrophe. If this basic premise were admitted, perhaps further bonds could then be forged between the two great powers that might deepen their perception of a common destiny. Once this process was set in motion, Soviet Russia and the United States might ultimately form a kind of partnership in the quest for a stable world order without which there was no real hope for peace.

For Henry Kissinger, America's relationship with Russia was absolutely basic to any policy that sought stability. Détente would depend, at least to some extent, on the ability of the United States to convert the Soviet Union from a "revolutionary" power with unlimited ambition, to a "legitimate" state with more circumspect objectives. A "legitimate" state, in Kissinger's view, could still remain a dictatorship vis-à-vis its own people. This was not his main concern. What mattered enormously to him was that the *external* goals of Soviet Russia would have to be adjusted to the overall imperatives of a stable world order. If he succeeded in this task, all else, he hoped, would fall in place. Of Kissinger's numerous pronouncements on détente with Soviet Russia, the following statement, made in April 1974, conveyed this central message with the greatest clarity:

> Détente is not rooted in agreement on values; it becomes above all necessary because each side recognizes that the other is a potential adversary in a nuclear war. To us, détente is a process of managing relations with a potentially hostile country in order to preserve peace while maintaining our vital interests. In a nuclear age, this is in itself an objective not without moral validity —it may indeed be the most profound imperative of all.

Without stability, no peace was possible. Without the Soviet Union's participation in this quest, there could be no stability and there might be no survival. These were the twin premises on which Kissinger set out to build détente with Soviet Russia.

I once asked Henry Kissinger in 1975 what he considered to be his most significant achievement in office up to that time. "SALT," he answered without hesitation, "without a question, SALT."

To appreciate this statement, one has to understand that, when Kissinger assumed office in 1969, a quarter of a century had elapsed since the end of the Second World War. This twenty-five year span had witnessed the most relentless arms race in the history of man. By then, the money devoted each year by the Soviet Union and the United States to military expenditures amounted to nearly three times what all the world's governments were spending on health and nearly twice what they spent on education. The record of disarmament negotiations was one of total failure. Despite endless conferences, both bilateral and multilateral, not a single weapon, either conventional or nuclear, had been scrapped as a result of a Soviet-American agreement. Mutual mistrust simply was too deep.

By the 1960's, the frustrations over disarmament had led some thinkers to approach the problem in a somewhat different way: arms *control* rather than disarmament. While the disarmer was primarily concerned with the actual scrapping of existing weapons, the arms controller was more interested in stabilizing the climate in which these weapons existed and in the prevention of additional arms build-ups. The emphasis here was less on hardware and more on psychology. The hope was that progress could be made on issues related to disarmament that might act as confidence-builders and ultimately lead to actual disarmament agreements. The partial nuclear test ban of 1963 was an example of this approach; the nuclear non-proliferation treaty of 1968 was another. Whatever breakthroughs had been made between the superpowers had taken place in arms control rather than disarmament.

Kissinger, too, was impressed by the arms control approach. Its emphasis on stability appealed to him. But there was a more fundamental reason for his preference. He had always shunned the technical approach by formula to problems that he considered basically political in nature. He simply did not believe that nations went to war because they had arms but, rather, that they had arms because they deemed it necessary to fight. Hence, he was convinced that efforts at disarmament were bound to fail unless they were preceded by more fundamental political accomodation. The way to begin, in his view, was not to seek the magic disarmament formula but to concentrate instead on the acceptance, and possible settlement, of political differences.

To put it somewhat differently, Kissinger believed that the problem of disarmament was not disarmament at all, but rather the problem of forging détente between the Soviet Union and the United States. Moreover, it was his conviction that not even the more modest search for arms control could take place in a political vacuum, but would have to proceed within the broader context of a general narrowing of differences in other areas as well. He saw a vital connection, for example, between progress in arms control and simultaneous progress on the defusing of the Indochina war. This linkage approach was absolutely basic to Kissinger's conception of détente. Every problem between the United States and the Soviet Union was linked with every other problem; progress on one would affect progress on all. Kissinger was determined to move on as broad a front as possible. Détente, like peace, was seen by him as indivisible.

When Richard Nixon, in his inaugural address on January 20, 1969, declared that the United States was prepared to enter "an era of negotiations", the Soviet Union responded within hours that it was ready to "start a serious exchange of views" on the problem of arms control between the two superpowers. There were several reasons for

Brezhnev's eagerness. In the first place, the tensions between China and the Soviet Union had reached a level of potentially explosive danger; second, Eastern Europe was showing signs of increasing turbulence. Only a few months earlier Brezhnev had sent Soviet tanks into Czechoslovakia to crush the Dubcek heresy; and finally, the Soviet Union needed American technology and credits in order to infuse new life into the sluggish Russian economy. The Soviet leader seemed to have staked his entire reputation on détente with the United States. He had even been responsive to overtures from West Germany's Chancellor Willy Brandt, and had shown increasing willingness to settle the vexing German problem through a diplomacy of compromise. A "serious exchange" about the two superpowers' nuclear arsenals, in Brezhnev's view, was therefore both timely and desirable.

Kissinger was aware of Brezhnev's urgency. While he was equally eager for détente, he wanted to link the beginning of strategic arms limitations talks (SALT) to progress on other issues that divided the two countries. Specifically, he believed that the Soviet Union held the key to peace in Indochina and in the Middle East. Kissinger hoped for a kind of diplomatic barter whereby he could make Brezhnev pay for American concessions on SALT and trade by helping him defuse Vietnam and restore tranquillity to the Middle East.

To Kissinger, the linkage concept was a good test of Soviet sincerity on détente. If the Soviet Union was now willing to engage in the "give and take" of diplomatic barter that linkage diplomacy implied, then this would indeed be evidence that Soviet Russia had at last accepted the legitimacy of the existing international order and abandoned its goal of global conquest.

Nixon, by inauguration day, was a respectful student of Kissinger's philosophy. He had read most of Kissinger's books and had even scanned, at Kissinger's request, Spengler's *The Decline of the West*. The linkage concept appealed to him, and, after only a week in office, he subscribed to it in a statement of his own:

What I want to do is to see to it, that we have strategic arms talks in a way and at a time that will promote, if possible, progress on outstanding political problems *at the same time*—for example, on the problem of the Middle East and on other outstanding problems in which the United States and the Soviet Union, acting together, can serve the cause of peace.

If Kissinger was able to convince the President of the wisdom of linkage diplomacy, he was unable to persuade the secretary of state, or for that matter, the Soviet ambassador. Rogers was eager to forge ahead on SALT regardless of progress in other areas. A bitter feud erupted between him and Kissinger over linkage. Dobrynin, with whom Kissinger had established a cordial relationship, regarded linkage as a form of extortion bordering on blackmail. Kissinger became alarmed and on February 6, 1969, in a press briefing, declared that there was "no attempt to blackmail the Soviet Union into a disadvantageous settlement in one area in order to give something in another area." Linkage diplomacy was to be a symmetrical proposition.

Kissinger believed that there was increasing evidence, during 1969, that the Soviet Union was serious about détente. As a result of Brandt's *Ostpolitik* policy of rapprochment with Soviet Russia, the two Germanies were finally beginning to move toward compromise with one another. The vexing German problem, for so long, at the center of the cold war in the heart of Europe, finally seemed to be accessible to reasonable settlement. Kissinger watched these developments with keen interest. While he felt encouraged and was inclined to go ahead with SALT by late 1969, he wanted to make sure that the United States entered these negotiations impeccably prepared. He assembled a staff of first-rate experts, yet made sure that control was concentrated in his own hands. Next to Vietnam, no other issue absorbed his time and energy as much as SALT during 1969. Dobrynin soon realized that it was Kissinger, not Rogers, who set the date on which the negotiations would begin. When the first session of SALT finally convened in Helsinki on November 17, 1969, Kissinger was ready.

Kissinger's overall philosophical approach to SALT was consistent with his quest for a stable world order. He had never believed that American nuclear superiority over the Soviet Union would be helpful. As he had written in *Nuclear Weapons and Foreign Policy:*

> It is no longer possible to speak of military superiority in the abstract. What does "being ahead" in the nuclear race mean if each side can already destroy the other's national substance?

In his judgment, a rough equilibrium in nuclear arsenals was most desirable. Superiority would be destabilizing and exact parity might be impossible to attain because of the differences in American and Soviet weapons systems. The term he preferred was "sufficiency." Nixon, who in earlier years, had been an ardent advocate of American superiority, now echoed Kissinger's opinion. "I think *sufficiency* is a better term", the President declared shortly after he took office, "than either *superiority* or *parity.*"

The American and Soviet negotiators both knew from the start that it would probably be hopeless to aim for actual physical disarmament. There was simply not enough trust or good faith between them to justify such an ambitious goal. Thus, Kissinger's more modest objective of stabilizing the existing balance of terror was preferred by both sides as more realistically feasible. Kissinger assumed, and the Russians agreed, that the balance would have to be stabilized with each side retaining invulnerable retaliatory power. This meant that neither side—even if it struck first—could destroy the other's ability to strike back. The logic of Kissinger's position was the somewhat Machiavellian assumption that the safety of weapons would increase the safety of people. If each side knew that no blow, however massive, could destroy the other's capacity to return the blow, stability would prevail. Mutual deterrence, therefore, rested on the awareness by each side of the other's retaliatory—or second-strike—capacity. The common recognition of this basic premise became the point of departure for the SALT negotiations.

The talks focussed on weapons that approached the outer limits of man's propensity for self-destruction. Both sides had offensive weapons of such stupendous destructive power that the Hiroshima bomb virtually paled into insignificance. These intercontinental ballistic missiles (ICBM) could be launched from a base on land or sea and guided with a fair degree of accuracy to an enemy target an entire continent away. As if this were not enough, the United States had developed a new technology whereby each missile was able to release individual warheads at varying times and angles. Thus, each individual missile could be assigned multiple targets. For a while, this multiple independent re-entry vehicle (MIRV) was regarded as the ultimate weapon against which no defense was possible. It seemed like the Hydra-headed monster of Greek mythology come back to haunt mankind in modern form.

By 1969, however, both the Soviet Union and the United States were experimenting with a possible defense against the MIRV—an anti-ballistic missile (ABM)—that would function like a bullet aimed to shoot down another bullet. Each side believed that the perfection of an ABM system would give it a decisive edge in the power balance since it could then risk a first-strike against the enemy without having to fear the consequences of retaliation. Needless to say, the cost of an effective ABM system was prohibitive and its dependability was considered far from certain. Nevertheless, by 1969, both superpowers were already spending billions of dollars on the research and development of the ABM.

When the SALT talks opened in the fall of 1969, the Soviet Union had ICBMs with bigger "throw-weight", or, as Pentagon jargon put it, "more bang for a buck." The American ICBMs, however, were purported to have greater accuracy. Besides, the United States had "MIRV'd" a considerable number of its ICBMs, and was also working on the ABM. The Soviet Union was striving feverishly to catch up with the United States in MIRV technology.

Kissinger perceived MIRV and ABM as two sides of a single coin, each justifying the existence of the other. He believed that, if the nuclear balance was truly to be stabilized, there would have to be a simultaneous agreement on both offensive and defensive missiles. One without the other was unacceptable to him.

Kissinger's approach to SALT was quite imaginative. Rather than tie himself down to a specific proposal or even to a number of proposals, he was prepared to accept, as a basis for negotiations, any proposal put forward by the Russians, *provided* it would ultimately yield a balance that was roughly even. It did not matter to him whether an agreement would permit a hundred or a thousand missile launchers; his goal was symmetry. Nor did he care whether an ABM would be limited to the defense of only a single city or of ten; equilibrium was what counted. This emphasis on flexibility saved much valuable time since it avoided bickering over specific proposals advanced by one side or the other. Kissinger's flexibility, however, never extended to the principle of equilibrium itself. He believed that any nuclear imbalance would be a threat to the stable world order that he was pursuing. "Flexibility", as he had written long ago," (was) a virtue only in the purposeful."

Despite Kissinger's profound knowledge of the subject and extraordinary negotiating skill, the initial phase of the SALT process of achieving equilibrium was a long and arduous one. SALT I, as it was later designated, went through eight stages (SALT 1 to SALT 8) and lasted almost three years. John Newhouse, in his authoritative study of SALT, *Cold Dawn,* described the process as "probably the most fascinating episodic negotiation since the Congress of Vienna."

SALT 1 held in Helsinki in November 1969, was exploratory, without any formal proposals submitted by either side. SALT 2, held in Vienna from April to August 1970, got down to specifics. The two superpowers agreed in principle on the terms of a defensive missile treaty that would have limited each side to one hundred missiles each around Moscow and Washington. But several months later, Kissinger, under heavy Congressional pressure, had to back away and advance a new proposal which would have given the United States

a 4–1 advantage. This was angrily rejected by the USSR, and it took
a few more months before the original two-site 200 missile compromise was reaffirmed. SALT 3, held in late 1970, broke up in disagreement over offensive arms. SALT 4, held in Vienna from March to
May 1971 could not reach agreement on a linkage between offensive
and defensive weapons. The Soviets did not want to place a limitation
on offensive missiles since they were behind the United States in
accuracy of targeting. When Kissinger, however, visited Peking in
July 1971, the Russian negotiators suddenly became more tractable.
Triangular diplomacy was paying dividends. Fearful of the American
rapprochement with China, the Soviet Union was willing to make
concessions on an ABM freeze. These concessions were reflected in
SALT 5, held from July to September 1971 in Helsinki. SALT 6, in
late 1971 and early 1972, produced the outlines of an ABM treaty
and SALT 7, the last round before the Moscow Summit, led to the
inclusion of submarine-based missiles in the final accord, reached in
Moscow in May 1972.

Kissinger was clearly in command of the negotiating process
though he delegated many of its technical aspects to a group of
specialists headed by Gerard C. Smith, an official with extensive
experience in the field of arms control. At crucial moments however,
when deadlock threatened, Kissinger would move the negotiations
forward, usually by persuading the President to make numerical
concessions without impairing the objective overall balance. For example, he permitted the Russians to keep a larger number of missile
launchers because he knew that the United States had more individual warheads.

Finally, on May 26, 1972 in Moscow, Nixon and Brezhnev signed
two historic arms control documents which signified the end of the
first phase of SALT. What was achieved that day was that the United
States and the Soviet Union renounced the defense of most of their
territory and people against the other's nuclear weapons. This was the
historic essence of SALT I.

The first document was an ABM Treaty of unlimited duration

which placed limits on the growth of Soviet and American strategic nuclear arsenals. The treaty established a ceiling of 200 launchers for each side's defensive missile system and committed both sides not to build nationwide anti-missile defenses. Each country was limited to two ABM sites, one for the national capital and the other to protect one field of ICBMs. Each such site would consist of one hundred ABMs. The United States already had a protected ICBM field in North Dakota and thus, under the terms of the treaty, could add an ABM site around Washington. The Soviet Union already had an ABM site for the defense of Moscow and thus was permitted to add an ABM site to protect an ICBM field. At the time of the agreement, the Soviet Union had a total of 2,328 missiles: 1,618 land-based ICBMs and 710 on submarines. The United States had a total of 1,710 missiles: 1,054 land-based ICBMs and 656 on submarines.

The second document was an interim agreement limiting ICBMs to those under construction or deployed at the time of the signing of the agreement. Kissinger and Soviet Foreign Minister Gromyko had held a number of nocturnal meetings in order to define what was meant by "under construction." They finally managed to agree that a missile was deemed to be "under construction" after its parts had been riveted to the hull. This meant the retention of 1,618 ICBMs for the Soviet Union, and 1,054 for the United States. The agreement also froze the construction of submarine-launched ballistic missiles on all submarines at existing levels—656 for the United States and 710 for the Soviet Union. However, each side could build additional submarine missiles if an equal number of older land-based ICBMs or older submarine missile launchers were dismantled. This "trade-in" provision had been a major stumbling block because the Soviet and American nuclear arsenals were so asymmetrical. How many old missiles were worth one new missile? Once again, Kissinger recommended a numerical concession to Nixon which finally broke the deadlock.

SALT I placed no limitations whatsoever on the qualitative improvement of offensive or defensive missiles, nor were ceilings imposed on the number of warheads that could be carried by offensive missiles or on strategic bombers permitted to each side. Modernization of missiles, including the emplacement of new missiles in new silos, was permitted. Both sides pledged "not to interfere with the national technical means of verification of the other party," and each side retained the right to withdraw from either agreement if it felt that its supreme national interest was in jeopardy.

SALT I thus managed to freeze a rough balance into the nuclear arsenals of the two superpowers. There remained "missile gaps," of course, in specific weapons. The United States, for example, retained the lead in MIRV technology while the Soviet Union possessed a larger quantity of missile launchers. Nevertheless, the overall effect was the achievment of a rough equilibrium, Kissinger's main objective in the first place.

Kissinger's skill and flexibility were indispensable qualities in bringing SALT I to a successful conclusion. But fortunately for him, he could be flexible without endangering his goal of overall stability. The higher degree of accuracy of the American missiles and the generally more advanced development of American MIRV technology made it possible to concede an advantage in overall missile numbers to the Russians. It is most unlikely that the Soviet Union would have agreed to SALT I without this numerical advantage. They pursued it with single-minded tenacity. It provided an illusion of superiority for the hard-line members of the Soviet Politburo who had challenged Brezhnev's commitment to détente with the United States.

The heavy-handed approach of the Soviet leaders stood in striking contrast to Kissinger's flexibility and nimble sense of humor. Brezhnev told Nixon and Kissinger repeatedly that "the terrible things" the Western press had said about him simply were not true. He had shaved down his bushy eyebrows for the Moscow summit and wanted to be reassured by Kissinger that he did not look brutal. He also seemed to be quite eager to be accepted as a fellow-Westerner. "For a European mind like mine," he said to Kissinger, "the Chinese are impossible to understand." The Kalb brothers report an amusing exchange between Kissinger and Podgorny at the Moscow airport after SALT I had been signed. A Soviet plane that was to take Nixon and Kissinger to Kiev simply would not start. Kissinger, eager to ease Podgorny's embarrassment, asked the Soviet president if he had ever heard of the "Law of the Wickedness of Objects." "No," Podgorny answered, looking puzzled. "Well," Kissinger explained, "if you drop a piece of buttered bread on a new carpet, the chances of its falling with the buttered side down are in direct relationship to the cost of the carpet." Podgorny's face looked vacant; he did not get the joke. Kissinger decided he would provide another example of his "law." "If you drop a coin on the floor," he said, "the chances of it rolling away from you rather than toward you, are in direct relationship to the value of the coin." Podgorny still looked blank. Finally, he said: "Whenever I drop coins, they roll toward me." Kissinger who had had C students before briskly changed the subject. On one occasion, however, during one of the all-night meetings between Kissinger and Gromyko, the Soviet foreign minister stole a march on Kissinger. Teasing Gromyko, Kissinger wanted to know whether he should speak closer to an apple or to an orange in a bowl of fruit, implying that one of them probably contained a miniature microphone. Gromyko, glancing at the ceiling indicated a sculpture of a buxom woman. He pointed to one of her breasts. "I believe it is in there," he said.

Kissinger was ecstatic about the success of SALT I. He thought of it as a great historic step toward a saner world. To his delight, less than a week after the Moscow summit had ended, the United States, together with the Soviet Union, Britain, and France, signed the final protocol of an agreement on the status of Berlin. In addition, the final instruments of a peace treaty between West Germany and the Soviet Union were exchanged. It seemed that the German problem, for so long at the center of the cold war, had finally yielded to a rational solution.

Détente was sinking roots at last. In the summer of 1973, the two Germanies were admitted as separate sovereign states to the United Nations. In June 1973, a second Nixon–Brezhnev summit was arranged by Kissinger, this time in Washington. On that occasion the two leaders agreed to continue negotiations on the limitation of strategic offensive arms. They also reached an accord on the avoidance of nuclear conflict with each other or with a third nation, pledging restraint on the use of force or the threat of force and agreeing to consult with one another if potentially dangerous situations should arise. Nixon visited Moscow once more in July 1974, only one month before his resignation, but by then his position had been eroded too much by Watergate to permit any further substantive progress.

SALT I had placed no restrictions of any kind on the qualitative improvement of missiles. During 1973, the Soviet Union made rapid strides in the evolution of MIRV technology, and threatened to catch up with the United States. As a result, Kissinger began to feel that it was a matter of great urgency for the United States to reach a second SALT accord with the Soviet Union which would include offensive weapons. He and Secretary of Defense James R. Schlesinger, however, developed profound differences over the most effective way in which this all-important negotiation should be approached.

Schlesinger favored either a dramatic mutual reduction in offensive missiles, or, if the Russians did not agree, and all-out arms race. Kissinger maintained that the Soviets would not agree to drastic cutbacks since they were still behind the United States. Hence, the Schlesinger proposal would result in an unchecked arms race which the United States would be unable to win. Kissinger thus argued for an agreement which would establish an equilibrium at high force levels, to be followed by step-by-step reductions over a period of time. The Joint Chiefs of Staff agreed with Kissinger since high force levels would permit them to complete their missile modernization programs. They also contended that Schlesinger's alternative of an allout arms race was not politically feasible since Congress would be reluctant to appropriate the necessary funds.

When President Gerald Ford met with Leonid Brezhnev on the Soviet Pacific coast in Vladivostok in October 1974, in order to discuss the possibilities of a SALT II agreement on offensive missiles, he was accompanied by Secretary of State Kissinger as his main adviser. Once again, the bargaining was tough. Kissinger, after a marathon negotiating session with the Soviet leader, got Brezhnev to drop his demand for numerical superiority. In exchange, Kissinger agreed to a higher ceiling for all kinds of missiles for both countries. This overall ceiling was set at 2,400 missiles for each side with 1,320 of these permitted to be MIRV'd. No restrictions were set on further qualitative improvements such as missile flight tests to increase accuracy or on the development of land-mobile and air-mobile intercontinental ballistic missiles. Nor were any restrictions placed on the development of cruise missiles launched from submarines.

Ford and Brezhnev did not sign a final accord, but reached agreement only in principle. Kissinger, however, expressed the hope that SALT II, once signed, would "put a cap on the arms race" for ten years "between 1975 and 1985." "In terms of permanent achievements, "Kissinger said in December 1974, "I would rank the outline for SALT II near the top."

Actually, Vladivostok was a rather modest achievement. The "cap" on the arms race did not signify a reduction of existing weapons stockpiles, but merely a quantitative limitation on the development of further weapons. The United States would have fairly good assurances of the maximum number of Soviet missiles over the next decade. On the crucial matter of verification, however, a major asymmetry prevailed. Since the United States was an open society with weapons systems subject to constant public scrutiny from their research and development phase to their actual deployment, the Soviet Union could have a high degree of confidence in American compliance with any limitation agreement. This was, of course, not equally true of American faith in Soviet honesty. The verification problems was now particularly crucial since it was important to know, under the Vladivostok accord, whether a missile was MIRV'd or not.

The verification issue began to haunt Kissinger in 1975 and placed in serious question further progress toward SALT II. Admiral Elmo R. Zumwalt, retired chief of naval operations, declared in December 1975 that the Soviet Union had committed "gross violations" of the SALT I accord of 1972 and that Kissinger had not properly informed President Ford. He charged that the Soviets were constructing launch silos for additional missiles and thus were surreptitiously up-grading their ABM defensive potential. He also accused the Soviets of converting "light" ABM missiles into "heavy" ones and thus violating the spirit of SALT I. Kissinger heatedly denied the charges and was supported in his defense by the Central Intelligence Agency. By this time, however, the ire of the Soviets was aroused. *Pravda* not only denied any violations of the 1972 accord, but in turn voiced serious doubts about American compliance. It now blamed the United States for the delay in reaching a final SALT II agreement which Brezhnev had hoped, would be sealed by the time the 25th Communist Party Congress was to convene in February 1976.

Progress toward SALT II was also stalled over two new weapons which the United States and the Soviet Union wanted to add to their respective arsenals. The Pentagon had developed a "cruise missile" which was a long-range, jet-propelled, extremely accurate guided nuclear bomb that could be launched from a bomber, a ship, or a submarine. Pentagon spokesmen declared that since the cruise missile traveled through the atmosphere, it should not be included in the SALT II ceiling of 2,400 ICBMs which travelled through space. The Soviet Union insisted that the "cruise missile" be included in the ceiling. At the same time, the Soviets had developed a new "Backfire" bomber which, they declared, should be excluded from SALT II because of its limited range. The Pentagon, insisting that air-to-air refueling could enable it to reach the United States and return, demanded its inclusion in the ceiling.

Kissinger, convinced that "ninety percent of SALT II had been completed" and that an agreement was essential in order to maintain the momentum of détente, clashed more and more with Schlesinger. The defense secretary, in turn, accused Kissinger of making disadvantageous agreements with the Soviets in order to preserve a dubious illusion of détente. While Ford's dismissal of Schlesinger in late 1975 left Kissinger in primary control of foreign policy, the position of Assistant for National Security Affairs was taken away from him. Thus, by early 1976, the future of SALT II was very much in doubt. The allegations of cheating by the Soviet Union, the dispute over the inclusion of newly developed weapons in the overall ceiling and a deepening suspicion of Soviet behavior in Angola and in the Middle East made Kissinger's position on SALT II extremely vulnerable. It seemed that despite the breakthrough on SALT I, the safety of the superpowers still depended, first and foremost, on their capacity for mutually assured destruction. SALT had made a dent into the balance of terror, but it was little more than a beginning.

In May 1976, the two superpowers agreed on a treaty that limited the size of underground nuclear explosions set off for peaceful purposes and, for the first time, provided for on-site inspection of compliance. While this treaty bore no direct relationship to SALT, it helped to keep alive the momentum of détente.

As we have seen, Kissinger conceived of détente as a relaxation of tensions along a broad front. It was not to be judged piece by piece; a stable international order would emerge from the web of mutual involvements being spun as part of an indivisible process.

Trade was to be an element of the fabric of détente from the very beginning. Kissinger was not so naive as to believe that trade *per se* with the Soviet Union would forge the bonds of peace. As a historian he knew that the nations that had gone to war against each other in

Europe had also been the closest trading partners. History provided little assurance that trade ensured peace—Russia's history least of all. But Kissinger believed that the Soviets needed American trade, technology, and credits and hence he hoped that, once having become dependent on these capitalist benefits, the Soviet Union might "become more conscious of what it would lose by a return to confrontation." Besides, trade was a vital element in Kissinger's linkage concept.

Kissinger's assessment of the Soviet position in 1972 was essentially correct. Not only had American overtures to China made the Soviet leadership eager to quicken the momentum of détente, but serious shortages in vital sectors of the Soviet economy had made a rapid trade expansion with the United States highly desirable. Moreover, the Soviet leaders faced immense problems in developing the vast resources of oil, gas and minerals located in Siberia. For this, American capital and technology were needed. And finally, in times of poor domestic harvests, the Soviets wanted access to the American grain market.

On the American side, the timing, too, was favorable. Nixon and Kissinger had benefited from some Soviet help on the Indochina problem and anticipated future favors in this vital area of concern. In February 1972, the Soviet Union informed the United States that it was willing to reopen negotiations, suspended for twelve years, on the repayment of the outstanding Soviet World War II lend-lease debt.

This Soviet initiative triggered a flurry of activity, making 1972 a record year for Soviet-American agreements. In July, an accord was signed which made it possible for the Soviet Union to purchase $750 million of American grain. In August, it was announced that the Soviet purchases would exceed the $1 billion mark. It was also revealed that the Occidental Petroleum Company had concluded a $3 billion arrangement for the exploitation of Siberian natural gas. In October, the negotiations on the lend-lease issue were successfully concluded with a Soviet agreement to pay $722 million over twenty-nine years to settle the outstanding debt.

Progress, however, was not destined to be smooth. A comprehensive trade agreement which Nixon and Kissinger signed with the Soviet Union in October 1972, ignited a debate in the United States on the entire issue of détente. In the first place, the Soviet grain purchases contributed to a dramatic rise in food prices in the United States, and angry American consumers were complaining bitterly about the "great Russian grain robbery." Second, and more important, the trade agreement of October 1972 had granted the Soviets most-favored nations status. This meant, in effect, the restoration of normal trade relations which had been suspended at the height of the cold war in 1951

Senator Henry M. Jackson led the forces that were skeptical about détente in general and were reluctant to grant most favored nations status to the Soviet Union without getting something in return. What Jackson sought, however, was not a concession in the economic field but a commitment from the Soviet government on freedom of Jewish emigration from the Soviet Union. He proposed an amendment to the Soviet trade bill requiring such a commitment. This demand touched off a bitter and protracted conflict between Kissinger and Jackson over the merits of détente, a conflict that was exacerbated greatly by the outbreak of war in the Middle East in October 1973.

Jackson and his followers attacked Kissinger's concept of détente as a kind of one-way street in favor of the Soviet Union. The Russians, he argued, were always getting the better bargain. "We sell the Soviets cars," exclaimed a critic of détente in a Detroit plant, "and they sell us parking places in Siberia." In addition, the critics maintained, the Soviet Union had violated the spirit of détente by encouraging the Arab assault on Israel in October 1973. Instead of consulting with the United States and looking for ways to stave off the conflict, the Soviet leadership had aided and abetted Egypt and

Syria in mounting their surprise attack. It was plain that the Russians were reaping the benefits of détente, but not living up to their obligations. Hence, the United States should insist on a major concession: the lifting of restrictions on Jewish emigration from Russia to Israel.

Kissinger opposed the Jackson amendment to the Soviet trade bill strenuously, not because he approved of Soviet domestic policies, but because he thought that the weapon was inappropriate and counterproductive. Its use denied the possibility, in his opinion, of normal commercial contacts so long as certain basic ideological conflicts remained unresolved. As he put it in 1974:

> Thus, the major impact of the continued denial of most-favored nations status to the Soviet Union would be political, not economic. Most-favored nations status was withdrawn in 1951, largely as a political act. Our unwillingness to remove this discrimination now would call into question our intent to move toward an improved relationship.

In short, if the United States rattled the skeletons in the Soviets' political closet, the Russians would probably respond in kind. Once the skeletons emerged from both closets, détente would be endangered. And as Kissinger never tired of pointing out, the overriding goal of détente was the avoidance of nuclear war. Besides, the Soviet attitude toward the leading capitalist nation had changed. Khrushchev had come to the United States in 1959, saying "we shall bury you." Yet when Brezhnev visited the United States in 1973, not a word was said about the burial of capitalism. Instead, Brezhnev's approach was more along the lines of "We want to borrow from you." Trade, in Kissinger's opinion, could serve to promote political détente only if trade was in fact kept politically neutral.

The Kissinger–Jackson feud ended inconclusively. Kissinger had to settle for a trade act that required periodic review of freedom of Jewish emigration from Russia by Congress on whose approval the continued Soviet most-favored nations status would depend. At the same time, Congress placed a limit of $300 million on government loans and guarantees which could be granted to the USSR without specific Congressional approval. The result of these steps was an angry Soviet rejection, in January 1975, of the entire trade agreement on the grounds that such interference in Soviet internal affairs could not be tolerated. Nevertheless, Soviet-American trade continued, though at somewhat more modest levels.

In the summer of 1975, the Russians again entered the American market to buy large quantities of grain. A deal was concluded under which, beginning in October 1976, the Soviets agreed to buy a minimum of six million and a maximum of eight million metric tons of wheat and corn each year for five years. Kissinger tried to introduce linkage into this business partnership. Specifically, he attempted to link grain with oil, and thus to drive a wedge between the Soviet Union and the Arabs. The Soviet Union, however, agreed to sell the United States only a small amount of oil at prices slightly below those charged by the oil cartel.

The trade relations between the United States and the Soviet Union had made Kissinger's approach to détente a subject of intense domestic controversy. Détente was no longer discussed solely by strategists of power politics; it now affected the daily economic lives of millions of Americans. Farmers wanted greater exports to the Soviet Union, resulting in higher prices for their products; consumers hoped for lower food prices and criticized the Soviet grain purchases; and politicians suddenly had to become sensitized to these cross-currents in American politics. In this debate, Henry Jackson preferred to confront the Soviets bluntly with conditions: concessions on Jewish emigration in return for concessions on trade. Kissinger preferred to deal with the question of Jewish emigration through quiet diplomacy. He pointed out that 35,000 Jews had left the Soviet Union for Israel in 1973 but that the rate of emigration had turned down sharply in 1974 and 1975 because the Soviet Union would not accept such humiliating conditions. In his judgment, it was a serious mistake to try to influence Soviet practice in domestic matters. He thought that it would be far better to try to induce changes in Soviet foreign policy. He did, in fact, attempt to use American grain sales in 1975 as a lever on Soviet foreign policy when he sought Soviet acquiescence to his diplomatic step-by-step initiatives in the Middle East. But he remained convinced that any attempt to change the domestic behavior of the Soviet Union would have a boomerang effect. Linkage, in short, was a concept that was meaningful only in international diplomacy. If misapplied to internal policies, it would set back, rather than advance, the process of détente.

To Henry Kissinger, the pursuit of détente could not be confined to the Soviet-American relationship bilaterally. SALT and trade were important building blocks, but they were not enough. Should the Soviet Union tamper with the overall equilibrium in other parts of the world, stability—Kissinger's prerequisite to peace—would be in jeopardy. Thus, the Soviet-American relationship, in Kissinger's mind, was analogous to the hub of a wheel. Action at the rim would automatically be transmitted to the center. Détente, to Kissinger, was always a global proposition.

Détente was tested quite severely on at least six occasions in different parts of the world. In 1970, the Soviets supported a Syrian drive into Jordan and threatened to upset the balance in the Middle East; at almost the same time, they tried to build a nuclear submarine base at Cienfuegos in Cuba; in the India-Pakistan confrontation over Bangladesh in 1971, the Soviet Union and India were military allies in Indira Gandhi's dismemberment of Pakistan; during the entire Indochina war, the Soviet leadership supplied Hanoi with vital war matériel; during the Arab-Israel conflict of October 1973, the Soviet Union threatened unilateral intervention on the Arab side, which triggered a global military alert on the part of the United States; and in 1975, the Soviet leadership and Castro's Cuba gave considerable support to one of three political groups fighting for control in Portugal's former colony, Angola. Kissinger's responses to these six challenges are well worth examining.

For Kissinger, the Middle East had always been a dual problem. On one level, there was the deep and violent conflict between Israel and her Arab neighbors. By 1970, three wars had been fought and the passage of time had done little to heal the festering wounds. Each side had done things that the other could neither forgive nor forget. Superimposed upon the Arab-Israeli conflict was the ever-present threat of a Soviet-American confrontation, since, over the years, the United States had supported the Israeli cause while the Soviet Union had sided with the Arabs.

Kissinger, on Nixon's orders, had left the Middle East to Rogers and the State Department. Not only was Kissinger deeply involved in Vietnam and the SALT negotiations, but he also did not wish to become a target for Arab extremist anti-semitic propaganda. His Jewish background, while essentially secular in nature, nevertheless gave him a sense of special commitment to Israel's survival. Having lost many relatives in Hitler's concentration camps, he regarded the Jewish state as a place of refuge for survivors of the Nazi holocaust.

In the summer of 1970, Kissinger's sympathy for Israel and his concern for the maintenance of an overall Soviet-American balance coincided, when the Soviet Union, in a dramatic and unexpected move, decided to support a Syrian invasion of Lebanon and Jordan with advisers, airpower, and tanks. Kissinger viewed the Soviet move as a potentially disastrous disruption of global equilibrium. He reasoned that if the Soviet Union succeeded in emplacing radical Arab governments in Lebanon and Jordan, Saudi Arabia's vast oil reserves might be vulnerable to similar encroachments. Israel would then be encircled and might be driven into the sea, with the global balance shifted, perhaps irrevocably, in Russia's favor.

Kissinger concluded that a move should be made without delay to expel the Soviet military presence, especially Soviet combat pilots and combat personnel from the Middle Eastern scene. He recommended to the President that, unless the Syrian tanks were withdrawn from Jordan, Israel should be encouraged to intervene on the side of King Hussein. When Israel's Ambassador Yitzhak Rabin asked Kissinger whether the United States would come to Israel's aid if the Soviet Union escalated its support to Syria, Kissinger prevailed on Nixon to promise such American support. When Israel reported that Syrian tanks were "pouring across the Jordanian border" and that Hussein was fighting for his life, Kissinger climbed up another step on the escalation ladder. Israeli forces would move against Syria in Jordan, he warned, unless the Syrians withdrew; if Egyptian or Soviet forces then moved against Israel, the United States would intervene against *both*. "You and your client started the war," Kissinger curtly told Soviet Ambassador Dobrynin, "and you now have to end it."

The Jordanian crisis of 1970 was Kissinger's first opportunity to manipulate America's nuclear arsenal in a major showdown. Eyewitnesses relate that he thoroughly enjoyed the experience. "Henry adores power, absolutely adores it; to him, diplomacy is nothing without it," exclaimed one Pentagon official. Apparently, the World War II sergeant had no difficulty in assuming the responsibility of generals and admirals during the crisis. He perceived the Soviet move as a direct challenge to stability and thus was determined to resist it at considerable risk.

Kissinger's crisis management was successful. The Soviet Union called off the Syrian invasion. Kissinger, though pleased, decided to warn the Soviet leadership not to strain the fragile fabric of the developing détente. "Events in the Middle East and in other parts of the world," he declared on September 16, 1970, "have raised questions of whether Soviet leaders as of now are prepared . . . to forego tactical advantages they can derive from certain situations for the sake of the larger interest of peace." It seemed that the Soviet answer to Kissinger's question was negative because, at that very moment, half a world away, the Soviet Union was constructing a nuclear submarine base on the southern coast of Cuba in clear violation of an understanding reached by President John F. Kennedy and Premier Nikita Khrushchev after the missile crisis of 1962.

It began almost like a replay of the missile crisis. A U-2 spy plane, flying over Cuba in September 1970, photographed a soccer field near the naval base of Cienfuegos. Cubans do not play soccer, but soccer is the Soviet national sport. Further pictures revealed that a Soviet nuclear submarine base was under construction at Cienfuegos. The 1962 agreement between Kennedy and Khrushchev had permitted Soviet defensive military installations. In Kissinger's view, a nuclear base was clearly offensive and would constitute yet another threat to global balance. He recommended to the President that a firm stance should be taken on the matter. Nixon agreed with Kissinger.

Kissinger, unlike Kennedy, decided to use quiet diplomacy. He arranged a private meeting with Dobrynin and informed the Soviet ambassador that the United States was aware that Russia was constructing an offensive base in Cuba. Unless the construction was stopped immediately, Kissinger warned, the new détente would be imperiled. Two weeks later, construction slowed down and soon thereafter stopped completely. Apparently, Brezhnev was not willing to follow in the footsteps of his predecessor whom he had described six years earlier as a "hare-brained schemer." Besides, the prospects of SALT, technology, and trade far outweighed the value of a naval base in Cuba. Thus, once again, Kissinger tested détente by a combination of diplomacy and force, and once again, the combination worked.

In August 1971, one month after Kissinger's trip to China, Prime Minister Indira Gandhi of India signed a twenty-five year friendship treaty with the Soviet Union which had all the earmarks of a military alliance. The pact which, in the words of an Indian parliamentarian, "put some meat into India's vegetarian diet of non-alignment," was intended as a clear warning to Pakistan and as a deterrent against the possibility of Chinese intervention in the escalating conflict between Mrs. Gandhi and Yahya Khan, the President of Pakistan.

Yahya Khan was then engaged in a brutal civil war with the Bengalis of East Pakistan who were separated from West Pakistan by one-thousand miles of hostile Indian territory. He had decided to cancel the results of an election that would have given the presidency of Pakistan to a Bengali, Sheikh Mujibur Rahman. The Easterners had rebelled and the result was a campaign of reprisal against them which was so pitiless that 10 million Bengalis had fled for their lives into neighboring India. Mrs. Ghandhi, weighing whether it was cheaper to feed 10 million starving Moslem refugees or to go to war against Yahya Khan in the hope of dismembering India's traditional enemy, decided on the latter course. On December 1, 1971, she issued an ultimatum in which she demanded that Yahya Khan withdraw all his forces from East Pakistan. Yahya Khan ordered an air strike against India which not only turned out to be a fiasco but gave Mrs. Ghandi the necessary pretext to order the Indian army to march on Dacca, the capital of East Pakistan.

Kissinger had watched the events on the Indian subcontinent with growing concern. He believed that Mrs. Ghandi intended to destroy Pakistan and that, if she succeeded, India and the Soviet Union would dominate the subcontinent completely. Hence, in order to balance the Soviet-Indian alliance, the United States would have to side with Pakistan. Nixon not only agreed but, as the "Anderson Papers", revealed later, Kissinger "got hell from the President every ten minutes for not being tough enough on India." The United States "tilted" toward Pakistan because Kissinger and Nixon believed that Mrs. Ghandi not only intended to detach East Pakistan from the West, but to dismember her old rival altogether. Even though State Department officials, in particular Undersecretary of State Joseph Sisco, disagreed with this analysis, Kissinger's view finally prevailed. He accused India of aggression and warned the Soviet Union that détente might be "jeopardized" if the Soviet-Indian offensive continued. A naval task force of eight ships, led by the nuclear aircraft carrier *Enterprise*, was dispatched to the Bay of Bengal. It was "gunboat diplomacy" in nuclear form. When there was no immediate response from Moscow, Kissinger declared that, unless the Soviet Union began to exercise a restraining influence on India very soon, the plans for the President's trip to Moscow might be changed and "the entire United States-Soviet relationship might well be reexamined."

The Soviet leadership, unwilling to jeopardize the Moscow summit, apparently decided to restrain India. At any rate, the war ended on December 16 with Pakistan split into two separate states. Kissinger claimed that his warning to the Soviet Union had prevented Mrs. Gandhi from dismembering West Pakistan as well. Sisco doubted whether she ever had such plans and many critics now began to accuse Kissinger of siding with a corrupt dictatorship against the world's largest democracy, and ignoring, in the process, the human tragedy of 10 million helpless Bengali refugees who had been the victims of Yahya Khan's brutality. Moreover, the critics pointed out, the Soviet-backed democracy won and the American-supported dictatorship lost, which did not exactly enhance American prestige throughout the world. Kissinger himself was so depressed by this episode that he briefly considered resignation. But he held on to his conviction that his policy of toughness against the Soviet Union had preserved stability on the Indian subcontinent.

An analysis of the Indochina war reveals that the United States tested the limits of détente much more than did the Soviet Union. Nixon and Kissinger decided to mine Haiphong only a few days before they were to visit Moscow in May 1972, and yet Brezhnev chose not to cancel the summit talks. Later that year, the Soviets applied pressure on Hanoi and cut back arms deliveries to their ally. These moves compelled the North Vietnamese leadership to make its first serious concessions to Kissinger in Paris. And even the bombings of Christmas 1972 did little to disrupt détente. In Brezhnev's calculus of power, the fear of China and the hope for arms control agreements, technology, and trade with the United States were overwhelming practical considerations. Détente conferred some very real benefits which the ideological alliance with Hanoi simply could not match. Kissinger's belief that China was the key to Russia, and Russia was the key to an Indochina settlement made sense in 1972 and 1973. Hanoi's final victory in 1975 stemmed more from its own enormous staying power and from Saigon's total military collapse than from Soviet violations of détente. On the whole, the Soviet Union showed remarkable restraint during the final years of the Indochina war.

The record is more mixed if one examines Soviet policy in the Middle East. There is no doubt that the Soviet leadership supplied the arms that made it possible the Egyptian-Syrian surprise attack on Israel in October 1973. Moreover, the Soviets were clearly aware of the impending attack, but chose not to warn the United States. This was clearly in violation of the understanding reached between Nixon and Brezhnev in 1973 in Washington under which the two leaders had pledged to consult with one another if potentially dangerous situations arose. Two weeks later, however, when, with American help, the Israelis had turned the war around and had entrapped 100,000 Egyptian soldiers, Brezhnev threatened the United States with "unilateral steps" in order to prevent an Arab military defeat. In response, Kissinger recommended to the President that a general "alert" of American military forces be announced. Backed up by this show of force, Kissinger resorted to diplomacy. "If the Soviet Union and we can work cooperatively", he said "first, toward establishing a cease-fire, and then toward a durable settlement in the Middle East, then détente will have proved itself." Shortly thereafter, the Soviet Union and the United States agreed on a face-saving formula through the United Nations. Once again, Kissinger had talked the Russians out of a confrontation after having alerted American military forces to prepare for one. And once again, the two superpowers returned from the nuclear brink to the safer terrain of détente.

Kissinger's "step-by-step" approach to a Middle Eastern settlement in 1974 and 1975 which will be examined in a later chapter remained virtually an American monopoly. The two disengagement agreements between Israel and Egypt, and Israel and Syria were triumphs of Kissinger's personal diplomacy. And the Sinai agreement reached by Israel and Egypt in September 1975 was yet another success for Kissinger. The Soviet Union grudgingly acquiesced in Kissinger's diplomatic solo performance. It had little choice because only the United States, by exerting pressure on Israel, was in a position to recover territories for the Arabs, while the Russians could only supply the weapons for another war. Besides, not only was the triangular policy with China still effective, but the lures of SALT, technology, and trade still proved too great for Brezhnev to resist.

Thus, for two years, the United States was the peacemaker in the Middle East while the Soviet Union was largely confined to the sidelines. And while the quest for peace continued, Kissinger was able to dominate Middle East diplomacy and yet maintain détente with Russia. Only when the "step-by-step" approach ran out of steps and the Palestinian question moved to the center of the stage, in late 1975, did Kissinger's diplomatic monopoly end.

Thus, in the Middle East, détente was strained by both the Soviet Union and the United States. The Soviet Union tested it in times of war, Kissinger through his unilateral diplomacy of peace. On several occasions détente was bruised, but managed to survive, though its critics gained in influence and power, especially in the United States.

The testing of détente was extended to the African continent in 1975 when the Soviet Union backed one of three political factions contending for the control of Angola, which had just gained its independence from Portugal. Calculating that the memory of the Indochina war and Congressional aversion to a new American involvement in a civil war would probably deter the United States from intervention, the Soviet Union supported the Luanda faction in Angola with war matériel and twelve-thousand Cuban combat soldiers.

Although Kissinger's power by that time was severely circumscribed by Congress in virtually every area of foreign policy, he nevertheless attempted, once again, to apply the leverage of linkage. He declared that the conclusion of a SALT II agreement might be in jeopardy and also added that trade concessions that he had recommended for the Soviet Union might founder on opposition in the Congress. Once again, he was quite explicit about the need to preserve détente, stating that there was "no question that the overall relationship (would) suffer if we do not find an adequate solution to the Angola problem."

This time, however, the Soviet leadership was no longer quite so eager for trade with the United States since it had been able to satisfy many of its needs through purchases in Japan and Western Europe. Besides, Gerald Ford who faced an election in 1976, needed an arms pact at least as much as Brezhnev. Most important, the Russians could readily see that Kissinger's leverage was limited by congressional opposition. As the Soviet-backed faction edged closer to military victory, Kissinger, in deepening frustration, pleaded with the Congress to match the aid provided by the Soviet Union and Cuba. The Congress refused flatly and Gerald Ford accused the legislative body of "having lost its guts." Finally, in February 1976, the Organization for African Unity (OAU) placed its official approval on the Soviet-backed Luanda faction by recognizing it as the official government of Angola. Once again, détente had undergone a strenuous test as both the Soviet Union and the United States had violated each other's assumptions about its meaning. The Soviet leadership had always regarded the support of "national liberation movements" as permissible within the confines of détente and was therefore somewhat baffled by Kissinger's response. Kissinger, in turn, believing that détente meant the avoidance of such confrontations in peripheral areas, had been ready to back diplomacy with force.

In 1975, the Soviet Union took the initiative in Europe. That summer, thirty years after the end of World War II, the heads of thirty-five nations met in Helsinki, Finland, and signed a declaration that committed them to "broaden and deepen" the process of détente. Specifically, the conference ratified the post-war frontiers in Europe, a goal that had long been sought by the Soviet Union. The signatories also pledged not to resort to force in disputes among themselves and to increase trade and other contacts between East and West. Unofficially, Helsinki ratified the principle of permanent spheres of influence in Europe for the Soviet Union and the United States. Kissinger welcomed the Helsinki accord because it helped to institutionalize the principle of equilibrium in Europe and thus would stabilize détente in the geographic area that had once been the very center of the cold war.

The record of the six occasions on which détente was tested in peripheral areas suggests that the mixture of diplomacy and force worked quite successfully, particularly when combined with linkage. When the Soviet Union tested détente in Jordan and in Cuba in 1970, diplomacy and force were applied in such a way that the Soviet Union was able to withdraw before its prestige had become irrevocably involved. In the Middle East, once again, after the "alert" of October 1973, Kissinger offered a face-saving device through the United Nations. In the Indochina war, the use of linkage resulted in quite extraordinary Soviet restraint; only in Bangladesh and in Angola does the evidence seem negative.

It appears that the critics and supporters of détente alike made claims that are essentially unprovable. It cannot be demonstrated that more pressure would have produced even greater concessions from the Soviet Union; nor can it be demonstrated that Soviet actions would have been even more aggressive without the restraining fabric of détente. On balance, however, it seems clear that, despite periodic setbacks, no significant segment of American opinion desired a return to the cold war policies of the pre-détente era. When Gerald Ford, in March 1976, expunged the word "détente" from his vocabulary and substituted "peace through strength," this did not signify an actual change in policy. The same can presumably be said of Soviet opinion. When one considers the fact that not too long ago, Soviet Russia and the United States almost went to war over missiles in Cuba, the détente achievement seems enormous. War between the superpowers seemed a remote possibility in the 1970s, but was not at all unlikely in the 1950s and 1960s. Objective changes in the global power constellation, in particular the rise of China, provided the initial impetus to détente. But it was equally important that the leading personalities on both sides had the intelligence and courage to seize the opportunity. Such moments are rare indeed in history. They seldom offer themselves a second time. And in their recognition, as Kissinger himself had written, lies the secret of historic statesmanship.

Kissinger's conception of détente was a synthesis of all that he had learned from his study of nineteenth century history. *Si vis pacem, para bellum*—"If you wish peace, prepare for war," was the credo that had been emblazoned on the ministry of war of imperial Austria. Kissinger's insight lay in his ability do translate that motto into the setting of the nuclear age. The old Roman maxim no longer quite sufficed; a whole network of linkages and agreements had to be created in order to gain leverage over the Soviet Union. But this, too, was not all that different from what Metternich and Castlereagh had done. They, also, had attempted to exercise control over the revolutionary power through manipulations and alliances. But in their time, no mistake was irretrievable. No outcome was completely fatal. There was no sense of ultimate catastrophe. It is this basic difference that haunted the conscience of Henry Kissinger. It is the reason why he believed with absolute conviction that there was no meaningful alternative to détente.

The credo of the cold war years had been updated since the times of imperial Austria. For the generation of the cold war, the appropriate motto might have been *Si vis vitam, para mortem*—"If you wish to live, prepare for death." For Henry Kissinger, this simply was not good enough.

10

China: Toward Reality

"I felt like Marco Polo."

Henry Kissinger
July 1971

It is a melancholy truth that men do not easily abandon misperceptions through rational analysis, but primarily through trauma and catastrophe. Most national leaders will not examine their prejudices and stereotypes until they are shaken or shattered into doing so. Man, in short, learns and grows largely through suffering.

When Mao Tse-tung took control of China in 1949, there were few objective quarrels between him and the United States that could not have been resolved through a policy of compromise. There was no defense treaty with Chiang Kai-shek, there were no American ships in the Taiwan straits, there was no Korean conflict yet and the Indochina war was years away. But Americans and Chinese had memories of one another that prevented compromise. More than a century of tragic history made reconciliation difficult. The Chinese remembered America's policy of the "Open Door" as a pretext for plunder and exploitation. They had never opened the door, they thought, but rather the Americans had crashed it in. Americans in turn, believed that they had played the role of China's benevolent guardian, and now China had been lost, as if China had been America's to lose. Both nations thus felt utterly betrayed and regarded one another as deadly enemies. It would take more than twenty years of hate, two bitter wars on Asian soil, and suffering on a horrendous scale, before China and America were to make fact, not fear, the basis of their policy.

A word should be said about those decades of frozen hate, before the great turning of 1971. For an entire generation, two great nations perceived each other through dark screens that often produced caricatures out of realities. They learned to fashion images of one another that were based on their deepest fears. To both Chinese and Americans, during the 1950s and 1960s, "the other side" was not quite human. There were times when these fears almost called forth a reality as terrible as the most anguished nightmare.

The Sino-American relationship during the 1950s and 1960s consisted of four such misperceptions: first, each nation's self-image; second, each nation's perception of the character of its adversary; third, each nation's perception of its adversary's intentions; and finally, each nation's perception of the other's power and capabilities.

In the matter of respective self-images, it is important to recall that both nations had quasi-religious, almost crusading, views of themselves. Each side's view of the other's character came close to Cotton Mather's conception of the Devil. The image projected on both sides was that of an opponent with whom there can, and must be, no compromise and whose very touch brought contamination and defilement. When Secretary of State John Foster Dulles, for example, encountered China's Premier Chou En-lai in Geneva in 1954, he refused to shake hands with the Chinese statesman. Little wonder that these images created an atmosphere of conflict that tended to exacerbate specific incidents. If you believe that the "other side" is your enemy long enough and hard enough, you will eventually be right.

Perceptions of each other's intentions always conjured up the worst. Thus, the Chinese leadership came close to believing in 1950 that General Douglas MacArthur was planning a full-scale invasion of China. The Chinese intervention in Korea and the bloody war that followed, were perceived in China, at least in part, as a defensive action. Two years later, the Americans expected a Chinese intervention, on the Vietminh side, against France in Indochina. This expectation was so powerful that it defied all evidence to the contrary. Neither the fact that the anticipated invasion failed to materialize nor the lack of evidence that it was actually planned lessened American apprehensions. Instead, the very strength of the expectation proved its own substantiation. Time and time again, quite unfounded rumors were accepted as proof of impending intervention. The result was a recurrent pattern of false alarms. Thus, the American support of France in the Indochina war in the early 1950s was at least partially intended to counter an impending Chinese military intervention.

Finally, misperceptions of the power of "the other side" courted disaster. General MacArthur, for example, had a curious contempt for the Chinese soldier. He believed that China neither would nor could intervene in the Korean war. This lack of respect was to cost him dearly. In late 1950, the Chinese attacked in overwhelming force and turned the American advance to the Yalu River into a bloody rout.

The Chinese and American peoples were not encouraged to learn new facts about each other. Instead, they had to offer up their bod.s in defense of shadows. For two long decades, there was little creative statesmanship. Shop-worn slogans dominated policy. For more than twenty years, the history of China and America was written in ignorance, tragedy, and blood.

As a graduate student at Harvard, Kissinger's attention was riveted on Europe and the Soviet Union. His knowledge of China was minimal and his interest virtually non-existent. When Senator Joseph McCarthy descended upon Harvard and attacked Professor John K. Fairbank, the dean of America's China scholars, most of us were shocked. In our discussions, many of us thought that there must be two sides to the conflict between China and America. Kissinger was not receptive. He regarded China as the classic "revolutionary" state of the atomic era. Even after he left Harvard, he continued to retain this attitude. His references to China in *Nuclear Weapons and Foreign Policy* were limited to Mao Tse-tung's strategic thought. He was preoccupied with "the threat of the Sino-Soviet bloc" and his reasoning followed the classic pattern of cold war analysis.

When the rift between China and the Soviet Union erupted into the open in 1959, Kissinger's sympathies were with the Soviet Union. He believed that the Russians might be "co-opted" into a stable global order, but he feared that the Chinese were unregenerate revolutionaries. When China exploded her first atomic bomb in 1964, Kissinger was deeply troubled. And when two years later, the Red Guards of the Cultural Revolution rampaged through the countryside and closed down universities in order to "purify the revolution," Kissinger's worst fears seemed to come true. He believed that China was bent upon aggression on a world scale. His thinking about China before 1967 exhibited none of the feeling for nuance and history that was so striking about his analyses of Russia and Europe. It is probably accurate to say, that Kissinger's approach to China, before he helped Rockefeller in the 1968 campaign, was more or less in harmony with the conventional wisdom of the time.

Kissinger was Nixon's teacher on how to build détente with the Soviet Union. In contemplating an American opening to China, however, both men reached similar conclusions at approximately the same time. Nixon, in October 1967, had written in *Foreign Affairs*, that "any American policy must come urgently to grips with the reality of China. There is no place on this small planet for a billion of its potentially most able people to live in angry isolation." He also was the first to see the possibility of leveraging the widening rift between China and the Soviet Union to the advantage of the United States. One week after Inauguration Day, Nixon sent a memo to his

new Assistant for National Security Affairs asking him to explore
discreetly the possibility of rapprochement with China. Kissinger
promised to do so, though he believed that it might take some time
to build a bridge to China. In the meantime, most of his energies
were devoted to two immediate problems: SALT and the war in
Indochina.

In March 1969, shooting broke out along the Ussuri River near the
Chinese–Soviet border. Tensions over disputed territory that had
been escalating for some time, finally erupted into open conflict. The
"fraternal unity" of the two colossi of the Communist world now lay
shattered in ruins.

Kissinger's view of China was altered fundamentally by these
events. He called upon his old colleagues from Harvard as well as
other China scholars to help him understand. Suddenly, it became
clear to him that there were two sides to the Sino-Soviet conflict. He
had always thought that China was more likely to attack Russia than
Russia was to attack China. Now he learned that the Soviet Union
had developed a formidable military buildup on the Chinese border,
complete with missiles, tanks and air power. In view of Brezhnev's
invasion of Czechoslovakia less than a year before, it was not impossible that the Soviet leader might be planning a surprise attack against
the Chinese nuclear installations.

Kissinger now believed that China's fear of Russia might be greater
than her fear of the United States, and that China, therefore, might
respond to an American gesture of reconciliation. It was not until
1967 that Kissinger had considered such an opening a realistic possibility. But now that he was sure, he quickly made it a centerpiece of
his entire policy. Rapprochement with China would give the United
States enormous leverage over the Soviet Union. So long as the
hostility between China and the Soviet Union prevailed, Kissinger
could thrust the United States into the position of the balancer.
America, in short, would then be wooed by both the leading powers
of the Communist world. The possibilities of this new constellation

suddenly seemed limitless. Kissinger made up his mind to rediscover China for himself.

Kissinger decided, as a first initiative, to resuscitate the Sino-American talks in Warsaw which had been suspended since January 1968. The talks had never been productive, but instead had often degenerated into mutual insults. Kissinger cabled the American ambassador in Warsaw, Walter J. Stoessel, Jr., instructing him to contact the top Chinese official in the Polish capital and to propose a resumption of the Warsaw talks. Stoessel, who was a Rogers man, chose to ignore Kissinger's instructions twice, but finally did meet with the Chinese chargé d'affaires in December 1969. In January 1970, the talks resumed. The atmosphere was businesslike and even cordial, far from the "stupefying boredom", as Kissinger characterized them, of earlier years. At a second meeting in February, the Chinese announced that the American delegation would be welcome in Peking. Kissinger considered the proposal seriously, but his new interest in China was deflected temporarily by the invasion of Cambodia. A third Warsaw meeting, scheduled for May, was cancelled by the Chinese three weeks after the invasion had begun on April 30.

Nixon was now concerned that Mao Tse-tung and Chou En-lai might interpret the Cambodian "incursion" as a hostile action aimed at China. Accordingly, he reassured the Chinese leadership privately through "third party" channels that the United States had not changed its intentions of leaving Indochina and of improving relations with Peking. A number of minor unilateral concessions had already been approved by Nixon. Scholars, journalists, and students were now permitted to travel to China; naval patrols in the Taiwan Straits had been suspended; and a one-hundred dollar ceiling on the purchase of Chinese goods by Americans had been rescinded. The president emphasized that these concessions would be allowed to stand and that others were under active consideration.

During the summer of 1970, the power struggle in the Chinese leadership between Premier Chou En-lai and Defense Minister Lin

Piao came to a head. Chou urged moderation in domestic policy and favored rapprochement with the United States. He believed that the Americans were sincere in their intention to withdraw from Asia while the Soviet Union, in his view, was determined to remain in occupation of Chinese territory. Lin Piao regarded the Americans as the greater peril and urged reconciliation with the Soviet Union. Mao Tse-tung leaned toward Chou's more pro-American position and on China's National Day, October 1, 1970, chose as his honored guest in the reviewing stand atop the Gate of Heavenly Peace in Peking, an old American friend, Edgar Snow. Snow had formed a friendship with Mao during the bitter fighting days in the 1930s, when the Chinese Communists were living in the caves of Yenan. The American journalist had been so impressed with their staying power and determination that he had predicted their ultimate victory in *Red Star Over China,* a book destined to become a classic. Now, the two aging men stood side by side once more, a signal to Nixon and Kissinger that China still desired reconciliation.

Kissinger used the occasion of the United Nations' twenty-fifth birthday to convey a confidential message to Mao. He told President Nicolae Ceausescu of Rumania that the United States would be interested in considering talks "at a high level" with the Chinese in Peking. On the occasion of a reception given for Ceausescu at the White House, Nixon delivered a toast to Rumania's good relations with the United States, the Soviet Union, and the People's Republic of China. When Soviet Ambassador Dobrynin asked Kissinger whether Nixon's unprecedented phrasing had any special significance, he received an evasive answer. After all, the Russians too, were referring to China as the People's Republic, Kissinger replied.

Kissinger also informed Yahya Khan, the President of Pakistan, of his new interest in China. During the next few months, Yahya Khan served as Kissinger's confidential courier to Peking. The Pakistani President was received by Mao in November 1970. Kissinger received unsigned notes from Peking at periodic intervals, all handwritten on white paper with blue lines, and each more cordial than the preceding one. Edgar Snow's memoirs revealed that Mao and Chou openly discussed the possibility of a presidential visit to Peking. "Mao would be happy to talk with Nixon," Snow reported, "either as a tourist or as president."

In February 1971, the Indochina war interfered once more with these delicate maneuvers. Nixon had just approved a South Vietnamese invasion of Laos. Since Laos had a common border with China, Mao and Chou became alarmed. For six weeks, no handwritten notes from Peking reached Kissinger. The Chinese leaders instead announced a military alert. MacArthur's drive to the Yalu River twenty years before was still a troubling memory for them. Perhaps another American general might try to escalate the war despite Nixon's good intentions. Nixon decided to reassure the Chinese leaders. On February 17, he declared that the Laos operation "should not be interpreted by the Communist Chinese as a threat to them." Two weeks later, Chou informed the Hanoi leadership that China would not intervene in the Vietnam war because Peking believed that the Americans were sincere in their promise to withdraw from Indochina. The exchanges via Pakistan resumed. Finally, in March 1971, another unsigned handwritten note was delivered to Kissinger by Pakistan's ambassador. The note extended an invitation for an "American envoy" to come to Peking. Two names were mentioned in the note: one was Rogers, the other Kissinger.

There was never any question in Nixon's mind that it would be Kissinger who would go to China. While the two men were discussing plans for the trip, taking careful precautions to prevent any leaks, the Chinese decided to make their first public gesture of conciliation. On April 6, 1971, during the finale of the international table-tennis competition in Japan, the Chinese team invited the American team to visit China. Four days later, the U.S. players crossed the border into China, the first official American group to do so in twenty-two years. The Americans, after being received by Premier Chou En-lai, reciprocated by inviting the Chinese team to the United States. Later that month, Nixon hinted that the United States might change its twenty-two year old posture in the United Nations from all-out support for Taiwan to a two-China policy. In the meantime, Kissinger asked the CIA to send him full biographies of Mao Tse-tung, Chou En-lai, and other Chinese leaders. Late at night, after the day's work was done on SALT and Indochina, Kissinger tried to fill the gap in his education by avidly reading about China.

Indochina threatened, at one point, to interfere once more with Kissinger's plans. In June, *The New York Times* began its publication of the "Pentagon Papers," a classified history of the American involvement in Indochina through early 1968. Kissinger feared that the disclosures would jeopardize the trip since the Chinese might feel that they could not rely on American discretion. His apprehensions, however, turned out to be groundless. The Chinese, much more fearful of the Soviet military threat than of possible American indiscretions, firmed up the date for Kissinger's visit to China: July 9 to 11, 1971.

Kissinger left Washington on July 1, allegedly on a round-the-world trip. Yahya Khan who was privy to his plans, helped him camouflage the real purpose of his global tour. When Kissinger arrived in Islamabad, the Pakistani capital, it was announced that he had come down with a slight case of intestinal flu and would have to rest for a few days in a mountain resort near the capital. Actually, Kissinger was in excellent health. Shortly after 3 A.M. on July 9, a Pakistani International Airlines jet took off from Islamabad's airport for China. Kissinger was on board, scheduled to arrive in Peking at noon.

I could not resist the temptation, one day in 1976—almost five years after Kissinger's first meeting with Chou En-lai—to ask him about those two days in July 1971, that had changed so dramatically the world's power constellation. I remembered the occasion when another scholar-diplomat had flown to China on a secret mission. In

1954, Dag Hammarskjold, then United Nations Secretary-General, had visited Peking in order to negotiate the release of American airmen who had been interned in China since the close of the Korean war. Hammarskjold had been deeply impressed with Chou En-lai's erudition. The two men had talked more philosophy than politics and shortly after Hammarskjold's return to Sweden, on his fiftieth birthday, the American airmen were released as a gesture of goodwill. I was curious to know what impact Chou En-lai had made on my fellow-student at Harvard who had once shown so little interest in China.

"I had no idea what the Chinese were like," Kissinger admitted frankly. He had taken a "briefing book" with him to China, which he brought with him to his first meeting with the Chinese leader. "Put your book away," said Chou En-lai, "and let us talk."

Kissinger spent more than twenty hours of his two-day visit in conversations with Chou En-lai. The experience had a profound and lasting effect on him. The two men discovered very quickly that, despite the gulf of time and culture that separated them, they were very much alike. Both had powerful intellects, with a penchant for philosophy and history. They engaged in a wide-ranging discussion of Sino-American relations without attempting to place blame on either side for the two decades of estrangement and hostility. Both men shared an elitist disdain for bureaucracy and mediocrity though they recognized the importance of pragmatic adjustments to reality. Both men had had their share of domestic opposition. During the Cultural Revolution in 1966, Chou En-lai's residence had been besieged by 100,000 Red Guards who had accused him of being a "cosmopolitan traitor." Chou had debated with the students for forty-eight hours before the throng had finally dispersed. Kissinger had his own memories of debates with students and professors during the Cambodian invasion of a year before. Finally, both men had survived adversity and achieved great power. Chou En-lai had been a member of the "Long March" which had decimated the Chinese

Communists to a remnant of 10,000 men seeking refuge in the dank caves of Yenan in the 1930s. Kissinger's own refugee background and meteoric rise from obscurity to power gave him a measure of empathy for the Chinese leader. In Fritz Kraemer's felicitous analogy, both men knew what it had been like to be "hunted men on the docks of Marseilles." Thus, Kissinger and Chou En-lai developed a genuine respect for one another which became the basis for a real friendship. Insofar as two world leaders separated by light years of culture and tradition can become friends, Kissinger and Chou En-lai formed such a bond. As Kissinger told the Senate at the confirmation hearings on his appointment as Secretary of State in September 1973: "I have been accused of perhaps excessive admiration for Prime Minister Chou En-lai, and it is true that I have very high regard for him." When the older man succumbed to a long illness in January 1976, Kissinger felt a keen sense of loss. "There is turmoil under the heavens," Chou En-lai had said to him in 1971. "And we have the opportunity to end it." Certainly that first encounter began the process of reconciliation. Fact gradually began to replace fear as the major basis of America's China policy.

Only a single specific agreement was reached between Kissinger and Chou during that first visit. Chou extended an invitation to Nixon to visit China in early 1972. Beyond that, the two negotiators reached a meeting of minds in two important areas that had caused Sino-American tensions in the past. They agreed in principle that Taiwan should be considered as a part of China and that the political future of the island should be settled peacefully by the Chinese themselves. The precise circumstances of such a future settlement were left purposely ambiguous. Kissinger, who knew when to be precise, but also when to be ambiguous, proposed that no specific plan be adopted for Taiwan except that the process of change be a peaceful one. Chou En-lai agreed to this vague formulation and expressed his admiration for Kissinger by saying, only half in jest, that his American visitor had a "Chinese mind." The second principle on which the two men managed to agree was that the political future of South Vietnam would have to be settled by the Vietnamese without outside intervention. Since this was not inconsistent with Nixon's latest offer to Le Duc Tho, Kissinger found it easy to concur.

When Kissinger prepared to leave Peking on July 11, he did so with a feeling of elation and accomplishment. Chou En-lai, too, was greatly pleased. Taiwan was important to the Chinese and the United States was about to revise her policy. Vietnam was important to the United States, and China might now be induced to help end the Indochina war. Lastly, the agreement on a Nixon visit in 1972 was important to both men since it would provide further leverage over Russia—for China as well as for the United States.

At 10 P.M. on July 15, Nixon made the following historic surprise announcement to the nation.

> Premier Chou En-lai and Dr. Henry Kissinger, President Nixon's Assistant for National Security Affairs, held talks in Peking from July 9 to 11, 1971. Knowing of President Nixon's expressed desire to visit the People's Republic of China, Premier Chou En-lai on behalf of the Government of the People's Republic of China has extended an invitation to President Nixon to visit China at an appropriate date before May 1972. President Nixon has accepted the invitation with pleasure. The meeting between the leaders of China and the United States is to seek the normalization of relations between the two countries and also to exchange views on questions of concern to the two sides.

The response to the announcement was almost uniformly favorable in the United States. Kissinger was heaped with praise and now came to be regarded by most Americans as Secretary of State in everything but name. The President, too, was grateful. It was revealed that, when Kissinger was forced to give up his tenured professorship at Harvard a few months earlier in order to continue in his post with Nixon, the President had written his National Security advisor that he could not imagine what the government would be like without him. The "inscrutable Occidental," as the *New York Times* had dubbed him a few days after his return from China, now enjoyed a rare occasion in his pressure-burdened life: a moment of undiluted joy.

Kissinger spent most of the rest of 1971 in preparations for the Nixon trip to China. Recalling the cancellation of President Eisenhower's visit to the Soviet Union in 1960 because of the downing of an American spy plane over Russia, Kissinger suspended all overflights of Chinese territory. He also took some tentative first steps that were to implement the main concession that had been made to Chou En-lai: that Taiwan ultimately was to be a part of China. Nixon issued orders to reduce the 9000-man American garrison on Taiwan, and Secretary Rogers declared in August that henceforth the United States would change its China policy in the United Nations. It would support Peking's admission, even its being seated on the Security Council as a veto-wielding permanent member, but it would oppose the ouster of Taiwan from the UN's General Assembly or from UN membership.

In September, Lin Piao made a desperate bid for power in China which, had it succeeded, might have nipped the growing rapprochement between China and America in the bud. He failed, however, and died under somewhat mysterious circumstances in a plane crash over the Gobi Desert on his way to Russia. In October, Kissinger announced that he would return to China in order to make concrete arrangements for the Nixon visit. Kissinger was to be in Peking in late October, which was precisely the time for the annual debate on China in the General Assembly of the United Nations.

The China vote in the United Nations took place on October 25. Kissinger was supposed to have left Peking on October 24, but he postponed his departure by two days. Thus, while George Bush, the American ambassador to the United Nations, tried to rally votes to keep Taiwan's seat in the General Assembly, Kissinger was cementing the new relationship with Chiang Kai-shek's bitterest enemy. The signal was obvious to the majority of UN delegates. After twenty-two years of diplomatic warfare, the United States would no longer oppose Peking's admission to the world organization. Despite intensive last-minute lobbying by George Bush to keep Taiwan in as well, the United Nations decided to make a clear-cut choice. By a vote of seventy-six in favor, thirty-five against, and seventeen abstentions, Peking was voted in and Taiwan was out. Anti-Taiwan delegates danced in the aisles and Nixon decided to reduce the American contribution to the UN's budget. Privately, of course, he was not surprised by the vote.

One month later, Nixon announced that he would visit China for a week, beginning on February 21, 1972. He also stated that, in his view, "The ultimate relationship of Taiwan to the People's Republic of China would have to be settled by direct negotiations between the two parties concerned." Chiang Kai-shek, in his exile on Taiwan, now felt utterly betrayed by Kissinger and Nixon. The Peking leadership, on the other hand, prepared to welcome the American president. Kissinger hoped that now, at last, he might have the opportunity to meet the aging, legendary leader of China's 800 million people, Chairman Mao Tse-tung.

Not everyone was pleased with America's new China policy. Japan's Prime Minister, Eisaku Sato, felt slighted and began to wonder what these two unpredictable Americans might do next. When the President devalued the dollar one month after Kissinger's secret trip to China, the Japanese reeled under the impact of "Nixon shock." Sato, shortly afterwards, was eased out of power and replaced by Kakuei Tanaka who promptly established diplomatic relations with Peking. Kissinger who was aware of Sato's plight and felt guilty for not having informed the Japanese leader of his plans before the China trip, later tried to make amends by supporting Sato for the Nobel Peace Prize. But Kissinger's relations with the Japanese were badly bruised. They never quite trusted him again.

The Soviet leadership too was, of course, alarmed. Kissinger had a soothing word for Brezhnev immediately upon his return from his first trip to Peking. "Nothing that has been done in our relations with the People's Republic of China," he declared on July 16, "is in any way directed against any other countries, and especially not against the Soviet Union." The Russians were not convinced. They were expecting Nixon in the Soviet capital in May 1972. Nixon decided to echo Kissinger's reassuring note. "Neither trip is being taken," he asserted, "at the expense of any other nation." The Russians did not believe him either and they were essentially correct. Both Kissinger and Nixon hoped that the opening to China would help end the Indochina war by exerting pressure on Moscow to exert pressure on Hanoi. But it would take almost an entire year before this strategy finally was to pay off.

When Kissinger and Nixon arrived in Peking on schedule on February 21, Chou En-lai was on hand to greet the two Americans. He and Kissinger were friends by now and were pleased that they had done their work so well. Another similarity the two men shared was their loyalty to their respective leaders. Chou, despite his superior intellect, saw himself as a subservient follower of Mao Tse-tung. And Kissinger, during the crisis of Cambodia, had been a loyal supporter of the President.

To Kissinger's surprise and delight, he and Nixon were invited to meet Mao immediately after their arrival. Rogers who had also come along, was specifically not invited. The two men spent an hour with Mao and Chou, and once again as on the occasion of Kissinger's first visit, the subjects were philosophy and history.

Almost five years later, I had the opportunity to ask Kissinger what he had thought of Mao Tse-tung. After all if ever there was a "revolutionary," the chairman certainly was such a man. He had helped to organize the Chinese Communist Party half a century before his encounter with Henry Kissinger. He had led the Long March in the 1930s and taken the remnants of the Red Army to a sanctuary more than 6,000 miles away. He had led his forces against Chiang Kai-shek, the Japanese, and finally against the Americans in Korea. In 1966, at the age of seventy-four, fearful lest China might emulate the ossified bureaucracy of Soviet Russia, Mao, always the adventurer, had set out to rejuvenate the revolution. I was most curious to hear what the author of *A World Restored* thought of this authentic twentieth century revolutionary.

Again, Kissinger admitted that he had been wrong. His description of Mao Tse-tung bordered on awe. "Wherever he sat or stood," Kissinger said, "there was the center of the room. Even though his voice was weak with age and each word was a struggle, he was quite lucid and in absolute command. Chou En-lai fell silent in his presence." Kissinger saw Mao as a modern visionary, a heroic figure, but also as a man who could be co-opted into a stable international order. "Here was a statesman", Kissinger said, "who combined revolutionary ardor with a sense of pragmatism, a man who had a vision for his people, but who had remained in touch with the practical realities as well." It was clear to me that both Mao and Chou appealed enormously to Kissinger's own romanticism, and resonated with his admiration for the solitary figure in adversity. In 1971 and 1972, Kissinger, as we have seen, developed a genuine fondness for one Chinese Communist leader and a profound admiration for the other.

The next few days in Peking were devoted to serious deliberations. On the American side, Nixon and Kissinger were the main negotiators on matters of principle, such as Taiwan and Indochina. Their two opponents were Chou En-lai and Chiao Kuan-hua, a deputy foreign minister. Parallel negotiations were being held between Secretary Rogers and China's Foreign Minister Chi Peng-fei on questions of travel, tourism, and trade. The evenings were taken up with banquets, table-tennis exhibitions, and a performance of *Red Detachment of Women*, hosted by Mao Tse-tung's wife, Chiang Ching. The theme of the ballet was the victory of a young peasant girl over Chiang Kai-shek's troops. Nixon found the performance "excellent theater and superb acting." Kissinger and Chiao worked late into the night in an effort to put together a joint communiqué.

Both sides wanted a positive statement about the visit. Nixon had made the occasion into a television spectacular and needed a successful outcome for the voters at home. The Chinese wanted to justify Nixon's presence to their people and also to impress the Russians with proof of tangible Chinese-American cooperation. Yet it became increasingly obvious as the talks progressed, that it would not be possible to draft a joint statement to which both sides would be able to subscribe. Some of the differences, especially on the problems of Taiwan and Indochina, could not be simply papered over by a document of studied ambiguity.

Kissinger and Chou came up with an idea that broke the deadlock. Both sides would agree to write separate sections into the communiqué, one expressing the American view of a particular problem and the other setting forth the Chinese position. This technique enabled the negotiators to focus honestly on differences rather than cover them up with diplomatic double-talk. On two occasions, Kissinger and Chiao worked until dawn in order to formulate a communiqué that would set forth the differences between the two nations without making them appear to be unbridgeable. In four areas— Indochina, Korea, Japan, and India-Pakistan—the difficulties were manageable. On the matter of Taiwan, however, the two positions were so far apart that even the technique of drafting separate statements ran into virtually insuperable difficulties.

On Indochina, the United States declared its long-range goal of self-determination for the Indochinese people, while the Chinese affirmed their support for the Provisional Revolutionary Government; on Korea, Nixon underlined his support for South Korea, while Chou supported North Korea; on Japan, the United States affirmed its alliance with that nation, while the Chinese declared their opposition to a revival of Japanese militarism; and on the Indo-Pakistani war, the United States evenhandedly supported the cease-fire, while the Chinese declared their firm support for Pakistan. In essence, the four statements were little more than agreements to disagree.

Kissinger spent most of his negotiating time and skill on the problem of Taiwan. The Chinese pressed him hard to concede Peking's sovereignty over the island. Implicit in their position was the demand that the United States must abrogate its defense treaty with Chiang Kai-shek since, the Chinese argued, a province could not legitimately maintain a pact with a foreign country. Kissinger, in turn, refused to scrap the Taiwan treaty and insisted that Peking renounce the use of force against the island. Both sides realized that full-fledged diplomatic relations between their two countries would have to be postponed until some mutually acceptable formula could be agreed upon.

Finally, on February 26, Kissinger and Chiao reached agreement on two paragraphs that set forth the two opposing positions with a minimum of rhetoric. In the American paragraph, Kissinger acknowledged that there was "but one China and that Taiwan (was) a part of China," but insisted on "a peaceful settlement of the Taiwan question by the Chinese themselves." He also pledged "the ultimate withdrawal of all U.S. forces and military installations from Taiwan," and a gradual reduction of American forces "as the tension in the area diminish(ed)." The implication was that the United States would gradually withdraw as the Vietnam war drew to a close, but would pull out completely only after Peking had renounced force as a way of "liberating" Taiwan. The Chinese paragraph asserted that "the Taiwan question was the crucial question obstructing the normalization of relations between China and the United States," and reasserted the position that the island was a Chinese province. It also implied, however, that Taiwan's ultimate absorption into China would not take place by force. This was about as far as the two sides were able to move toward a compromise.

These were the major problem areas that Kissinger and Nixon covered in a communiqué issued in Shanghai one day before they departed from Chinese soil. Neither side was very happy with the Taiwan statement, but both agreed that a solution by force was to be ruled out. Thus, this delicate issue was neatly transformed from a problem to be solved immediately into a process to be managed over a period of time.

In addition, Rogers and Chi Peng-fei had worked out some initial agreements on travel, tourism, and trade. It was also agreed that a "senior U.S. representative" would be stationed in Peking. At the final banquet, Nixon proclaimed that his visit to China had been "a week that (had) changed the world." Kissinger's euphoria was almost greater. "What we are doing now with China is so great, so historic," he stated at a news conference, "that the word 'Vietnam' will be only a footnote when it is written in history."

Kissinger and Nixon returned to Washington to heroes' welcomes. In Moscow, the reaction was one of sullen anger and suspicion. In Tokyo, the Sato government collapsed, and on Taiwan, Chiang Kai-shek declared that the United States could no longer be trusted as an ally. One thing was clear to all, however: the bi-polar world was clearly over. A triangular constellation now loomed on the horizon.

Nixon and Kissinger had every intention of broadening and deepening the new understanding with China. In March 1972, the Chinese table-tennis team visited the United States, and in April the first American businessmen were invited to visit the Canton spring trade fair. Then, however, the blossoming relationship was temporarily halted because of the Haiphong mining of May 1972 and the "Christmas bombing" in December. On February 15, 1973, however, less than a month after the Paris accords on Indochina, Kissinger once again visited Peking. Eager to pursue the further normalization of United States-China relations, but frustrated in this quest by the American defense treaty with Taiwan, Kissinger and Chairman Mao settled on a compromise. The United States and China agreed to open liaison offices in Washington and Peking. In addition, each nation made another concession to the other. In exchange for China's release of two captured American pilots and review of the sentence of John Downey, a CIA agent held prisoner in China since the Korean war, the United States agreed to negotiate the settlement of American claims against China and the release of Chinese assets "blocked" in the United States since Korea. In March 1973, David Bruce was appointed to head the United States liaison office in Peking and Huang Chen, China's former ambassador to France, was named to fill the Washington post. The liaison offices were formally opened in May 1973. In practical terms, they fulfilled most of the functions of regular embassies, without, however, stumbling over the divisive issue of Taiwan. Kissinger was greatly pleased with this compromise solution.

In late 1973, however, a "mini-cultural Revolution" in China slowed down the process of rapprochement. The ancient sage Confucius came under severe attack for his "bourgeois" philosophy. The music of Beethoven and Schubert was compared unfavorably to *The White-haired Girl*, a Chinese opera that had put Kissinger to sleep during his previous visit. Richard Bach's *Jonathan Livingston Seagull* was denounced for its "reactionary" tendencies, and Michelangelo Antonioni was attacked as a "decadent" filmmaker. Both Huang Chen and David Bruce went home for about a month before taking up their posts again. The "mini-Cultural Revolution," however, was far milder both in scope and content than the upheaval of 1966. It apparently was an expression of bitter disagreements between those forces in the Chinese Politburo led by Madame Mao, who considered the United States as the principal threat to China, and those of Premier Chou En-lai, who preceived the Soviet Union as the greater danger. Both groups agreed on the philosopher Confucius and on Defense Minister Lin Piao—both "unpersons" and dead—as convenient symbols for the reactionary enemy.

Kissinger steadily encouraged intellectual exchange and trade, but the Taiwan problem kept these contacts at a fairly modest level. On the issue of academic exchange, for example, China retained virtually exclusive power to decide who would visit, for how long, to see what and to meet whom, and under what circumstances. In fact, the

Chinese restrictions on American contacts were more severe than those imposed by the Soviet Union.

The trade pattern followed an erratic course. Two-way China-American trade approached the $1 billion mark in 1974. During that year, the United States became China's second most important trading partner. In 1975, however, the figure was slashed in half and the Chinese abruptly cancelled a large order for American wheat and corn. Taiwan's trade with the United States in 1975 was almost ten times as large and Hong Kong's was four times as large. The evidence suggests that the Taiwan issue inhibited a more rapid expansion of commercial contacts. Financing problems, the American refusal to grant China most-favored-nations status, and the lack of a formal trade agreement could all be traced back to the absence of full diplomatic relations. Thus, Kissinger's "liaison office" solution did not resolve the Taiwan problem, but merely circumvented it. By 1975, rapprochement between China and America had reached a fairly stable plateau. There was little, if any, forward movement. Even a trip to Peking by Kissinger and Ford in the fall of 1975 did not restore the old momentum.

In February 1976, exactly four years after his first visit as President, Richard Nixon again went to China, this time in the role of tourist. The Chinese government had extended the invitation to the former President apparently as a signal to Ford and Kissinger that the United States was paying too much attention to détente with the Soviet Union and not enough to China. Chairman Mao hoped that the meaning of an invitation to the architect of the American opening to China would not be lost on his successor. Kissinger, who denied any part in the plans for Nixon's China visit, nevertheless decided to "debrief" his former chief who had not only been entertained by Chairman Mao personally but also by Chou En-lai's successor, Hua Kuo-feng.

By 1976, a chill wind was blowing out of China in Kissinger's direction. While he was not an "un-person" in Peking, Chou En-lai's successors regarded him with growing mistrust and ambivalence. They felt that he had overplayed the Soviet card and that the time had come perhaps to turn the tables on the United States. They sensed that Kissinger's triangular policy was vulnerable. In politics as well as love, triangles were inherently unstable. There was no guarantee that the United States would always remain the "lady."

What had brought Henry Kissinger to Peking for the first time in 1971 and what brought him back seven more times by the end of 1975 was, first and foremost, the possibility of using this odd Sino-American coupling as leverage on the Soviet Union. Kissinger made sure that he would hold the best position in the triangle, as the only point with lines to the other two. He was careful to keep the United States in a position of equidistance between the two Communist powers. Yet, his triangular policy was based on one fundamental assumption that was absolutely essential for its success: the permanent hostility between China and the Soviet Union. His thinking on this crucial subject is therefore vital to any examination of his foreign policy.

Kissinger, the historian, was quick to point out that the decade of the 1950s was the only period in the entire history of Chinese-Russian relations in which the two nations were closely allied. This ten-year aberration from a century-long pattern of nationalist tension and territorial competition, was in essence, a response to a common enemy that, temporarily, was perceived as the greater threat: the United States. As this threat receded in the wake of détente, the historical animosities between China and Russia resurfaced and the relationship reverted to its fundamental hostility. The end of the Indochina war removed the major policy issue on which the two nations had found themselves in agreement in the past.

Kissinger believed that it was idle to speculate about the relative importance of traditional nationalism and Communist ideology in the Sino-Soviet constellation. The crucial point to be made was that both forces were destabilizing elements in the picture.

On the question of traditional nationalism, Kissinger emphasized that China considered Russia to be the last Western state that still occupied, without consent, territories that China regarded as her own. The fact that Russia showed little if any inclination to accede to these irredentist claims continued to maintain tension at a high level.

As for sharing a common ideology, Kissinger believed that communism had long since ceased to be a unifying factor. On the contrary, the strident claims made by each leadership in aspiring to the role of exclusive torchbearer of Marxism-Leninism widened the gulf even further. It was unlikely, in Kissinger's view, that these powerful forces making for tension and discord were easily reversible.

Kissinger believed that both China and the Soviet Union had a fairly accurate perception of each other's military power. It was for this reason that a major war between them was certainly not inevitable, or even very likely. The Chinese were aware that they were no match for the vastly superior Soviet military apparatus, and the Soviets seemed to have learned sufficiently from history, including recent American history, the possible calamitous consequences of a major land war in Asia.

Kissinger has predicted the most likely pattern of future Sino-Soviet relations to be a kind of cold war. He did not believe that the succession to Mao in China or to Brezhnev in the Soviet Union was likely to affect this pattern in any fundamental way. The subjective impact of new leadership personalities might, of course, result in temporary rapprochement, but it was most unlikely, in Kissinger's opinion, that any single individual could decisively reverse a long-established negative historical encounter, only briefly interrupted for a decade by the perception of a common enemy.

Hence, while rapprochement with the United States was likely to come under periodic attack in China, Kissinger was confident that the long-run trend was for the continuation of such a policy. This trend was the result of objective changes in the global power constellation. America's withdrawal from Vietnam, the Soviet presence on the Chinese border, and the American decision to balance its relations with China and the Soviet Union but to remain equidistant from them both, were primarily responsible for this great turning. Yet it was also true that both China and America had been fortunate to have as leaders men of the caliber of Henry Kissinger and Chou En-lai, both equipped with realistic perceptions of themselves and of each other, a rare knowledge of history and an even rarer gift for empathy. This personal dimension had no doubt accelerated the movement away from fantasy and fiction toward rapprochement and reality. Kissinger and Chou En-lai had recognized the objective conditions necessary for a turn-for-the-better in the relations between China and America. They had seized the crucial moment at one of history's great junctions and helped to make it happen. By this recognition and determined action, Chou En-lai and Kissinger made their claim to historic statesmanship.

11

Europe: The Troubled Partnership

> Nations that cannot agree on common negotiating
> positions are not likely to be able to concert a
> common strategy for an apocalypse.
>
> Henry Kissinger
> *The Troubled Partnership*, 1965

Henry Kissinger has always spent more time and energy on adversaries than on friends—until the friends turned into adversaries. This has been the paradox of his relationship with Western Europe and Japan. In his book, *The Troubled Partnership*, which was published four years before he came to power, Kissinger considered the forging of a common Atlantic policy with Europe as one of the most urgent tasks confronting American foreign policy. Many of the writings of Professor Kissinger during the 1950s and 1960s were devoted to Western Europe and to the North Atlantic Treaty. His analyses of the problems of the European continent, particularly those of Germany and France were impressive, often profound. Hence, it was not at all surprising that many Western Europeans in 1969 were pleased to see a fellow European in such a pivotal position on the other side of the Atlantic.

During his first three years in office, however, Kissinger paid little attention to America's allies in Western Europe and even less to Japan. Most of his time was taken up with Indochina, the Soviet Union, and China. The fate of Europe, which had occupied him so much during his earlier days, had virtually drifted from his range of vision. He was aware, of course, of serious strains in NATO, and criticized the new economic competitiveness, the selfishness, and the growing nationalism of the Western European countries. Many of Europe's leaders seemed weak and ineffectual to him, and when they were strong, like Charles de Gaulle, they appeared opposed to the United States. To Europe, in turn, the United States seemed to have lost its sense of priorities and gotten bogged down in a suicidal war in Indochina. Many European leaders found Kissinger's attitude high-handed and accused him of placing the interests of U.S.-Soviet détente before the interests of Europe. By 1973, it was quite clear that America's main military alliance was in serious disrepair and that the relationship with Western Europe was drifting from respect and friendship into mutual resentment and hostility.

For a single moment, in the spring of 1973, Kissinger decided to concentrate on Europe. On April 23, 1973, in a major national address, he announced a "Year of Europe." His diagnosis of the shortcomings of the transatlantic dialogue was a perceptive one. "There have been complaints in America," he stated, "that Europe ignores its wide responsibilities in pursuing economic self-interest too one-sidedly and that Europe is not carrying its fair share of the burden of the common defense. There have been complaints in Europe that America is out to divide Europe economically, or to desert Europe militarily, or to bypass Europe diplomatically." He then explained that the focus on America's adversaries had been necessary "to lighten the burdens of fear and suspicion," but that the time had now arrived to "gain the same sense of historical achievement by reinvigorating shared ideals and common purposes with our friends." Finally, he called upon the Europeans to "join in a fresh act of creation, equal to that undertaken by the postwar generation of leaders of Europe and America."

Kissinger's call for a "new Atlantic Charter" had none of the impact of the historic speech, given by Secretary of State George C. Marshall at Harvard more than a quarter-century before, that had launched the American program for the recovery of Europe. The reason for this was not the lack of a design or plan. Kissinger, in fact, had persuaded the President to meet with Western European leaders during the summer and fall of 1973, and he meant quite earnestly to move Europe to the center of his concerns. But two traumatic events that he could not predict laid waste his European plans. The Yom Kippur war which erupted in the Middle East in October and the peace-making efforts that ensued, absorbed most of his diplomatic energies. And by early 1974, Nixon was too sticken by Watergate to carry out his European tour. The impeachment controversy by then had almost totally engulfed him. Kissinger himself, had not been left untouched by Watergate and was under personal attack for his alleged role in the wiretapping of government officials and journalists. In a moment of despair, in June 1974, he threatened to resign his office unless the Senate vindicated him. Thus, it came about that Europe, once again, was relegated to the periphery of Kissinger's attention.

As fate would have it, however, Europe thrust itself upon Kissinger at the very moment when Nixon was politically *in extremis.* A full-blown crisis erupted on the island of Cyprus in the summer of 1974 that threatened not only to wreck the southern flank of NATO, but pitted Greece and Turkey against each other in a frenzy of bewildering confusion and hostility. At the same time, a leftist revolution overtook Portugal and it seemed, for a while, that the country might succumb to a Communist dictatorship. Kissinger, beset with the problem of the Middle East and besieged by Watergate, dealt with Cyprus cavalierly and haphazardly, alienating both Greece and Turkey in the process. His decisions on Portugal were so erratic and so contradictory that they almost brought about the very victory of communism that he attempted to prevent. Reluctant to delegate responsibility, he made crucial decisions personally by transatlantic telephone, only to discover on more than one occasion afterwards, that he had been misled.

"When sorrows come, they come not single spies, but in battalions," Shakespeare had written. Even for a man of Kissinger's resourcefulness and stamina, Cyprus and Portugal in 1974 were two sorrows too many. The "Year of Europe" thus became a casualty of the Arab-Israeli war abroad and of Watergate at home. "Opportunities cannot be hoarded; once past, they are usually irretrievable," Kissinger had written ten years earlier. This statement was to sum up well the predicament and tragedy of his European policy.

Since Cyprus had become independent of Britain in 1960, the relationship between the Greek and Turkish communities on the island had been a perennial problem. Periodic flare-ups and protracted communal strife at times had often threatened to involve Greece and Turkey in a wider conflict and thus to jeopardize the cohesion of NATO. The eruption that was to demand Henry Kissinger's attention began on July 15, 1974 with a military coup that toppled the president of Cyprus, Archbishop Makarios. For fifteen years, the wily Makarios had been a tightrope walker between the hammer and the anvil of Greek and Turkish power. The coup was carried out by the Cypriot National Guard but had been masterminded by the military junta then ruling in Athens. The junta's aim was *enosis,* or union between Cyprus and Greece, to which Makarios had been stubbornly opposed. The new president of Cyprus, installed by the Greek military junta, was Nikos Sampson, a young Greek fanatic and self-confessed killer who had once been sentenced to death by the British for his terrorist activities. Sampson immediately proclaimed his goal of union between Cyprus and Greece.

When the news of the coup on Cyprus reached Kissinger, his attention was divided between the Middle East and Watergate. He had always been impatient with the endless feud on Cyprus and had not regarded Makarios' acrobatics of survival with unalloyed enthusiasm. In one conversation, he had referred to the Cypriot president, with heavy irony, "as a man who (was) much too big for so small an island." Many high State Department officials had shared his view about Makarios. One bureaucrat, upon having learned that Makarios had survived the coup, had reportedly remarked, "How inconvenient." Even George Ball, who was severely critical of Kissinger's Middle East diplomacy had once been known to rage at the Archbishop, exclaiming: "God damn it, Your Beatitude. . . ."

"Who is Nikos Sampson?" Kissinger asked the Cypriot ambassador on the day of the coup in Nicosia. Ambassador Dimitriou replied that Sampson was considered a paranoid and an egomaniac. "But I have been called an egomaniac too", Kissinger responded, with a smile. "You should not compare yourself to Sampson, Mr. Secretary," the Cypriot ambassador replied.

Kissinger attached little importance to the events in Nicosia. He did not criticize the violent act of intervention from Greece nor did he express the usual words of regret about the attempt to assassinate Makarios. This created the impression that he was tilting toward a *de facto* recognition of the new Sampson government. A State Department spokesman pointedly announced that Kissinger was going to meet the following Monday with *Archbishop* Makarios. Two days later, the *New York Times* reported that "high American officials indicated that the Nixon Administration was leaning more toward Sampson than Makarios." Kissinger, in fact, believed that Makarios was politically finished, and could never return to Cyprus unless the Greek military junta was deposed in Athens. The Soviet Union, on the other hand, eager to prevent the transformation of Cyrpus from a neutral state into a NATO bastion, continued to recognize Makarios as president.

On July 17, Kissinger dispatched Undersecretary of State Joseph Sisco to the Mediterranean on what turned out to be a hopeless mission: to prevent the Turks from invading Cyprus. The Turks had been waiting for ten years for such an opportunity. As one senior Turkish official put it later: "The Greeks committed the unbelievably stupid move of appointing Sampson, giving us the opportunity to solve our problems once and for all. Unlike in 1964 and 1967, the United States leverage on us in 1974 was minimal. We could no longer be scared off by threats that the Soviet Union would intercede." Turkey's Prime Minister Bulent Ecevit put it even more succinctly in a conversation with Sisco: "We have done it your way for ten years," said Ecevit, "now we are going to try it our way." Shortly after dawn on July 20, Turkish warships steamed toward the coast of Cyprus, and Turkish paratroopers began to land on the island. Greek warships from Piraeus left for Cyprus in order to cut off the Turkish fleet. A Greco-Turkish war seemed in the making.

The escalating crisis was not without its moments of black humor. Kissinger, for example, likes to recall the occasion when he was woken up by Ecevit in the early morning hours of July 21. The Turkish premier complained that an entire Greek armada was steaming toward Turkey. "Those perfidious Greeks, you know what they are doing? They are flying Turkish flags to fool us!" Ecevit shouted over the transatlantic telephone. "Why don't you tell him to shut up and sink the goddamned things," Nancy Kissinger was reported to have grumbled sleepily. As it happened, the Turks did precisely that, only to discover that they had sunk several of their own ships. The suspected Greek ships had been Turkish after all. The Pentagon, fearful of damage to American ships in the vicinity, began a frantic inventory of all U.S. vessels in the area. American naval authorities, however, discovered very quickly that all Greek, Turkish, and American ships in the region had been made in U.S. shipyards and thus were indistinguishable from one another.

To add to the confusion even further, the Greek military junta now began to founder. A consensus had emerged in Athens that only a man of recognized national stature could lead Greece out of its immediate chaos. On July 24, the junta generals in Athens reluctantly agreed to recall former president Constantine Karamanlis from his exile in Paris. Karamanlis who had been waiting for years for this moment, returned to Athens immediately and constitutional government was restored after seven years of military rule.

In the meantime, the Turks had gained a modest territorial foothold on the coast of Cyprus. Sampson, on command from Karamanlis, abdicated and it seemed that a settlement was now in sight. Kissinger was pleased with the return of democracy to Greece and now hoped to produce an inter-communal settlement on Cyprus between the two main negotiators: Glavkos Clerides for the Greek Cypriot majority and Rauf Denktash for the Turks. He thought that his telephonic persuasion and a bit of luck had saved the situation. What he did not know was that the Turks were bent on pressing their military advantage.

Premier Bulent Ecevit, who had been a member of Kissinger's international seminar at Harvard, chose not to be receptive to his former mentor. Slowly, but steadily, Turkish forces continued to advance in a low-level prolongation of the war. Ecevit, determined to end the Greek domination of Cyprus and using his military advantage as a trump card, continued to violate a military cease-fire that had been agreed upon at Geneva. On August 14, with sudden ferocity, the Turkish troops advanced with reinforcements and cut the island virtually in half. Within the new Turkish sector were confined 200,000 Greek Cypriots who now formed a tide of refugees fleeing southward. Two days later, the Turks had gained all the territory they wanted. They now occupied forty per cent of Cyprus and, with consummate lack of tact, referred to the new border as the Attila Line.

Most of Kissinger's energies during the final phase of the Cyprus denouement were absorbed by Watergate. The agonies of the presidential transition had left him virtually spent. During this period of depression and uncertainty, he was unable to muster his usual determination and vitality. Thus, he did not apply strong pressure on the

Turkish government nor did he take measures that might have made Ecevit somewhat more compliant, such as a cutoff of military aid. In effect, he acquiesced in the Turkish territorial conquest. He also reasoned that, in overall strategic terms, Turkey was more important to the United States and NATO than the unpredictable government that had just been installed in Greece. As one State Department official put it later: "Let's say that Greece is Denmark and Turkey is Germany. We may be fonder of the Danes, but we *need* the Germans more."

The response to Kissinger in Athens was immediate and predictable. "For seven years the Americans had supported the military junta, and now for seven days they could not support Karamanlis," a Greek parliamentarian said bitterly. Greco-American relations soon reached a new nadir and, at home, Kissinger was confronted with a hostile Congress which insisted on a cutoff in military aid to Turkey. Kissinger, who chose to fight the Congress on this issue, did so from a position of considerable vulnerability. His critics accused him of an abiding tendency to identify American national security with authoritarian governments dominated by military oligarchs. Kissinger not only lost the fight with Congress, but the debate was only the beginning of a succession of severe restrictions that the legislative branch would impose upon him in the future.

It is difficult to say with certitude what motivated Kissinger's policy in Cyprus. No doubt, the denouement of Watergate was a serious distraction. But there was also the calculus of balance and stability. Turkey simply was perceived as a more important asset to the North Atlantic Treaty than was Greece. The fact that Greece was now a democracy did not change Kissinger's position. If forced to choose, stability, not justice, remained the goal of his policy.

In his doctoral dissertation, completed exactly twenty years before his involvement in the Cyprus crisis, Kissinger had chronicled an interesting episode in the history of nineteenth century Europe. In 1821, during Greece's war of independence, the Turks had committed terrible atrocities. They had hanged the Greek patriarch outside the door of his cathedral in Constantinople. Tsar Alexander was tempted to intervene on the side of Greece. He was deterred from doing so, however, by a dispatch from Viscount Castlereagh which contained the following fateful paragraph:

> If a statesman were permitted to regulate his conduct by the counsels of his heart instead of the dictates of his understanding, I really see no limits which might be given to the impulse. . . . But we must always recollect that his is the grave task of providing for the peace and security of those interests immediately committed to his care, that he must not endanger the fate of the present generation in a speculative endeavour to improve the lot of that which is to come. . . .

On April 25, 1974, when a group of rebellious officers calling themselves the Armed Forces Movement (AFM) ousted Antonio Salazar's successor, Premier Marcello Caetano, in a bloodless coup in Lisbon, joy erupted in the streets of Portugal's cities and flowers were tossed at the military "liberators." After nearly a half-century of heavy-handed dictatorship, it seemed that the people of Portugal were at last going to speak out freely at the ballot box. After almost half a millennium of overseas empire, they were going to be relieved at last of the burdens of their restless African territories.

On May 15, a provisional government was formed under the leadership of a popular general, Antonio de Spinola. The new premier was Professor Adelino de Palma Carlos, a sixty-nine year old liberal. The cabinet included several Socialists—in particular Mario Soares as foreign minister—and two Communists. The Communists were Alvaro Cunhal as minister without portfolio and Arelino Goncalvez as labor minister. Spinola had approved the inclusion of the Communists and Soares and the Socialists had posed no objections.

In June 1974, Kissinger met Soares for the first time at the NATO ministerial meeting in Ottawa. On that occasion, Kissinger expressed his hope that Portugal would adhere to her NATO obligations and maintain her cordial relationship with the United States. A few days later, Nixon stopped at the Azores Air Force Base for a meeting with Spinola, emphasizing the continued importance of that strategic base for the United States.

July and August 1974 were dreadful months for Henry Kissinger. Not only was he beset by Watergate, the Middle East, and Cyprus, but he now discovered also that the situation in Portugal was deteriorating rapidly. Cunhal's Communist Party had taken control of hundreds of municipal councils throughout Portugal and had also taken over the newly created labor confederation. Kissinger, distracted and in a deep depression, plunged into an almost Spenglerian pessimism with regard to Portugal. He had little faith in Soares' Socialists or in the moderate elements in the Portuguese army. When Cunhal declared that "there (would) be no bourgeois democracy in Portugal," Kissinger took his statement at face value. By the time Gerald Ford assumed the presidency, Kissinger had become convinced that a Communist victory in Portugal was unavoidable.

On September 16, when Soares came to Washington to ask for economic aid, Kissinger refused. There was no purpose in helping a government that he considered doomed. On September 30, Spinola resigned and the presidency passed to General Costa Gomes. Kissinger saw no reason to revise his pessimistic forecast. On October 19, Gomes and Soares were Kissinger's luncheon guests in Washington. Kissinger took the opportunity to lecture his guests about the dangers of Communists in coalition governments. Tad Szulc recollected the occasion in an article in *Foreign Policy* in December 1975:

> There were 14 persons at the table: seven Americans and seven Portuguese. Turning to Soares, the Socialist, Kissinger said: "You are a Kerensky . . . I believe your sincerity, but you are naive." Soares shot back, "I certainly don't want to be a Kerensky." Kissinger said, "Neither did Kerensky."

Kissinger suggested that Gomes and Soares expel the Communists from their cabinet. A heated exchange ensued in which the two Portuguese explained that such an action would lead to a major crisis and, most likely, to a surge of sympathy for the Communists who had suffered grievously at the hands of the Salazar dictatorship. The Communists, Soares tried to assure Kissinger, would be gradually eliminated as the revolution evolved and gained maturity.

Kissinger was not convinced, but decided to give the Portuguese a chance. In December, he recommended an amount of $20 million in housing loans as "a positive demonstration of United States support and confidence in Portugal's future." He also appointed Frank Carlucci, an experienced Foreign Service officer, as ambassador to Lisbon. In March, 1975, however, there was another coup which dramatically increased the power of the Communists. Kissinger's pessimism quickly returned. He was now convinced that Portugal was just a step away from an Eastern European-type Communist state. Carlucci in the Lisbon embassy, however, still seemed confident that all was not lost. It appeared that the ambassador's hopes were at least temporarily justified. The elections in April 1975, resulted in a Socialist victory and a Communist defeat. Shortly afterwards, however, the pendulum swung again, when the Communists took over the nation's most influential socialist newspaper. Kissinger's patience with Portugal by now had run out completely.

In May 1975, Ford, on Kissinger's advice, questioned whether Portugal still deserved to belong to NATO. "I am concerned about the Communist element and its influence in Portugal", the President stated, "This is a matter that I will certainly bring up when we meet in Brussels." Kissinger believed that a threat to push Portugal out of NATO would make the government mend its pro-Communist ways. Most NATO members disagreed with this strategy. As a British diplomat put it heatedly: "Doesn't Kissinger realize that the Portuguese problem is an internal one—not one of foreign policy—and that the Portuguese are responsive to internal pressures, not to international blackmail? Why is Kissinger so set on internationalizing the Portuguese crisis? Does he want to turn it into a NATO confrontation?"

The Soviet Union, actually, was quite restrained in its support of Portuguese Communism. While the two countries had opened full diplomatic relations and were engaged in brisk and profitable trade, the Soviet ambassador in Lisbon, Arnold Kalinin, went out of his way to reassure Carlucci that the Soviets had no interest in absorbing Portugal. Moscow was apparently content with the pro-Communist drift of the government in Lisbon, and did not wish to risk détente. If Moscow had been forced, however, to choose between Portugal and détente with the United States, the temptation to swallow Portugal might have been difficult to resist. As it turned out, that choice did not present itself.

Kissinger now planned to "isolate" Portugal in NATO. This policy was to be a kind of quarantine whereby Portugal was to be denied access to nuclear planning and vital military information by the other NATO members. The Lisbon government avoided a public showdown by simply refusing to attend the July 1975 meeting of NATO's Nuclear Planning Group. Also, Lisbon did not abrogate any of its standing bilateral agreements with the United States. In fact, it showed particular concern not to antagonize the United States in any way despite its virtual exclusion from NATO.

In the summer of 1975, an all-out power struggle erupted between the Socialists and the Communists of Portugal. Cunhal, the Communist party leader, had concluded that the time had come for a bid for total power. Ironically, this old-line, Moscow-trained Communist was challenged by Italian and French Communists who told him that revolutionary power goals had become obsolete. The Italians and French had broken with Moscow over the 1968 invasion of Czechoslovakia. They believed that the "road to socialism" in Western Europe had to be a gradual process in which the Communists would have to collaborate with Socialists in order to acquire a share of power. Cunhal disagreed. He was convinced that he could bring the Communist Party to victory in Portugal by force. Henry Kissinger shared that view.

In August, in a final gamble, Cunhal staked the future of his Party on a military *putsch*. However, he discovered that the moderate military officers fought back. The Socialists, too, rose against him. Suddenly on the defensive, Cunhal volunteered to collaborate with the Socialists in order "to save the revolution." A new moderate cabinet was installed in September 1975, with only a single Communist. Carlucci had been proven right and Kissinger wrong.

Several conclusions can be drawn from this vignette. In the first place, Kissinger's excessive pessimism about Portugal was not so much based on Portuguese realities, about which he knew little, but was apparently caused by extraneous circumstances such as Watergate and the denouement in Indochina. Moreover, Kissinger feared that a Communist victory in a European country would seriously disturb the U.S.-Soviet equilibrium. Hence, hard measures would have to be taken to prevent such a blow to overall stability. In fact, Kissinger's policy of "insulating" Portugal from NATO and thus internationalizing what was primarily a domestic crisis, almost precipitated the very outcome that Kissinger so desperately wanted to prevent: a Communist Portugal. It was not Kissinger who saved the Portuguese from communism; it was the Portuguese themselves who cut Cunhal down to size. And the Soviet Union valued détente with the United States too much to come to Cunhal's rescue. No single individual, not even a man of the enormous talent and intellect of Henry Kissinger, could deal effectively with multiple crises simultaneously without delegating at least some responsibility to others.

Cyprus and Portugal were unsettling experiences for Kissinger. But neither confronted the American Secretary of State with the far-reaching challenge that was posed by the "historic compromise" reached by two Communist parties of Western Europe in 1975.

The leader of the Communist Party of Italy, Enrico Berlinguer, evolved a new strategy in 1975. He committed his party to independence from Moscow and to the preservation of a parliamentary system in Italy. Unlike Alvaro Cunhal in Portugal, who had vowed to prevent a "bourgeois democracy", Berlinguer pledged that his party would preserve democratic liberties, a mixed economy, and membership in NATO and the Common Market. He even promised that he would leave office quietly if defeated at the polls. In short, he promised genuine collaboration with the ruling Christian Democratic Party if he came to power. Despite much skepticism by non-Communists, these claims paid off handsomely in the Italian elections for municipal and regional offices in June 1975. The Communists emerged with striking gains, winning 33.4 percent of the popular vote, placing them only two points below the Christian Democrats.

George Marchais, the secretary-general of the Communist Party of France, was encouraged by the success of Berlinguer. In November 1975, he committed his party to "the Italian way." A joint Marchais-Berlinguer statement pledged the two Communist Parties to respect "the liberty of thought and expression, of the press, of meeting and association, the right to demonstrate, the full movement of persons inside and outside their country, the inviolability of private life, of religious liberties, the total freedom of expression of currents of thought and of every philosophical, cultural and artistic opinion." And in a complete break with past Communist practice, Marchais and Berlinguer added the following key paragraph:

> The French and Italian Communists favor the plurality of political parties, the right of opposition parties to exist and to act, the free formation of majorities and minorities and the possibility of their alternating democratically, the lay character and democratic functioning of the state and the independence of justice. Their position is not tactical.

In February 1976, Marchais went even further and declared that he would pursue communism "under French colors."

Echoes of this "historic compromise" reached even the distant shores of Japan. Not only did the Japanese Communist Party announce its adherence to the parliamentary system, but a party theoretician explained that Karl Marx's embarrassing statement about religion being the opiate of the people meant only that religion should be a "comfort" to people in trouble, not a poison.

Berlinguer and Marchais engaged in polemics with the Soviet leadership. They criticized the 1968 invasion of Czechoslovakia and even defended the behavior of dissident Soviet intellectuals. They also successfully resisted a Soviet effort to incorporate the French and Italian parties at a "unity" meeting of European Communist parties. At least in some areas, Marchais and Berlinguer seemed to follow up their promises with action.

Henry Kissinger's response to the developments in Italy and France was one of deep suspicion of Communist intentions. He told European leaders in late 1975 that the alignment of the Western world's two most powerful Communist parties on virtually a Social Democratic platform was a tactical ruse to bemuse the voters and to give the Communists a chance to enter governing coalitions. But, Kissinger pointed out, the historically-based possibility existed that, once in office, the Communists would probably repudiate their former promises, seize power, leave NATO, and unite with Moscow in a Communist alliance from Asia to the Atlantic. Any such trend would seriously destabilize the overall balance of power between the United States and the Soviet Union. Hence, in Kissinger's opinion, it was essential for Western European countries to do everything possible to exclude the Communists from power. They should be quarantined, and dealt with only when it had become unavoidable to do so. Any other course would invite the destruction of NATO and the piecemeal erosion of democracy in Western Europe.

European critics of Kissinger evoked a different prospect. Santiago

Carrillo, for example, the leader of the Spanish Communist Party, declared that Moscow feared nothing more than the emergence of a "bloc of European socialist countries" independent of the Soviet Union, with Western-style freedoms. Such an evolution, in Carrillo's view, would become a magnet for attraction for Eastern Europe and the entire working-class movement. Ultimately, it might endanger the Soviet form of communism and encourage schisms within the Communist movement reminiscent of the breakaways of Yugoslavia and China.

The leader of Italy's Republican Party, Ugo La Malfa agreed with Carrillo. He asserted that nothing would unsettle the Soviet Union more than a truly independent European Communist movement. If European Communist parties came to practice as well as preach the doctrine of "socialism with a human face," that is, a combination of Western democracy with Marxist economics, this would inevitably have a broadly subversive impact on Eastern Europe. It was, after all, in order to prevent just that kind of dilution of authority for a ruling Communist Party that Brezhnev had ordered the invasion of Czechoslovakia in 1968.

Kissinger remained totally unimpressed by these arguments. His pursuit of overall stability led him to resist the expansion of Communist influence in Western Europe. His usual feeling for nuance did not extend to the European situation. So single-minded, in fact, did his pursuit of stability become that a British editor, in late 1975, compared Kissinger to John Foster Dulles. "There has been nothing so vehement since Dulles' time", this Englishman remarked. "Kissinger has proposed a new domino theory: the Italian Communists would enter the Rome Government, leading to Communists sharing power in France as well as Portugal and Spain, provoking a withdrawal of American troops from Europe, and the collapse of the North Atlantic Treaty Organization."

Actually, Kissinger's position on European communism was not inconsistent with his position on communism elsewhere. He had always taken a harder line with Communists in peripheral areas than with the Soviet Union itself, since, in his view, these peripheral areas had the potential of destabilizing the central relationship with the Soviet Union. He had followed the same approach in Indochina, Portugal and Cuba. The developments in Western Europe, however, confronted Kissinger with a new dilemma. In Italy and France, Berlinguer and Marchais might indeed be the harbingers of genuine progress and social reform, not the instruments of Soviet-led subversion. If that were so, Kissinger's defense of the status quo would not make him an apostle of order and stability, but, in the end, like Metternich, a defender of an obsolescent empty shell.

The evolution of European communism, with its dangers as well as its possibilities, underlined again what Kissinger had earlier described as the most difficult and tragic aspect of foreign policy: the problem of conjecture. How could he be sure that the European Communists were sincere? If he trusted them, and they deceived him, the consequences might be catastrophic for the building of a stable global order. If he resisted them, they might be prevented from reaching power. He believed that his warnings against Communism had helped the Christain Democrats achieve their narrow victory in the Italian elections of June 1976. And if the Communists ultimately came to power anyway, he would discover the truth of their sincerity soon enough. To Kissinger's conservative mind, the latter course offered the smaller risk. His judgment perhaps was questionable, but not his philosophical consistency. As he had written in 1973:

> The policy-maker has to act in a fog of incomplete knowledge without the information that will be available later to the analyst. He knows—or should know—that he is responsible for the consequences of disaster as well as for the benefits of success.

12

The Third World: Toward North-South Rapprochement

> The most solid block in the world today is, paradoxi-
> cally, the alignment of the non-aligned. This divides
> the world into categories of north and south, develop-
> ing and developed, imperial and colonial, at the very
> moment in history when such categories have be-
> come irrelevant and misleading.
>
> Henry Kissinger
> Milwaukee, July 14, 1975

It was customary for most doctoral students in Harvard's Department of Government in the 1950s to register for a course or two in economics and to follow developments in the United Nations. Henry Kissinger was virtually allergic to the former and quite uninterested in the latter. He agreed wholeheartedly with Carlyle's description of economics as the "dismal science" and dismissed the United Nations as a kind of "international social service agency" with only the most tangential political value. He also showed little interest in the problems of Africa, Asia, the Middle East, and Latin America—not yet known in those days as the Third World. All his intellectual energies were invested in the problems of the European continent, past, present, and future.

These omissions in Kissinger's academic training were long reflected in his policies. He left little room for innovative moves toward the new nations of the Third World, most of which had been born in Kissinger's own lifetime. His interest in the United Nations remained minimal, and he shied away consistently from the interrelated issues of food, population, energy, raw materials, and development. In his opinion, they were barely relevant to his main concern: the creation of a stable global order.

All this, however, changed with dramatic suddenness shortly after Kissinger became Secretary of State in September 1973. The October war in the Middle East and the oil embargo and price rises that followed, resulted in massive power dislocations on the world scene. Never before in history did a few states that had been weak for so long, suddenly become so powerful, and never before had states that had been traditionally powerful, suddenly become so vulnerable. When Kissinger assumed office in 1969, the United States and the industrialized world, including Japan, had clearly controlled the international economy. For practical purposes, the global economy then *was* the economy of the Western world. By 1974, however, the economies of the developed nations were reeling under the impact of the policies of a relatively small group of thirteen nations in the Third World which had formed an oil cartel and quadrupled the price of that vital product.

The price rise had the effect of a huge tax on the economies of the oil-importing countries, both rich and poor. As a result, a "Fourth World" had emerged from the Third. Its members were those nations which lacked all resources or economic power. They had neither oil nor food nor money, only rapidly growing populations. But the developed countries, too, were sharply affected, especially Japan. Even the United States, which imported less than fifteen per cent of its energy supply from the Middle East, found the price rise galling. In the meantime, the producing countries enjoyed surplus revenues of $60 billion in 1974.

The price increases contributed to inflationary spirals in the West that, in some cases, threatened the very fabric of its liberal democracies. In Britain, France, West Germany, and Italy serious concern arose over whether democratic institutions could survive such economic strains. The poorest countries of the Fourth World found themselves in desperate straits and there was a serious question whether some of them would be able to survive at all.

On balance, the oil crisis of 1974 had created a situation for which Kissinger's training simply had not prepared him. A handful of countries which had little *but* oil had managed to hold hostage most of the military and political power wielders of the modern world. Countries with almost none of the traditional elements that made up national power found themselves able to influence the policies of the nations with the most formidable military arsenals. Weakness had suddenly become strength and strength weakness.

Kissinger perceived the oil crisis within the framework of a power struggle. He approached the challenge with the perspective of a strategist, not that of an economist. Having structured it in such a manner, his response was quite traditional. Now that the world's power struggles were shifting from an East-West to a North-South line of confrontation, the building of a stable world order would have to be broadened to include relations between North and South as well. In order to build North-South détente, the oil-consuming nations of the North would have to learn to stand together just as the NATO nations had learned to stand together against the Soviet Union. A mixture of diplomacy and toughness, once again, as in the past, would be the most effective road toward a balanced equilibrium between producer and consumer nations. Any frightened *sauve-qui-peut* within the camp of oil-consuming states would only enhance the "blackmail" capabilities of the opposing side.

In a speech before the United Nations General Assembly in September 1974, Kissinger employed a balanced mixture of toughness and conciliation. "What has gone up by political decision," he asserted, "can be reduced by political decision." The implication was clear enough. The price rises were not justified on economic grounds, hence the United States expected prices to come down. Elsewhere in his speech, however, Kissinger was more conciliatory. He recognized that "oil producers [sought] a better life for their peoples and a just return for their diminishing resources."

The OPEC countries took offense at Kissinger's suggestion that the price increases had been motivated by political considerations. They maintained that, in the past, cheap oil had been a major factor in the growth of the industrialized countries. In fact, the West had achieved its present status as a result of a parasitical relationship with the oil-producing countries. Oil prices had simply caught up with the inflationary amounts that the industrialized nations had demanded for their technology and skills. When considered in that light, the oil producers argued, the price of energy had been depressed for far too long.

Kissinger was not impressed. On one occasion, he declared that "if the West should face the threat of strangulation, even the use of force could not be ruled out altogether." This comment touched off a spate of speculation about whether the United States might contemplate the forcible seizure of oil fields in the Middle East. Professors debated the pros and cons of such military action in journals of national prominence.

By 1975, however, the energy crisis had subsided somewhat and Kissinger began to blend his power-political approach with economic considerations. He quickly grasped that energy would pose long-range, complex problems and that his thinking would have to become more multi-faceted. For the first time in his career, he now took economics seriously and formulated a new four-part policy on energy.

In the first place, he continued to believe in the need for the solidarity of the consumer nations in order to render them less vulnerable to embargo threats and the dangers of financial collapse. Second, he recommended a systematic effort at energy conservation of sufficient magnitude so as to lessen the West's dependence on the producer countries. Third, he proposed common institutions of financial solidarity so that individual consumer countries would not be so obsessed by their sense of weakness that they would negotiate on the producers' terms. Finally, he proposed a concerted policy of developing alternate sources of energy so that the combination of new discoveries of oil, new oil-producing countries, and new sources of energy would create a situation in which the oil cartel would find it impossible to operate.

By 1976, OPEC was in trouble. An oil glut, not a shortage, faced the producer countries. They now were forced to share production cutbacks, rather than enjoy the prospect of even higher prices. A modest rise of ten percent decided upon in late 1975 had come unstuck. Most OPEC nations were selling oil at considerable discounts. The worst seemed to be over for consumers, at least for a while.

Kissinger was not so naive as to believe that his policy had been successful. The West had not held firmly together in the face of crisis. Energy conservation had not worked smoothly, common financial institutions had not been fully formed, and there were still no viable substitutes for oil. Kissinger knew that the consumer countries had escaped catastrophe by a combination of luck and circumstance. But he, too, had learned a lesson. Quietly, but with great determination, he gathered a staff of economists around him who helped him fill the void of earlier days. He sensed that he would need new intellectual weapons to hasten the process of reconciliation between the world's rich and poor.

Oil was not the only world product that was the object of a fierce power struggle during the 1970s. Food loomed equally large as an object of competition. Here, however, it was the United States which was in a commanding position. America controlled a larger share of the world's exportable food than the Arab countries' share of oil. The world of the early 1970s had become dependent for its well-being upon American agriculture. However, a dramatic surge in world food demand and huge Soviet grain purchases directly affected food prices in the United States. Crop failures in the Soviet Union and in India sent foreign buyers to the United States to compete directly with American bakers, cattlemen, and food processors for increasingly more expensive products. The relationship of many countries to the United States in food terms began to resemble the relationship, in energy terms, of much of the world to the OPEC nations.

Henry Kissinger had been aware of the potential of American "food power" for some time. During the crop failures in the Soviet Union in 1972, he had tried to use the sales of cheap grain as leverage on the Russians for help in Indochina. This linkage of food to power politics had worked relatively well, and was used again by Kissinger in influencing Soviet behavior in the Middle East. The impact of these policies on food prices in the United States was of little concern to him. If food power could be used effectively in the building of a stable international order, higher food costs would be a small price for Americans to pay. The economic implications of his larger strategy did not intrude a great deal into his range of vision.

By 1974, however, an ominous new element had entered the global food situation. Large-scale food deficiencies in India, Bangladesh, and several sub-Saharan African countries had claimed hundreds of thousands of lives. World food reserves were the lowest in a twenty-year period that saw global population grow by one billion. The rampant inflation of food prices everywhere threatened the livelihood of millions of people who literally could no longer afford to eat. The United Nations reported that thirty-two nations had been so seriously affected by food shortages that their very survival was at stake.

In the United States, there was considerable disagreement over possible approaches to the food crisis in the nations of the Third World. Farmers, eager for higher food prices, argued for greater exports. Consumers, disturbed over the inflated costs of staple foods, were less willing to make sacrifices for the sake of Asia's and Africa's starving millions. Some felt that America could not feed everyone and that, therefore, the concept of "triage" might have to be applied.

During the trench warfare slaughters of the First World War, a system of processing the wounded had been the custom in Allied medical tents. The groups involved consisted of those likely to die no matter what was done for them, those who would probably recover even if untreated, and those who could survive only if cared for immediately. With supplies and manpower limited, the third group alone received attention. The analogy of the medical tent to global famine became obvious to some Americans in 1974. If only one nation, the United States, had a surplus of food in a world stricken by famine, it would be the United States which would, with godlike finality, dispense food after systematically deciding which people were salvageable and should be fed, which would survive without help, and which were beyond hope and thus should be left to the ravages of famine.

While Kissinger was never attracted to the triage idea, the famine conditions in Africa and on the Indian sub-continent did present him with serious dilemmas. On the one hand, in the interest of détente, he had recommended the cheap grain sales to Russia in 1972. On the other hand, these sales had made food more expensive for the American consumer and had made the Department of Agriculture more reluctant to ship grain at reduced prices to famine–stricken India. Thus, after President Ford had approved the sale of 2.2 million tons of wheat to the Soviet Union in 1974, Kissinger informed Indian officials that the United States would be able to supply only 500,000 tons of low-priced grain to India, even though India needed at least seven million tons of grain to overcome the food deficit for 1974.

Kissinger tried to soften the harshness of the debate over the uses of American food for strategic linkage versus more openly humanitarian purposes. As early as September 1973, in his first speech as Secretary of State, he had proposed to the General Assembly of the United Nations the convening of a World Food Conference, to be held in Rome in November 1974. During the intervening year, as the crisis deepened, he had given the problem more than passing thought. By late 1974, he had reached the conclusion that a penurious food policy would lead the United States into a confrontation with the Third World. Famine might have dire political repercussions and threaten the fabric of world stability. The turmoil over Bangladesh in 1971 had been a case in point. Hence, in the interest of stability as well as humanitarian considerations, a generous policy on food would be in the national interest.

At the opening of the World Food Conference in Rome in November 1974, Kissinger declared that "We must act now and we must act together to regain control over our shared destinies. If we do not act boldly, disaster will result from a failure of will." He pledged substantial amounts of American food for the stricken countries and promised aid programs to help the starving nations increase their productive capacities; he also promised efforts to improve food distribution to the poor nations and to help finance their imports. Most important, he proposed a system of nationally held but internationally coordinated grain banks and the establishment of a World Food Council to serve as an umbrella organization to funnel food and money to needy nations. Taken together, these two proposals were reminiscent of the biblical Joseph's granary. Kissinger concluded by proclaiming that, "within a decade, no child should go to bed hungry, no family should fear for its next day's bread, and no human being's future and capacities should be stunted by malnutrition."

Kissinger's approach to food in world politics was quite successful. By 1976, the World Food Council coordinated the delivery of some ten million tons of grain to needy countries on an annual basis. In addition, it arranged for grains to be stockpiled in a food reserve and for an early warning system of potential food disaster areas. Kissinger also encouraged the oil-exporting states—most of which were food importers—to invest in food production in the less-developed countries. But, perhaps most important, Kissinger was lucky. The food crisis, like the energy shortage, had abated slightly by 1976 and this gave Kissinger the time to engage in long-range planning rather than short term emergency relief plans to alleviate disaster.

In his overall approach to food, Kissinger had to consider a number of conflicting strains. Not only did he have to balance political and humanitarian considerations, but divergent pressures within the United States made an integrated policy difficult to attain. Secretary of Agriculture Earl Butz, for example, made a policy statement in Rome that differed in some important respects from Kissinger's own. When asked at a press conference to explain the differences, Kissinger, before making his formal reply, was understood to say, under his breath, "I cleared my speech with Jerry Ford. I don't know who he cleared his with."

Kissinger's view that the United States should provide leadership on world food required a domestic farm policy geared to world needs, including a global grain reserve. This implied, in turn, a wholesale shift in farmers' attitudes, from fearing to favoring the surpluses that such a policy would produce. In his attempts to harmonize these pressures, Kissinger's newly acquired knowledge of international economics paid handsome dividends. But his basic policy objective—to shape consensus and to avoid collision with the world's poor—was merely an extension of his general design: the construction of a stable world order.

During the earlier years of Henry Kissinger's career, the United Nations had been dominated by the cold war. The United States, during the first two decades of the U.N.'s life, had enjoyed a large measure of control, both in the Security Council and in the General

Assembly, and the American delegation had seldom hesitated to use its "automatic majority" in the furtherance of its national interest. Gradually, however, as the admission of a newly sovereign state became virtually a monthly event, the major political controversies in the General Assembly began to shift from an East-West to a North-South axis. As a result of the liquidation of the colonial empires, the membership of the United Nations had almost tripled by the time Henry Kissinger reached power in 1969. More than one hundred new nations from the Third World now enjoyed an absolute mathematical majority in the General Assembly.

The major controversies over political, economic, and social issues now raged between fewer than forty developed countries and over one hundred developing nations in Asia, Africa, the Middle East, and Latin America. Since its inception in 1945, the United Nations had almost totally changed in character. During its first twenty years, it had served primarily as an instrument of American foreign policy. During its third decade, it gradually became a vehicle for the nations born since the end of World War II. Of these one hundred nations, over forty, with a population of almost 1 billion, belonged to the "Fourth World"—the poorest of the poor. Their people lived in situations so deprived as to be below any rational definition of human decency. Life expectancy was twenty years less than that of citizens of the industrialized nations. Over half of them never saw the inside of a classroom. Politically, most of these nations had been Western colonies. Now they were dictatorships.

A Chilean observer, Gabriel Garcia Marquez, had written in *Harper's Magazine* in May 1974 that Kissinger was totally indifferent to the plight of the Third World. "I am not interested in, nor do I know anything about, the southern portion of the world from the Pyrenees on down," Kissinger had allegedly remarked to Marquez. Even though this statement may never have been made, it did reflect an element of truth. The United Nations and the problems of the Third World were never prominent on Kissinger's agenda. The energy and food crises of 1974, however, forced him to pay attention. And even more important, the nations of the Third World had begun to act in concert. By 1974, they had formed a formidable power block in the United Nations. It was this new element of real power that finally forced Kissinger to take a closer look at the United Nations.

By the time Kissinger addressed the UN in September 1974, the radical wing of the new Afro-Arab-Asian nationalism had captured increasing control of the General Assembly. Various "national liberation" groups demanded and received legitimacy. The most prominent case in point was the decision of the General Assembly in 1974, by overwhelming vote, to invite Yasir Arafat, the leader of the Palestinian Liberation Organization, to address the world body. When Arafat appeared, he was accorded all the ceremonial honors usually reserved for heads of state. Only four nations out of the 138 that made up the Assembly's membership had opposed the invitation—the United States, on Kissinger's instructions, among them. When during the Palestine debate, Assembly President Abdelaziz Bouteflika of Algeria in effect curbed Israel's right to speak by limiting the debate to one speech from each country, this ruling was vainly opposed by the United States. And when the Assembly, in late November 1974, by yet another large majority, affirmed the right of the Palestinian people to be free and sovereign and, in a companion vote, awarded permanent observer status to the PLO, the United States again was on the side of the opposition.

In addition, to Kissinger's growing irritation, the Third World coalition confronted the industrialized nations with unprecedented economic demands. They called for a "new international economic order," which was to be nothing less than a redistribution of the world's wealth from the rich to the poor. In this fight, the new nations intended to make the United Nations their major vehicle. They argued that centuries of plunder and of colonial exploitation had condemned the non-white nations to a kind of global servitude. The time had now arrived for reparations. They, too, deserved their place in the sun.

With little regard for the opposition from the industrialized nations, the new majority easily mustered enough votes to adopt a Charter of Economic Rights and Duties of States. This Charter, in Kissinger's opinion, conferred duties only on the developed countries while all the rights were reserved for the Third World. The Charter permitted the expropriation of Western companies as a "national right" while prescribing the creation of a special fund for the poor nations to which the world's rich were to contribute generously. Clearly, the developing nations were attempting to impose their "new economic order" by majority.

Kissinger, not surprisingly, found this approach both irritating and naive. In a world of nation states, no new economic order could be imposed by majority vote; it had to be negotiated on a basis of mutual interest. If the United Nations was about to become a place where the developing countries had only rights and developed countries only obligations, the latter would abandon it in favor of other forums. In the end, in Kissinger's opinion, the indiscriminate use of the majority vote by the developing states was more likely to harden the heart of the rich than to produce the necessary concessions.

Thus, Kissinger used his persuasive powers to try to steer the Third World states away from confrontation politics. He made it clear to them that the developed countries, too, had raw materials that might be developed to achieve an independence from the poorer nations. The world was more dependent on the United States for food than it was on the Middle East for oil. Not a voice had been raised in the United Nations to question the Arab oil embargo though it had violated UN resolutions condemning economic coercion sponsored by the developing countries themselves. The ultimate consequence of confrontation politics by producer cartels would be to force the developed countries toward self-sufficiency and this would ultimately destroy the developing countries' best prospects for export-led growth. In addition, confrontation politics would doubtless cause a backlash in the developed countries that would make it impossible for them to pursue the generous trade and aid policies that the developing nations wanted.

Throughout most of the fall of 1974, the Third World coalition persisted on its collision course. Finally, in December, U.S. Ambassador John A. Scali, on Kissinger's instructions, delivered a somber warning to the General Assembly. He deplored the growing tendency "to adopt one-sided, unrealistic resolutions that cannot be implemented" and warned that the UN was in danger of fading into "the shadow world of rhetoric, abandoning its important role in the real world of negotiation and compromise." "The United Nations," Scali concluded, had fallen victim to "the tyranny of the new majority."

In the summer of 1975, Kissinger himself took over. Incensed by further Arab attacks against Israel in agencies such as UNESCO, and realizing that only toughness might deflect the Third World coalition from its proposed collision course, Kissinger delivered a major speech on the United Nations in Milwaukee on July 14. On that occasion, he pointed out the paradox that the most solid block in the United Nations, was "the alignment of the nonaligned." He proceeded to say that there were already "all too many incentives" for the United States "to depart the scene." "Those who seek to manipulate U.N. membership by procedural abuse," read a sentence that was left out of his spoken address, "may well inherit an empty shell." The concluding warning was unmistakable: "It is the smaller nations of the organization who would lose the most," Kissinger declared, "They are more in need of the U.N. than the larger powers such as the United States which can prosper within or outside the institution."

Kissinger had correctly diagnosed a mood of increasing disenchantment with the United Nations in the United States. "The American people," he declared, "are understandably tired of the inflammatory rhetoric against us, the all-or-nothing stance accompanied by demands for our sacrifice which too frequently dominate the meeting halls of the United Nations." It was time to go on the offensive. Kissinger had been impressed with an article by the former ambassador to India, Daniel P. Moynihan, entitled "The United States in Opposition." In it, Moynihan advocated that the United States "unfurl the banners of the liberty party" in the world forum and speak out loudly and energetically against injustice, tyranny, and abuses of the UN Charter. Kissinger conferred with Moynihan and asked him to replace the ineffectual Scali. Moynihan made his debut at a special session of the General Assembly which was convened in early September 1975 to discuss the "new international economic order."

The expected confrontation between the United States and the Third World coalition did not take place. By September, both sides had tempered their positions. Mexico's President Luis Echeverria Alvarez, a leading spokesman for the "new international economic order", advocated a "new equilibrium." Kissinger responded with a major speech entitled "Global Consensus and Economic Development," that contained a raft of concrete proposals ranging from preferential trade agreements to commodity price stabilization schemes. Kissinger had worked hard to coordinate his proposals not only with key Third World countries, but also with the Treasury Department at home. The speech which had gone through eight different drafts mirrored many of the demands of the U.N. majority. It did not, however, accept the principle of the necessity of a fundamental change in the world economic system. Basically, it was a "New Deal" type approach to adjust the old order to new global realities. Kissinger's effort at conciliation was acclaimed when at the closing of the special session, the General Assembly achieved enough agreement to adopt a sweeping final resolution by unanimous vote.

The truce was to be short-lived, however. By far the most dramatic and controversial event that took place during the Thirtieth Session of the General Assembly was a vote, taken on November 10, 1975, on a resolution defining Zionism as "a form of racism and racial discrimination." By that time, the membership of the world body stood at 142. The vote was seventy-two in favor, thirty-five against, with thirty-two abstentions and three delegations absent.

Moynihan, on Kissinger's instructions, had fought bitterly against the passage of this resolution. To both men, the resolution was a "big lie" that would make a mockery of the ideals of the United Nations

Charter. In his eagerness, however, Moynihan, had engaged in a bit of "overkill" that had irritated the more cautious Kissinger. In the context of a speech that he gave in California, Moynihan had cited approvingly an editorial from the *New York Times* that had described Uganda's President Idi Amin as a "racist murderer." Kissinger had no objection to that description, but became incensed when he learned that Moynihan had gone on to say that "it was no accident that the Organization of African Unity had elected Amin as their president." Actually, the presidency of the OAU was decided by rotation and it was Uganda's turn. Hence, Amin's election *had* in fact been an accident and Moynihan's comment was resented by a number of African delegates whose votes on the anti-Zionist resolution might have been shaded by their pique.

Kissinger told Moynihan to be more circumspect but discovered very quickly that his new ambassador, by the very bluntness of his rhetoric, had captured the mood of exasperation and impatience that many Americans felt toward the United Nations. In the end, neither Kissinger's diplomatic caution nor Moynihan's plain speaking prevented the adoption of the anti-Zionist resolution. The reasons for its passage were far from simple.

In the first place, a number of Third World votes were in effect bought with petrodollars. Second, several African states had supported the resolution for reasons of Third World solidarity without much substantive knowledge about either Israel or Zionism. As the delegate of Mauritius had said, "many people voted without knowing what Zionism is. I am confused." Third, many delegations had supported the anti-Zionism drive because they were against what the Palestinians told them Israel was: a white, imperialist military state, reminiscent of the colonial regimes established by the West in days gone by. Fourth, Israel, it was pointed out, had been settled largely by whites and its early leaders had been Europeans from Russia. Fifth, many states had voted for the resolution because of fear of Arab oil retaliation or had abstained for similar reasons, as in the case

of Japan. Finally, the Africans and Arabs had reached an "understanding." The Arabs and Communists had pledged to join the
Africans in their fight against South Africa if the Africans and Communists would join the Arabs in pushing through the anti-Zionist
resolution. Thus, the anti-Zionism vote of November 1975, signified
the confluence of a number of factors.

Kissinger was enraged and Moynihan was quick to point out
that those nations that had voted in favor of the resolution were
largely dictatorships, both of the left and of the right, while those
in opposition were largely, though by no means exclusively,
the Western democracies. To Kissinger it seemed that this vote
could not go unpunished. Accordingly he recommended that
the United States reduce its financial aid to those nations that
had shown hostility toward the United States in their voting behavior and increase aid to those that had been loyal and suppor-
tive.

All things considered, the events of 1975 were not designed to
revise favorably Kissinger's fairly low opinion of the United Nations.
In 1974, the UN had won his grudging respect when it had managed
to deploy two peace-keeping forces in the Middle East in the Sinai
desert and the Golan Heights. But now, Kissinger believed, the UN
had made his job more difficult. Even though he privately believed
that, sooner or later, Israel would have to negotiate with the Palestinians, Kissinger decided to make a common front with Israel in the
United Nations on the non-recognition of the PLO. He instructed
Moynihan to veto two Security Council resolutions that would have
modified previous resolutions to the detriment of Israel. Kissinger
perceived the Third World coalition of the United Nations in 1976
as an undisciplined collection of revolutionary states some of which
threatened the stable global order always uppermost in his mind. He
had tried to negotiate and compromise, but now, it seemed, the
radicals had won. Kissinger's response, predictably enough, was that
of a conservative.

If Kissinger's policy toward Western Europe showed that he paid little attention to friends until they threatened to become adversaries, then Kissinger's policy toward the nations of the Third World showed that he paid even less attention to neutrals until the neutrals gained a measure of power and threatened to become revolutionaries.

Latin Americans accused Kissinger of paying little attention to their continent until Chile had elected a Marxist to its presidency. It is true that Kissinger had postponed four visits to Latin America because of more pressing concerns. But, finally, in February 1976, he visited Brazil, Venezuela, Peru, Guatemala, Costa Rica, and Colombia. The high point of the trip was the signing of an agreement under which the United States and Brazil agreed to consult each other on all mutual and major international problems. This agreement considerably enhanced Brazil's aspirations to become a world power. In Peru, Kissinger declared that the United States was "fully sympathetic with Peru's struggle to create a social democracy" and in Venezuela he pledged American support for Latin American efforts to form regional organizations. Throughout his trip, Kissinger was confronted with demands to renegotiate the old Hay-Bunau-Varilla Treaty of 1903, which had ceded control over the Panama Canal to the United States.

While the visit improved the atmosphere somewhat, domestic strictures made practical progress difficult. The Congress was unwilling to lift trade restrictions that had been a source of friction between the United States and Brazil, Venezuela, and Peru. And the rhetoric of Ronald Reagan made the Panama Canal into a campaign issue during most of 1976. Kissinger found his freedom of maneuver severely circumscribed by events over which he had little or no control.

By 1976, African leaders had also become impatient with Kissinger. They pointed out that the American Secretary of State had never bothered to visit an African country. President Kenneth D. Kaunda of Zambia, on the occasion of a visit to the White House in April 1975, had declared that he was dismayed by America's policy toward Africa, "or the lack of it which, of course, can mean the same thing." It took a Soviet victory in Angola to persuade Kissinger finally to visit six black African countries in the spring of 1976. His tour took him to Kenya, Tanzania, Zambia, Zaire, Liberia, and Senegal.

In a major policy address in Zambia, Kissinger placed the United States firmly behind the goal of eventual black majority rule in southern Africa. "The United States," he declared, was "wholly committed to help bring about a rapid, just, and African solution" in Rhodesia. He avowed support "in the strongest terms" for Britain's proposals for negotiations leading to African majority rule in Rhodesia within two years. He seemed determined to crush any hopes of Rhodesia's white minority regime for American support "at any stage in its conflict with African states or African liberation movements." On the contrary, he stated that the Rhodesian whites would "face our unrelenting opposition until a negotiated settlement [was] achieved." As part of that opposition, Kissinger promised that he would urge Congress to repeal the Byrd Amendment, which authorized the importation of Rhodesian chrome in violation of United Nations sanctions against the Ian Smith regime.

On the matter of South Africa, Kissinger urged that nation to fix a timetable for self-determination in Namibia under United Nations supervision and insisted on the end of apartheid—the separation of the races—in South Africa itself. In Liberia, Kissinger declared that he was ready to normalize relations with Angola if the Cuban troops were withdrawn from that African country. And in Senegal, he called upon the world's industrial nations to join in a vast project to "roll back the desert" in drought-devastated West Africa. Finally, at a meeting of the United Nations Conference on Trade and Development in Nairobi, Kenya, Kissinger proposed the creation of a $1 billion International Resources Bank to "promote more rational, systematic, and equitable development of resources in developing nations." A majority of the UNCTAD membership, however, rejected this proposal, objecting to its emphasis on private enterprise.

On balance, Kissinger's African tour was an impressive if belated attempt to atone for past American blunders in Africa, and to establish a climate for mutually beneficial relations with a part of the world that the United States could no longer ignore in safety. Angola had shown the heavy price of the policy of neglect of previous years. Kissinger was in no mood to leave the field to the Soviet Union. He also had begun to realize the importance of building détente between the races and the world's rich and poor. The campaign politics of 1976 could not deflect him from that course.

In his overall approach to Third World problems, Kissinger tried to apply the same mixture of diplomacy and power that he had administered in his relations with the Soviet Union. On energy, he admonished the West to unite and to negotiate with the oil producers from strength. He was aware of the potential of food power though he was prepared to be forthcoming with food on humanitarian grounds as well. He went quite far to meet the demands of the emerging majority for a new international economic order, but he was not prepared to abandon the old order. In all cases, he strove for equilibrium and balance in the relations between North and South just as he had striven to attain these ends in the relations between East and West. The weapons, however, were different. In order to preserve the old economic order, Kissinger resorted, knowingly or not, to the policies of Franklin Roosevelt's New Deal. Roosevelt had saved the endangered capitalist system by adjusting it to the demands of a majority of dissatisfied Americans. Kissinger tried to save the old global economic order by making it more responsive to the demands of the world's poor and dispossessed.

There is one final irony, however, in this story. Kissinger may have prevented World War III by his policy of détente with Russia and China. He may be justified in his belief that the two colossi of the Communist world might no longer be "revolutionary" powers. Could it be, however, that the real "revolutionaries" might be those radical forces in the Third World to which, until recently, he paid the least attention? Kissinger might not be surprised by such a revelation. For he always suspected that history, though lacking a sense of justice, had a consummate sense of irony.

The Middle East:
The Thirty Years' War

> In all efforts for peace the overriding problem is
> to relate the sense of individual justice to the
> common good. The great tragedies of history occur
> not when right confronts wrong, but when two rights
> face each other.
>
> Henry Kissinger
> Geneva, December 12, 1973.

Once, on one of those rare occasions when Henry Kissinger reminisced about his youth as a Jew in Hitler's Germany, he mentioned that he had lost a number of his relatives in Nazi concentration camps. "And most of my Jewish boyhood friends also perished" he recalled. "But one escaped", he suddenly remembered, his face brightening. "He is living in England now, but it is his dream to visit Israel."

This conversation took place at Harvard in 1951. More than twenty years later, I discovered that Kissinger's friend had died in England without ever having seen the Holy Land. In 1971, Kissinger had sent a check to the Jewish National Fund. His instructions were to plant a grove of 300 trees near Jerusalem in memory of his boyhood friend from Fürth.

Kissinger has always been committed to the survival of the Jewish state. Like other German-Jewish intellectuals—Hans Morgenthau and Hannah Arendt for example—he perceived Israel not in religious terms but as a place of refuge for the Jews. As he put it to me once, "if there had been an Israel in Hitler's time, millions of Jews could have been saved." Despite his basically secular nature, Kissinger's concern for Israel's survival has been a genuine and deep emotion.

But how was Israel's survival to be secured? Here, Kissinger, the historian, took over. All that he had learned had taught him that a victor's peace was seldom lasting. Neither was total defeat. To be durable, a peace would have to be constructed on a measure of equality. The flush of victory, Kissinger believed, often made the victor hard and brittle. He then no longer understood the pain and anguish of the vanquished. His realism became another word for lack of empathy. This was the danger, in Kissinger's opinion, that Israel faced after her spectacular victory of 1967. The Arabs, on the other hand, unable to cope with a terrible reality, took refuge in their fantasies. Their dreams and their despair, rather than facts, determined policy. They learned in 1967 what the Jews had always known: the utter desolation of defeat. Their honor would have to be restored at all costs, even at the price of yet another setback. Thus, Kissinger was always sure that Israel's 1967 victory would be followed by another war.

Intellectually, Kissinger perceived the Arab-Israeli conflict as a tragedy of Aristotelian proportions. Such tragedies did not arise from encounters in which right clashed with wrong. They occurred when right clashed with another right. This, in Kissinger's opinion, was the heart of the conflict between Israel and the Arab states in Palestine. Jews, responding to centuries of persecution, had attempted to save themselves by creating a state of their own. They had established it in a land that had been occupied by Arabs for centuries, at the precise moment when the Arab peoples were emerging from the crucible of Western colonialism and were rediscovering their own national destinies. Thus, Jewish nationalism clashed head on with Arab nationalism in Palestine.

When Kissinger was sworn in as Secretary of State in September 1973, three wars between Israel and her Arab neighbors had been the result of this collision. The modern Middle East had been the scene of both irreconcilable hopes and aspirations, bitter hatreds and violent passions. The wars had been fought with the deepest emotion. Each contestant had regarded his rights as self-evident and firmly based upon the will of God, morality, law, and reason. As passions rose, irrationality had become commonplace. Desperate deed had been heaped upon desperate deed until right and wrong, responsibility and guilt, could no longer be distinguished. Each side had done things that the other could neither forgive nor forget.

Kissinger was also aware that time had not served as a healer of wounds. On the Arab side, the shock inflicted by the establishment of Israel had grown more, rather than less, acute as nationalism had gathered momentum. The trauma was accentuated by the fact that Israel—four times its original size since 1967—was seen as an ever-growing menace by the Arab world. Most Arabs were convinced that no hope existed to regain the lost territories except through war. They had abandoned all faith in diplomacy. On the Jewish side, in turn, time had turned Israel into virtually a garrison state. Here was a nation that was a viable democracy, yet forced to impose upon itself a Spartan discipline, living virtually in a state of siege, dependent for its very survival upon the policies of its one ally—the United States. Thus, it had come about that the Jews who had lived homeless in the Diaspora for two millennia should, within a quarter of a century, create a state with fearful military capability. Jews, to whom military matters had always been anathema, now had found it necessary to make them their first priority. This is what time had done.

To Kissinger, the Arab-Israeli conflict posed a dual challenge. On one level, there was the ever-present danger of conflagration in the region. But, on a global level, the situation, in his view, was also "murderously dangerous." Since the Soviet Union had decided to support the Arab cause, and the United States had tended to support the Jewish state, the danger of superpower confrontation was always present. All that Kissinger had tried to build could be destroyed on the Middle Eastern battlefield. Détente could be smashed and with it, the entire architecture of stability which Kissinger regarded as a prerequisite for peace. Hence, as he assumed his new duties in the fall of 1973, the Middle East caused him particular anxiety. He regarded the achievement of a peace of equilibrium and balance not only as his gravest responsibility as a statesman but also as his greatest diplomatic challenge. Yet he was mortally afraid that before there could be initiatives for peace there would have to be another round of war. He suspected that such a conflict would again begin with a surprise attack by Israel.

Two weeks after he had taken his oath of office, his worst fears had come to pass. The fourth Arab-Israeli war had broken out. But there had been no surprise attack by Israel. Instead, Syria and Egypt had begun a massive ground assault against the Jewish state on Yom Kippur, the holiest day in the Jewish calendar.

Kissinger had not expected war to come so soon. Despite repeated declarations by Egypt's President Anwar Sadat in 1972, that Egypt would launch a war against Israel "within a year" Kissinger had tended to dismiss these statements as empty threats. He believed that Sadat simply would not dare to attack Israel. Moreover, he had been reassured by Brezhnev's susceptibility to linkage and therefore hoped that the Soviet leader would not risk détente for the sake of a dubious military adventure in the Middle East.

In March 1973, Israel's Prime Minister Golda Meir received a pledge from President Nixon for a shipment of forty-eight Phantom jets over a four-year period. This American decision had convinced Sadat that only a war could regain his lost territories. He now decided to develop a common strategy with Saudi Arabia and Syria. President Assad of Syria could provide a large and well-trained army while King Faisal of Saudia Arabia declared that he was ready to use his oil as a weapon in the battle against Israel. Most important, the Soviet leadership decided that it could have both détente *and* a Middle Eastern war and it began to ship large quantities of war matériel to Syria and Egypt. By May, Kissinger had become concerned with these arms shipments and in one statement referred to them as "irresponsible". In early September, Kissinger's suspicions were aroused to the point that he asked Israel's ambassador, Simcha Dinitz, for an assessment of Arab troop movements. Dinitz replied that Israel had no conclusive evidence of Arab plans for an attack. Kissinger, who had considerable respect for Israeli intelligence activities, felt reassured that the Arabs would not go to war.

In late September an event took place that made Kissinger suspect that the Israelis, not the Arabs, were planning a surprise attack. On September 28, a band of Palestinian terrorists had ambushed a trainload of Russian Jews who were in transit in Austria on their way to Israel. Austria's Chancellor Bruno Kreisky gave in to the terrorists' demands and closed a transit center for Jewish emigrants to Israel. A visit to Austria by Mrs. Meir was unable to dissuade him. Feelings in Israel ran high and Kissinger feared a major move by Israel in retaliation, probably against Syria and Palestinian camps throughout the Middle East.

Kissinger, worried that an Israeli attack would lead to another inconclusive war and, moreover, would set the United States and the Soviet Union on a collision course, warned Ambassador Dinitz in the strongest terms "not to pre-empt." The American Ambassador Kenneth Keating declared in Israel that only if there was "irrefutable" proof that the Arabs were the aggressors in a war, would the United States feel morally obliged to help. If Israel struck first, she would have to fight alone.

Only on October 4, forty-eight hours before Sadat's D-Day, did some Israeli military leaders respond to the imminence of an Arab attack. Chief of staff, General David Elazar, pleaded with Mrs. Meir for permission to call up the reserves and urged her to consider a pre-emptive strike against Syria and Egypt. General Ariel Sharon predicted "war within one or two days." Mrs. Meir refused. She did not wish to go against Kissinger's solemn warning. Moreover, she did not want to provoke the Arabs by calling up the reserves or to disrupt the observance of Yom Kippur by putting the nation on a full alert. Thus, Golda Meir made a decision of historic importance: by refusing to permit a pre-emptive strike against Syria and Egypt, she decided that Israel would accept the first blows. The diplomatic advantage of being the victim outweighed, in her mind, the military advantage of being the attacker.

Kissinger was shocked and angered by the Syrian-Egyptian attack. He resented the duplicity of the Soviet leaders who had not only refused to warn him, but had actively conspired with the Arabs, in clear violation of the Soviet-American agreement reached in Washington only a few months earlier. He suddenly realized how wrong he had been. The Soviets obviously thought that they could help the Arabs without destroying détente with the United States. A chastened Kissinger met with Dinitz immediately after the attack. Dinitz informed Kissinger that Israel now faced 2,000 Egyptian and 1,000 Syrian tanks. He told Kissinger of Mrs. Meir's decision to heed his injunction against a pre-emptive strike. "But now," Dinitz added gravely, "that decision bestows a special responsibility on America not to leave us alone as far as equipment is concerned." Israel was now the victim of aggression and was urgently in need of planes, tanks, and ammunition so that she would be able to defend herself.

A domestic counterpart of the "six-day war" now erupted between Kissinger and Defense Secretary James R. Schlesinger. All accounts agree that the United States was terribly slow in supplying Israel with desperately needed planes, tanks, and ammunition—so slow in fact that Israel's survival hung in the balance. Two diametrically opposite versions however, exist about the precise reasons for this near-fatal delay. The Kalb brothers, in their biography of Kissinger, describe a secretary of state who was engaged in a one-man fight on behalf of Israel against a reluctant Schlesinger and a Pentagon fearful of an oil embargo. Finally, according to their account, Kissinger was able to overcome the defense secretary's presistent foot-dragging and, fortified by a clear-cut presidential order, extracted the needed war matériel from the inventory of the Pentagon.

The opposing version, related by Tad Szulc in an article in *New York* magazine in July 1974, and supported by Gil Carl AlRoy in his book, *The Kissinger Experience,* as well as by Matti Golan in a book, *The Secret Conversations of Henry Kissinger,* casts Kissinger into the role of Israel's nemesis. According to this latter interpretation it was really Kissinger who, in his eagerness to save détente with Russia and to forestall a crippling Arab oil embargo, had decided against quick and massive aid to Israel. Schlesinger only followed Kissinger's policy and the secretary of state cast Schlesinger into the role of "bad guy" in order to mislead Israel. Kissinger wanted to appear as Israel's ally, however, in order to prevent the Israeli ambassador from making a direct appeal for help to Congress. Finally, on October 13, Nixon overruled Kissinger's objections and the massive airlift that enabled Israel to turn the war around was set in motion.

The dramatic importance of these six days in October 1973 warrants a closer examination of the evidence. What was at stake during that period, was nothing less than the life or death of Israel.

According to the pro-Kissinger version, Schlesinger, on October 8, rejected a request by Kissinger that Israeli planes should be allowed to land in the United States to pick up ammunition and spare parts. Dinitz complained to Kissinger, who promised to help. Shortly afterwards Kissinger called Dinitz and reported that Israeli planes would be permitted to land at U.S. bases provided they would paint over their Israeli insignia. In addition, Kissinger reported that the President had given his approval "in principle" to replace Israeli plane losses. Dinitz expressed his gratitude, but wanted to know when he could count on the planes. Later that evening, Kissinger reported that he had run into "bureaucratic difficulties" with the Pentagon: all that Schlesinger was willing to release were two planes. Dinitz, near despair, exclaimed that Israel needed dozens. On October 9, Kissinger told Dinitz that he was engaged in "a one-man fight with the Pentagon to fulfill the Israeli requests." To reassure the Israeli ambassador, Kissinger had a "hot-line" installed to the Israeli Embassy.

On October 10, Dinitz informed Kissinger that a Soviet airlift had begun into Cairo and Damascus. "His enemies", Dinitz pointed out, "had no trouble getting help while the Israelis had to spend their time painting Jewish stars off their planes." Kissinger again offered rapid action and, according to the Kalbs, called Schlesinger and asked him to organize civilian charters to carry American military aid to Israel as quickly as possible. Dinitz made an appointment directly with Schlesinger for noon that day, but Schlesinger cancelled at the last minute. His deputy, William Clements, fearful of the oil lobby, had persuaded his chief to procrastinate. Later that afternoon, reports reached Kissinger that the Soviet airlift to the two Arab states had reached "massive" proportions.

During the night of October 10, according to this version, Kissinger reached the decision that the Russians would have to be stopped—not only to save Israel but to prevent another superpower confrontation. He now decided that the United States had to match the Soviet airlift by an equally massive American airlift to Israel. Kissinger had no doubt that, with such help, the Israelis could turn the tide of battle and restore a military balance in the area, thereby providing the United States with the diplomatic leverage to shape the postwar negotiations. He was also determined to demonstrate to Syria and Egypt that the Arab states could never win a victory with Soviet arms and that they would have to deal with the United States if they wished to attain any of their policy objectives.

On October 11, Kissinger argued heatedly with Schlesinger, demanding that twenty transport planes be chartered at once to carry supplies to Israel. Schlesinger resisted just as heatedly and argued that such an American airlift would so infuriate the Arabs that they would impose an oil embargo on the United States. He also offered to release six Phantoms. In view of the fact that by then Israel had lost an estimated seventy-five planes, Dinitz's despair was understandable. By the afternoon of October 11, he was seriously considering to "go public," to appeal directly to the Congress to help Israel in her desperate plight.

By the morning of October 12, Dinitz still had no decision on the twenty charter planes. Kissinger reported that Schlesinger had told him that he had failed to hire civilian charters. Most companies, said Schlesinger, did not want to get involved in the Middle East war. Kissinger "snapped" at Schlesinger to get the job done with military planes. There was no more time to lose.

That evening, Dinitz finally managed to see Schlesinger. Several of the defense chief's deputies were also present, including William Clements. Dinitz lamented the "unbelievably slow response of the Americans", warning that every hour had to be paid for in Israeli lives. Schlesinger explained that the United States did not wish to destroy its "position and image in the Arab world." Insofar as U.S. military transports were concerned, he would permit the pilots to carry the supplies to the Azores Islands, but no further. Israel would have to make her own arrangements to move the supplies from the Azores to Tel Aviv. Dinitz broke down in despair. He stated that, in that case, the supplies would not get to Israel "in time for this war." To make matters worse, Schlesinger disclosed that he would permit a rate of delivery of Phantoms of only "one and a half per day." After "a couple of days," the deliveries would be stopped so that "we could read Arab reactions before we decide on further shipments." In any case, no more than sixteen Phantoms, in all, were earmarked for Israel.

In desperation, Dinitz went to see Kissinger at midnight. "One and a half Phantoms a day, for a couple of days," Dinitz exclaimed, was "a mockery." He then played his ace. "If a massive American airlift to Israel (did) not start immediately," Dinitz declared, "then I will know that the United States is reneging on its promises and its policy, and we will have to draw very serious conclusions." The implication was clear to Kissinger. Unless massive aid was forthcoming immediately, Dinitz would "go public", and, with the Congress and the people sympathetic to Israel, such an appeal might topple the Nixon administration, already seriously weakened by Watergate. "We held our fire because Kissinger told us to," Dinitz would say, "And now you don't come through for us in our hour of need." Kissinger promised Dinitz that he would do "everything in his power" to bring the Pentagon into line.

Shortly after midnight, Kissinger reached Schlesinger and told him angrily that he was working against presidential orders. "The President," he told him, "would blow his top" when he learned of the Pentagon's footdragging. Immediately afterwards he requested an emergency meeting with the President. At that meeting, Kissinger complained bitterly about Schlesinger's obstructionism. Nixon took immediate action. Realizing that Israeli pilots were needed for combat duty, he ordered thirty transport planes to be flown directly to Israel. He also ordered the immediately delivery of ten more Phantom jets.

On Saturday morning, according to the Kalb version, Nixon summoned all his top advisors to an emergency meeting at the White House. Schlesinger tried to explain his difficulties in chartering civilian transport planes. "To hell with the charters," Nixon exploded. "Get the supplies there with American military planes! Forget the Azores! Get moving! I want no further delays!" That afternoon, a massive American airlift began. A fleet of planes was on its way to Israel. The planes and supplies arrived just in time. The Israeli army was running out of fighting machines and ammunition. Kissinger had won his "six-day war" with the Pentagon.

The "anti-Kissinger" version puts matters differently. In that account, Kissinger made policy while Schlesinger merely followed orders. According to this version, Kissinger believed that Israel could hold her own against Syria and Egypt without American help. Thus, détente could be salvaged and the oil lobby could be kept friendly while Israel would fight her way to a military stalemate. But such a policy necessitated an enormous deception. Kissinger would have to represent himself to Dinitz as his ally, while at the same time ordering Schlesinger to "drag his feet."

According to this version, Kissinger emerges as a masterful manipulator. He gained Dinitz's confidence by being accessible to him at any hour during the day or night. According to Szulc, Kissinger used the method known in police circles as the "Mutt and Jeff" routine, a technique intended to undermine the resolve of the victim by creating a false sense of solidarity. While one policeman is friendly and overly sympathetic, the other is harsh and brutal. This leads the victim to see the friendly policeman as an ally, to the point of confiding in him, especially since the friendly policeman intimates that he is doing all he can to help the victim against his brutal colleague. Thus, Kissinger was the sympathetic cop and Schlesinger the brutal one.

The anti-Kissinger version maintains that it was Kissinger who invented the idea of "civilian charters" while Schlesinger was prepared to use military planes. And it was Kissinger who wanted the American planes to fly to the Azores only, while Schlesinger was in favor of going all the way to Israel. Whenever Dinitz threatened to "go public", Kissinger offered more hope. Only when the Soviet airlift had reached massive proportions, did Nixon finally agree to intervene directly. He authorized Schlesinger to go ahead with a massive American airlift to which Kissinger, by October 13, gave his half-hearted consent. At that fateful meeting in Nixon's White House office, it was Schlesinger who won the fight for Israel, not Kissinger. So ends this second, anti-Kissinger version of the "six-day war" in the United States over the question of massive help for Israel.

It seems to me that the Kalbs' version is not quite accurate. Rather, the evidence suggests that Kissinger tried to use the war to promote a settlement. If neither side would win decisively, it would be easier for him to launch a diplomatic offensive. Thus, so long as the Soviet Union showed restraint, he would withhold *major* arms deliveries to Israel. He would deliver just enough to keep the balance. But when, by October 12, he had become convinced that the Soviet airlift had become so heavy that it threatened Israel's survival, he promptly decided to release a massive flow of arms to Israel.

The anti-Kissinger version, however, strikes me as even further off the mark. In the first place, during the meeting between Schlesinger and Dinitz, the defense secretary had made clear his opposition to the Secretary of State. Given the very real tensions between Schlesinger and Kissinger, it strains credulity to assume that Schlesinger would become a willing accomplice in Kissinger's alleged deception. Why should he do Kissinger the favor of playing the part of the "brutal cop" while giving him the credit for saving Israel? It seems more logical to assume that the differences between the two men were genuine and what Dinitz experienced was no elaborate charade staged by the Secretary of State. The anti-Kissinger version would have us believe that Kissinger had virtually Mephistophelean powers over the Secretary of Defense who was, after all, a man of considerable inner strength, integrity, and intellect. Second, if Kissinger had really acted in accordance with the second version, he would have been totally out of character. Not only would the logical conclusion of such a policy have jeopardized the very survival of Israel, but it would have permitted the Russians to score a major military victory. Even if, as AlRoy believes, Kissinger was indifferent to the fate of Israel—and I am not prepared to accept this assumption—he was certainly not ready to permit the Soviet Union to destabilize the global equilibrium in so absolute a fashion. Only *with* American help did Israel have any hope of turning the war around. Without American help, the conflict might have ended with an Arab military victory and as a major triumph for Soviet power. In my opinion, the military solution Kissinger wished to bring about was not an Arab victory, but a stalemate, a balanced equilibrium. He would match the Soviets plane for plane and tank for tank to create a balance in the Middle East. Such a balance would be the starting point for peace negotiations. This had been his policy from the beginning of the October war. To have us believe otherwise is to have us believe that Kissinger, in this single instance, did not behave like Kissinger.

Almost immediately after the beginning of the American airlift, the Israeli army went on the attack. During the second week of the war, Israel gradually gained the upper hand on both the Syrian and Egyptian fronts. After fierce tank battles in the Golan Heights, the Israelis not only threw back the Syrians but embarked on the road to Damascus. In the words of General Dayan: "We have to show the Syrians that the road leads not only from Damascus to Tel Aviv, but from Tel Aviv to Damascus." On the Egyptian front, the Israeli troops, in a daring tactical maneuver, crossed over to the west bank of the Suez Canal on Egyptian territory. Their aim was to encircle the Egyptian troops on the east bank and to cut off their retreat across the canal back to Egypt. After massive air and tank battles, the Israeli objectives were attained. The Egyptian troops were trapped in two large pockets and the Third Army was at Israel's mercy for its supply of food and water. By October 19, the military balance had definitely shifted in Israel's favor.

On October 19, Brezhnev invited Kissinger to come to Moscow for "urgent consultations on the Middle East." In view of Israel's rapid military advance, the Soviet leader was now eager for a cease-fire. Kissinger, after some reflection, decided to accept. By going to Moscow to negotiate, he would allow Israel at least another two to three days to improve her position. A rejection of Brezhnev's invitation, in Kissinger's view, might have led to Soviet military intervention on the Arab side.

On the eve of Kissinger's departure for Moscow, the President announced that he had asked Congress for $2.2 billion in emergency military aid for Israel. The war matériel would be given, rather than sold, to the Jewish state the President declared. While Kissinger was on his way to Moscow, King Faisal of Saudi Arabia finally decided to use the oil weapon against the United States. An oil embargo was Faisal's answer to American military aid to his Zionist enemy.

Kissinger was determined to exact a price for a cease-fire. Egypt had consistently refused to engage in direct negotiations with Israel. It was Kissinger's aim to exploit Brezhnev's nervousness about the Israeli offensive to arrange a cease-fire that would lead to direct talks between Egypt and Israel. He knew that the Israelis would chafe under a cease-fire that would be imposed on them when they needed only a few more days to defeat the Egyptian and Syrian armies. He therefore hoped to mollify them with the prospect of direct talks with Egypt. Kissinger prevailed on the Israelis to accept Brezhnev's proposal for a cease-fire in place and the Soviet leader won Sadat's agreement to direct talks with Israel. Kissinger was pleased. He had restored military equilibrium, and in addition, had used the war to force Egypt and Israel to take an unprecedented step. On October 22, the United Nations Security Council unanimously adopted a superpower call for a cease-fire in place.

On October 23, however, reports reached Kissinger that there had been massive violations of the U.N. cease-fire. The Egyptians apparently had committed the first violations and the Israelis had then taken advantage of them to extend their lines on the west bank of the canal. The Israelis were virtually in a position to capture Suez, giving them the power to encircle Egypt's Third Army of 100,000 men.

Kissinger now realized that, in order to save his policy of equilibrium, he would have to help Egypt rather than Israel. He was determined to prevent another decisive Israeli victory patterned on the 1967 model. Such a victory, in his judgment, would be sure to trigger yet another war. Finally, if he was to gain acceptance as a peacemaker between the Arab states and Israel, he would have to demonstrate his impartiality. The rescue of the Egyptian Third Army Corps would be a tangible demonstration of such a policy.

This time, it was Kissinger who put pressure on Dinitz and it was Israel which was slow to respond to American entreaties. By October 24, the Israelis announced that their forces had reached the outskirts of Suez and that the Third Army was completely surrounded. Kissinger was furious and urged Dinitz to permit humanitarian convoys of food, water, and medical supplies to reach the trapped Egyptian soldiers. He implied strongly that if the Israelis resisted the United States itself would supply the convoys. Kissinger was determined to stop the Israelis and to bring about a military stalemate.

On October 24, Brezhnev issued his threat of Soviet unilateral intervention. On October 25, Nixon and Kissinger responded with the "military alert" that has been discussed in a different context. By evening, the crisis had passed and the UN Security Council had approved a resolution setting up a UN Emergency Force that was to serve as a buffer and cease-fire observer between Israel and Egypt in the Sinai Desert. Israel's advance was stopped and Egypt was saved from another humiliating defeat. Kissinger's equilibrium had become a reality.

Kissinger now, for the first time, came under severe criticism in Israel. "If only he had given us a few more days," one Israeli official exclaimed bitterly, "we would have had another 1967 victory." "To be followed by yet another inconclusive war," Kissinger snapped back. Besides, he believed that had he not come down on Egypt's side, there would have been a "three out of four chance" that the Soviet Union would have intervened. Such an intervention in his judgment, might have led to the destruction of Israel and to a substantial shift in the Middle Eastern balance, and ultimately, to a world war.

Thus, Kissinger's role in the October war can neither be described as pro-Israeli nor as pro-Arab. In essence, it was pro-equilibrium.

Before the war erupted, Kissinger perceived Israel as the stronger side and thus warned the Jewish leaders "not to pre-empt." But when he turned out to have been mistaken and Syria and Egypt launched their coordinated surprise attack, Kissinger switched sides and provided American military aid to Israel in order to restore the military balance. And when the Israelis, with this American assistance gained the upper hand, Kissinger switched sides again and insisted on the rescue of 100,000 trapped Egyptian soldiers. When a cease-fire was finally proclaimed by the United Nations, both sides were exhausted and roughly even—exactly what Kissinger had wanted. It had always been his firm belief that only a war without victory or defeat could contain the seeds of peace.

As Kissinger surveyed the ravages of the October war, he conceived his plan for peace in the Middle East. He decided to subdivide the problem into manageable segments instead of addressing it in its totality. He would approach it step by step, beginning with the least forbidding obstacle and then, after having built a basis of trust between the rivals, he would try to negotiate the more formidable hurdles. A first tentative step had already been taken. Egypt had agreed to talk to Israel. If Kissinger could achieve a military disengagement between Israel and Egypt, a momentum toward peace might then be set in motion. It would perhaps then be possible to leap over yet another hurdle and to effect a military disengagement between Syria and Israel. If such military interim agreements were possible, perhaps one might be able to move the rivals toward political accommodation. Once Egypt and Syria had entered negotiations with Israel, Saudi Arabia might be persuaded to lift her oil embargo and, if luck held, it might even be conceivable to think about a compromise between Israel and the Palestinians and a Jerusalem settlement. Such was Kissinger's train of thought. The peace-making process would be like a steeple chase, with each successive hurdle higher and more treacherous. But at least, Kissinger believed, the step-by-step approach would yield some limited successes and should not be a total failure.

The objective that Kissinger had in mind, of course, was equilibrium. Israel would have to withdraw from some of the conquered territories, but within the context of her national security. The diplomatic re-emergence of the Arabs would be encouraged, but within a context of realism and responsibility. An effort would be made to woo the Arabs away from the Soviet Union. They would come to the United States because, in Kissinger's judgment, "they could get weapons from the Russians, but territory only from the United States." Thus, by delivering some real estate to the Arabs, Soviet power in the Middle East would be diminished and American influence strengthened. To achieve this objective, however, pressure would have to be applied on Israel. She would have to be encouraged to trade territory for security. And if Kissinger's reasoning was wrong, he would have to protect Israel by always being generous with arms.

Kissinger's step-by-step approach to peace was not greeted with general acclaim. The Soviet Union was highly critical and pushed for a general peace conference to be held in Geneva. There was also criticism in the United States. Numerous Middle East experts asserted that Kissinger's approach was that of a doctor who planned to stitch up only part of a wound while permitting a raging infection to continue unattended.

By concentrating on Egypt, these critics stated, Kissinger intended to woo the moderate Sadat away from the Arab camp. This would not only remove the most conciliatory voice from Arab councils, but it would postpone and ultimately make more difficult the moment of truth. The heart of the matter, Kissinger's critics declared, was neither Egypt nor Syria, but the problem of the Palestinians, which Kissinger had chosen to postpone indefinitely, not to mention Jerusalem which he had chosen to ignore completely. Thus, as George Ball, one of Kissinger's most trenchant critics put it, "the step-by-step approach was the work of a tactician when the times called for a strategist."

Kissinger was undaunted by these attacks. He believed that the aftermath of an inconclusive war was the best time for a concentrated peace effort. Shortly after the last shot had been fired, he decided to commit his skill, energy, and reputation to a highly personal diplomatic peace offensive in the Middle East. During the next few months, he would visit virtually every Arab capital, shuttle between Aswan and Jerusalem, and later between Damascus and Jerusalem. Sadat would call him "brother"; Faisal would welcome him even though he was a Jew; Hussein would pilot him in the royal helicopter; even Assad would learn to like him; and Golda Meir would have endless conversations with him in her kitchen. The end result of this extraordinary diplomatic *tour de force* was the successful negotiation of the first two hurdles. In January 1974, Kissinger was able to produce a military disengagement accord between Israel and Egypt and four months later, after immense effort, he was able to achieve a similar accord between Israel and Syria. Kissinger's "shuttle diplomacy" was so uniquely his own that it merits special consideration.

Kissinger was very careful throughout both negotiations not to take a firm, formal position on any issue under discussion. Such a role would have aborted the talks whenever one of the parties would refuse to go along with him. This was precisely the kind of predicament into which former Secretary of State Rogers had trapped himself when he had proclaimed the specific plan that came to be associated with his name. Kissinger, instead, allowed the negotiations to take their course and only when the differences had narrowed to a point when, in his judgment, an intervention was virtually certain to close the remaining gap, did he present "American proposals" which, in fact, were always accepted.

At first he was a high-class messenger in both negotiations. He carried proposals and maps between Aswan and Jerusalem and then between Damascus and Jerusalem. He never served as lawyer for either side, however, nor would he bargain on behalf of anyone. He simply promised to convey accurately to each the proposals of the other. Only when he recognized that both sides wanted an agreement but that, for reasons of prestige, neither side was able to accept a proposal by the other, did Kissinger offer his own proposals.

By this time, both parties had become so dependent on Kissinger that he was able to exert considerable leverage to move the sides to the desired compromise. Threats that he would have to return to Washington always produced additional concessions. The Syrian accord almost collapsed twice. But when Kissinger finally prepared to leave and was already at the door, Assad said quietly: "What a pity. We have come so far and we have not succeeded. Can't anything be done?" The Syrian leader asked Kissinger to stay on and, two days later, the deal was concluded. In the end, Kissinger had earned the gratitude of all the parties to the conflict. Sadat continued to acclaim "his brother Henry." Assad looked forward to Kissinger's visits to Damascus, and the aging Jewish prime minister would prepare dinner for the Jewish secretary of state who had wondered only half in jest "how one million Jewish mothers in Israel could collectively cook such awful food."

Kissinger's task with Syria and Egypt was considerably simpler than his task in Israel. In Egypt and in Syria, Kissinger negotiated with a single man. If he was able to gain Sadat's and Assad's approval, he had won. No one else had to be persuaded. In Israel, on the other hand, Mrs. Meir's approval, though essential, was not enough. The cabinet had to be won over. And even if the cabinet was friendly, the political opposition and the press were not. Many ordinary Israelis were deeply suspicious of Kissinger. Not infrequently, hostile demonstrators chanting "Jew boy, go home" disturbed his sleep at night.

Besides, it seemed to Kissinger, not without reason, that there was no such thing as privacy in Israel. Nothing seemed to be confidential. Almost his every word sooner or later became public knowledge. It seemed a lot more tidy to negotiate with two authoritarian regimes than with a multiparty democracy like Israel. Moreover, it was Israel that had to be persuaded to give up tangible territory conquered in a war that she had not begun. Kissinger was aware of this asymmetry. Yet he argued forcefully that occupation had not assured security. The Yom Kippur war, in his opinion, had disproved that popular Israeli assumption. He was now convinced that time was no longer on Israel's side, if indeed it ever had been. He urged the Israelis to exchange land for new and guaranteed borders. The time had come, in his opinion, for Israel to "take some risks for peace" while she could still negotiate from strength. If she chose to cling to all the territories, the combination of more sophisticated Soviet weapons, an Arab oil embargo, and a more ambivalent United States would gradually narrow Israel's options until she might have to accept a greatly inferior settlement. Kissinger's logic prevailed in the end and Israel withdrew its forces from both the east and west banks of the Suez Canal approximately twenty miles back into the Sinai. Israel also agreed to return the destroyed city of Kuneitra to the Syrians.

Thus, Kissinger's intensive diplomatic effort produced two interim military accords of disengagement. Moreover, an important precedent was set. On November 11, 1973, at Kilometer 101 on the Cairo-Suez road, an Israeli and an Egyptian general shook hands, the first such occasion in a quarter of a century. On December 21, the foreign ministers of Egypt, Jordan, Israel, the United States and the Soviet Union gathered in Geneva under the chairmanship of UN Secretary-General Kurt Waldheim in order to begin the long process of peace-making in the Middle East. On that occasion, Kissinger gave a short but moving speech. He had not yet concluded either of the two accords and Syria had decided not to attend the conference. Yet, he was undaunted. One passage recalled young Kissinger's rejection a quarter century before of Spengler's pessimism:

> We are challenged by emotions so deeply felt—by causes so passionately believed and pursued—that the tragic march from

cataclysm to cataclysm, each more costly and indecisive than the last, sometimes seems preordained. Yet our presence here today —in itself a momentous accomplishment—is a symbol of rejection of this fatalistic view. Respect for the forces of history does not mean blind submission to history.

"There is an Arab saying," he continued, *"Illi Fat Mat,* which means that the past is dead. There is justice on all sides, but there is a greater justice still in finding a truth which merges all aspirations in the realization of a common humanity." He concluded with a quote from Hillel: "It was a Jewish sage who, speaking for all mankind, expressed this problem well: he said if I am not for myself, who is for me, but if I am for myself alone, who am I?"

At long last, Israelis and Arabs had agreed to meet in a face-to-face diplomatic encounter. Even though Syria was absent, Kissinger was pleased with the result. As Abba Eban, Israel's foreign minister, had said one year earlier: "For something to be born, the parents have to meet at least once."

During the year that followed the second disengagement accord, events transpired, both on the world stage and in the Middle East, that almost killed Kissinger's step-by-step approach to peace. The summer of 1974 brought the Cyprus crisis and the denouement of Watergate, and in September, Kissinger's attention shifted to Portugal. In October, he finally managed to visit the Middle East again in order to explore a second-phase agreement between Israel and Egypt. But during that month an event occurred that would place a new hurdle in his path. At an Arab summit meeting held in Rabat, Morocco, it was decided to recognize the Palestine Liberation Organization as the sole legitimate representative of the Palestinian people. King Hussein of Jordan acquiesced in a decision that in effect ceded the west bank of the Jordan to Yasir Arafat, the leader of the PLO. Hence, from Kissinger's point of view, the radical PLO had now replaced moderate Jordan in the complex mosaic of the Arab-Israeli conflict. He had urged the Israelis in early 1974, to reach an accord with King Hussein over the west bank, but to no avail. Now it was too late. Kissinger visited the area in November 1974 and again in February 1975 in order to reaffirm the Egyptian-Israeli focus of the next step and to determine the possibilities for an agreement over Sinai. Sufficiently buoyed by these discussions, he returned again in March, hoping to be able to conclude an agreement. But he was mistaken. The Egyptian–Israeli negotiations broke down and Kissinger had to return to the United States, empty-handed and sorely disappointed. Relations between him and Israeli leaders reached an all-time low during the spring and summer of 1975. What had happened to ground the shuttle?

In the aftermath of the Yom Kippur war, the old leadership was crumbling. Golda Meir was accused of sharing the responsibility for Israel's military and psychological unpreparedness for war. She resigned in April 1974, and pulled down with her almost the entire top echelon of leaders who had steered the country for more than a decade. The post of prime minister, almost by default, went to Yitzhak Rabin who had distinguished himself in the 1967 war and who had been uninvolved in Israeli politics during the crucial months before Yom Kippur 1973. Rabin, though unblemished by the October war, was nevertheless elected only by a narrow margin. From the very start, his government recalled the memory of the Fourth Republic of France. Rabin would have to seek consensus among opposing views in order to keep the government from falling. It would be extremely difficult for him to make hard decisions that were bound to divide the nation. And yet, it was precisely those decisions that Israel, in Kissinger's opinion, now would be called upon to make.

Kissinger felt strongly that in order to prevent another round of violence, the diplomatic momentum would have to be maintained. After lengthy consultations with Kissinger, the Egyptian president had disclosed his "rock bottom" requirement for another interim agreement with Israel. He would grant a verbal assurance of non-belligerency in exchange for the return of two mountain ranges in the Sinai Desert—the Gidi and Mitla passes—as well as the return of the Abu Rudeis oilfields in the Sinai. In February, Rabin had indicated to Kissinger that he was confident that he could persuade his cabinet to agree to Sadat's conditions for a second-phase interim accord.

In March, however, when Kissinger began his second shuttle between Cairo and Jerusalem, it turned out that Rabin had made a serious misjudgment. He had overestimated his persuasive powers with the cabinet and his hairline majority in the Knesset threatened to disintegrate. "Words, words, words" was the opposition party's description of Sadat's non-belligerency offer. Its members accused Rabin of "delivering Israel into Kissinger claws" for nothing more than promises of dubious validity. Rabin reminded opposition leaders that giving back some territories in exchange for promises was inherent in the step-by-step approach. "Since when is Abu Rudeis a Jewish Holy Place?" he demanded angrily. But it had become apparent that Rabin would not be able to fulfill his pledge to Kissinger.

When Kissinger discovered during his shuttle trips in March that Rabin would not be able to deliver the oilfields and the mountain passes, he felt that he had been misled. He believed that Sadat's offer was a reasonable one. After all, Sinai was occupied Egyptian territory and the Egyptian president was willing to grant an element of peace for some territory. He could not be expected to sign a formal treaty with Israel while most of Sinai and all of Gaza were still under Israeli occupation. Kissinger believed that the Israelis were stubborn and unreasonable. Unless they had a change of heart and took some risks for peace, he felt, Israel was embarked on a suicidal course. Worst of all, however, Kissinger mistakenly believed that he had been misled intentionally. He mistook an honest error and misjudgment by Rabin for a deliberate design to embarrass him and to paralyze his step-by-step diplomacy. These misperceptions caused much unnecessary bitterness and anguish on both sides.

During the spring and early summer of 1975, Kissinger complained bitterly about Israel's refusal to be "more forthcoming." Ford sent an angry letter to Rabin. This letter was read to the Knesset and inflamed Israeli resentment even further. Israel, in turn, put pressure on the U.S. Congress which resulted in an open letter to the President, signed by seventy-six Senators, warning against any reduction in American aid to Israel. This intervention in domestic politics of course did little to assuage the anger in the White House and the State Department.

The disaster of the final American defeat in Indochina in April 1975 only deepened Kissinger's sense of gloom. The Spenglerian foreboding of the scholar almost submerged the statesman who had declared less than two years before that respect for history did not mean a blind submission to its forces. Ford, on Kissinger's advice, ordered a "reassessment" of Middle Eastern policy. The Geneva alternative was briefly considered but rejected by Kissinger as unproductive. Slowly, while Rabin and Kissinger cooled down, it became clear to all concerned that the step-by-step approach still offered the best hope for another interim agreement between Israel and Egypt.

This time Kissinger instituted a "reverse shuttle." He invited the two parties to send their views, and sometimes their representatives, to Washington. Only when he was absolutely certain that he could bridge the remaining differences, did he embark on yet another shuttle to the Middle East in August 1975. This time he was successful and an agreement over Sinai was signed in Geneva on September 4, 1975.

The Sinai agreement bore the typical *imprimatur* of a Kissinger settlement. Neither side was happy with it but neither side was able to produce a better alternative that was acceptable to both. The Israelis promised to return the two mountain passes and the oil fields. In exchange, they received pledges from Sadat to the effect that Egypt would refrain from the threat or use of force against the Jewish state. Sadat also agreed to continue negotiations toward a final peace agreement and to extend the mandate of the UN buffer force annually, for at least three years.

What finally made it possible, however, for Rabin to conclude the agreement was a specific American commitment that Kissinger had not made before. Kissinger offered to provide 200 American civilian technicians who would be stationed in the Sinai *between* the contending parties. They would serve as a kind of early warning system in case either side planned an attack upon the other, and they would report to both Israel and Egypt. In addition, Kissinger pledged that he would recommend an American aid commitment of $2.3 billion to Israel. Israel which did not trust the UN buffer force, found the pledge of a small, symbolic American presence reassuring. The aid package, too, was attractive and, furthermore, Rabin could tell the opposition that Israel still retained over eighty-five percent of Sinai and the entire Gaza Strip. Sadat received his coveted mountain passes and oilfields plus an American commitment for $700 million needed for the impoverished Egyptian economy. The 200 Americans were welcome too, since their presence only underlined Sadat's growing independence from the Soviet Union. Thus, Egypt gained some territorial allowances and Israel received political consessions. What could not be bridged between the parties directly was bridged by American commitments. Some Senators grumbled that the 200 Americans in the Sinai reminded them of the beginning of Vietnam, but Kissinger was quick to point out that the Americans in Sinai were civilians who were to aid both sides in keeping the peace, not soldiers who were to help one side to win a war.

On a deeper level, Kissinger was criticized, especially by Morgenthau and Ball, for side-stepping the central issue of the conflict, the Palestinian problem. Besides, Morgenthau asked, what if Sadat was a liar? Neville Chamberlain, according to Morgenthau, was supposed to have moaned on his death bed: "If only Hitler had not lied to me, all would have been well." Morgenthau expressed the hope that Kissinger would not find himself in a similar predicament with the

Egyptian president. Ball, who in an article in *Atlantic* magazine in February 1976, accused Kissinger of engaging in virtuoso diplomacy to satisfy "his elemental need for power and glory," also criticized the secretary for excluding the Russians from the entire diplomatic process. In Ball's opinion, Kissinger had reduced Moscow to "so humiliating a position that Soviet Foreign Minister Andrei Gromyko felt compelled to fly repeatedly to Damascus to see President Assad, each time arriving after Kissinger had left town—in the manner of the assiduous lover of a traveling salesman's wife."

Kissinger stated, in defense, that the Sinai agreement was good for both Israel and Egypt. If Sadat was lying, he would attack Israel with or without an agreement. Hence, an agreement, in Kissinger's opinion, was a net gain. Besides he perceived Sadat as a "moderate bourgeois nationalist," who was much more interested in rebuilding the Egyptian economy with American help than in another war with Israel. So far as the Soviet Union was concerned, the Russians would be included in the diplomatic process when the time came for a final settlement. On the whole, Kissinger was pleased with the second Sinai interim agreement. It was, after all, the first accord between Israel and an Arab nation that was not the immediate consequence of war. He knew that it was far from a genuine peace treaty, but he was convinced that his step-by-step approach was still the best way to proceed. And he was relieved that the "family quarrel" with Israel seemed to have subsided. In his judgment, most Americans were still willing to take great risks to preserve the state of Israel, but were *not* willing to take such risks to preserve Israel's conquests. He did not know, however, in the fall of 1975, that his step-by-step approach would suddenly run out of steps before the year was ended.

If the Sinai agreement was a victory for the moderate Arab forces, the anti-Zionist resolution passed by the UN General Assembly on November 10, 1975, signified a triumph of the radical elements.

Kissinger watched the developments at the United Nations with considerable concern. Syria refused to extend the mandate of the UN Disengagement Observer Force on the Golan Heights unless the PLO was invited to participate in an overall Security Council review of the Middle East situation scheduled for January 1976. Kissinger who had hoped to follow up the Sinai accord with a similar second-phase agreement between Israel and Syria, now discovered that Syria and the PLO had joined forces and made a united front in their battle for the recognition of the Palestinians. Faced with a choice between the demise of the UN buffer force and acquiescence in the seating of the PLO on the Security Council in January, Kissinger regarded the latter alternative as the lesser evil. Then, on December 2, in the first major military action by Israel since the Sinai accord, an air attack was launched on two suspected guerrilla sites in Palestinian camps inside Lebanon. On December 3, a Security Council meeting was called by Lebanon and Egypt. Egypt, embarrassed by the raids and under heavy criticism from Syria and the PLO since entering into the Sinai agreement with Israel, called for participation by the PLO. In a procedural vote, the PLO was seated, with Israel refusing to attend. When Israel, however was condemned for the raids, the United States, on Kissinger's instructions, cast its twelfth veto in thirty years. And when the council, at the end of its January deliberations, was ready to declare an independent Palestinian state and to demand that Israel withdraw from *all* the conquered territories, Kissinger again instructed Ambassador Moynihan to cast a veto. The two vetoes did much to alleviate the crisis of confidence between the United States and Israel, although differences of opinion continued to exist.

What had become clear by 1976, both to Kissinger and the Israeli leadership, was that the step-by-step approach had reached a dead end. The heart of the matter, it was now acknowledged, was the problem of the PLO. Deputy Assistant Secretary Harold Saunders, as early as November 1975, had placed the Palestinian issue at the heart of the search for peace. And in December, Kissinger had privately explored the possibility of an Israeli change in attitude if the PLO were to renounce terrorism and recognize Israel's existence. Within Israel, in December 1975, over one-third of Rabin's twenty-person cabinet, including Foreign Minister Yigal Allon, were willing to consider such a course. Nevertheless, when Rabin visited the United States in January 1976, he did not allow for any flexibility. Not even the fact that an election on the West Bank replaced moderate Arab groups with more radical elements that were sympathetic to the Palestinian cause changed Israel's position.

Kissinger knew, of course, that he was placing a dreadful choice before Israel. If she agreed to negotiate with the PLO and return some territories for the purpose of creating a Palestinian state, such a state would clearly be a dagger pointed at the heart of Israel. If, on the other hand, she refused to negotiate, she risked another war or another oil embargo, as well as slow economic strangulation and increasing isolation. Kissinger, the historian, believed that Arafat was the kind of revolutionary who could be co-opted into the established order. Once he ceased to be a revolutionary and became a statesman, he could be woven into the network of the give-and-take of diplomatic compromise. Despite the risks involved, Kissinger believed that, ultimately, Israel would have to face the Palestinians as a reality that would not go away, just as America, after more than two decades, had to adjust herself to the reality of a China that was Communist. The dangers of pursuing a rigid policy, in Kissinger's opinion, were always greater than a purposeful flexibility in the quest of a stable equilibrium. There were now three million Israelis and three million Palestinians. Both were permanent realities and, sooner or later, a compromise solution would have to be discovered.

To Kissinger, Zionism for the Jews was a necessary response to the need to save their lives. In their own plight, however, they had driven more than a million other human beings to despair by the creation of their state. Over the years, the Arab refugees became the Palestinian "freedom fighters." In Kissinger's opinion, of the two nationalities that clashed in Palestine, the Jewish was militarily superior but not politically stronger. The vanquished were yearning for redress. Time was on the Arab side. Zionism, to endure, would have to find the courage not to inflict on others what had been inflicted on the Jews in history. This would take a generosity of spirit that had seldom been extended to the Jews in their Diaspora. It was for this reason that Kissinger constantly exhorted Israel to "take risks for peace," and to exchange territory for security although, by 1976, he stated privately that he "no longer had the stomach to haggle with the Israelis." Yet, if Israel refused, Kissinger saw the future darkly for the Jewish state.

I have no doubt whatever that Kissinger was sincere in his quest for a Middle Eastern peace. It may be appropriate to question his judgment, but not his motivation or sincerity. He is objective about Israel, but not detached. "How could I, as a Jew," he told me once, "do anything to betray my people?" It would be a disservice to the cause of peace, however, simply to gloss over what remained a profound intellectual divergence between Henry Kissinger and many Israelis and American Jews. In their heart of hearts, most Israelis and even American Jews believed that Israel's security was best guaranteed by victory and the fruits of victory. Kissinger's entire life as an historian and statesman had convinced him of the opposite. Victories and defeats merely led to other wars. Only a settlement without victory or defeat could create stability. And without stability and balance, peace could not be born at all.

According to their faith, the Jews had been chosen to have an almost infinite capacity for suffering. Now, at long last, they were no longer chosen. They themselves were forced to choose.

Once, during that painful spring of 1975, I visited Henry Kissinger together with Hans Morgenthau and Elie Wiesel, to talk about the Middle East. Four Jewish refugees agonized about the future of the Jewish state. At the end, when the three of us prepared to leave, Elie

Wiesel asked Kissinger in parting: "Mr. Secretary, do you realize that Jewish history now goes through you?" "I know," Kissinger replied. His tone betrayed neither an improper vanity nor a false modesty. He had understood that the Jewish poet had simply said the truth.

Part III

The Anguish
of Power

14

The Anguish
of Power

I have been generally identified, or it has been alleged
that I am supposed to be interested primarily in the
balance of power. I would rather like to think that
when the record is written, one may remember that
perhaps some lives were saved and that perhaps some
mothers can rest more at ease, but I leave that to
history.

Henry Kissinger
News Conference, Salzburg, Austria
June 11, 1974

"I know I have a first-rate mind," Henry Kissinger once told me many
years ago, "but that's no source of pride to me. Intelligent people are
a dime a dozen. But I am proud of having character."

Henry Kissinger never had much patience with mediocrities or
fools. But when, in the rolling cadences of his Bavarian accent, he
would describe some luckless academic as a "characterless bastard,"
he meant to convey a bottomless contempt. Kissinger reserved this
ultimate epithet for those unfortunates who did not have the courage
to *act* on their convictions. A man who said one thing but did another
was even more certain to incur his wrath than someone who had no
convictions whatsoever. The move to Washington did little to

change Kissinger's opinion. "The worst kinds of bastards in this town," he declared three years after he had come to power," are those who hold high positions and then go out and say they really didn't believe in Administration policies. If anyone would ever say I didn't believe in what Nixon is doing, I would publicly dispute him. I like the President. I agree with him. We've gone through all this for three years, like two men in a foxhole. . . ."

"Character" to Kissinger, had little to do with intelligence. What he admired was a man's capacity to stand up for his convictions in the world of action, alone if necessary. When, in a rare unguarded moment, Kissinger had said, "I have always acted alone," he had revealed a deep emotional conviction. Even though his intellect reminded him that "a policy that was conceived in the mind of one, but resided in the hearts of none," was doomed to failure, this *emotional* preference for solitude remained. It is for this reason that Kissinger preferred Castlereagh to Metternich. Castlereagh had a grand design and, even though it had "outdistanced the experience of his people," he had found the moral courage to remain loyal to his vision. Metternich, on the other hand, despite his brilliance and his cunning, had never found the courage to "contemplate an abyss as a challenge to overcome or to perish in the process." Thus, he had ultimately doomed himself to sterility, and with him, Imperial Austria.

Among contemporary statesmen, Kissinger most admired those who had not only conceived a vision, but had found the courage to translate it into action, even in the face of anguish and adversity. The fact that most of the men who shared these qualities happened to be adversaries, did not deter him in the least. When as a scholar at Harvard, he was preoccupied with Europe, he had often expressed considerable admiration for the strength and steadfastness of Charles de Gaulle, the *bête noire* of the North Atlantic Treaty. After he had come to power, he spoke with genuine respect of Mao Tse-tung and Chou En-lai and of their courage in adversity. Among his fellow intellectuals, he was most drawn to Hans Morgenthau, even though the older scholar had often attacked his policies on Indochina and the Middle East. But he admired Morgenthau's vision in having been the first to oppose Indochina policy under Kennedy and Johnson and his courage in making that early opposition known despite official ridicule and even harassment.

In Kissinger's hierarchy of values, courage and decisiveness came first. Loyalty, too, was prized by him. Intelligence, even brilliance, he considered fairly commonplace. If they were coupled with indecisiveness and weakness in a man, that combination was sure to arouse Kissinger's contempt. Whether one chose to describe Kissinger's ideal in the romantic terms of Hegel's *Zeitgeist,* or in the more rustic image of an embattled cowboy in a Western town, its essence was the same: a man must know how to think and act *alone.*

A great deal has been written about Henry Kissinger's personal diplomacy. His insistence on conducting important negotiations personally and his habit of establishing close relationships with adversary leaders are well known characteristics of his statecraft. His low opinion of the bureaucracy has also been widely commented upon. This penchant for the solo performance has been variously attributed to Kissinger's "enormous ego," his "obsessive secrecy" or to his "elemental need for power and for glory."

I should like to submit another interpretation. I believe that, in order for Kissinger to succeed in his most historic diplomatic initiatives, he *had to* establish personal dominance over the bureaucracy. To establish such control moreover, he had to act decisively, often secretly, and, at times, alone.

Kissinger had never had much patience with bureaucracy. When a professor at Harvard, he had reserved his most acid comments for university administrators. His tolerance for bureaucracy in government was not much greater. After having studied the American "foreign policy-making apparatus" he had come to the conclusion that it was a kind of feudal network of competing agencies and interests, in which there was a "powerful tendency to think that a compromise among administrative proposals (was) the same thing as a policy." The bureaucratic model for making a decision, in Kissinger's opinion, was a policy proposal with three choices: the present policy bracketed by two absurd alternatives.

Kissinger had been a consultant to both the Kennedy and Johnson administrations. While he never said so publicly, he had been deeply disappointed. So much had been promised; so much less had been attempted and, in his judgment, so little had been done. He had had the opportunity to observe government decision-making from a fairly close perspective. What impressed him most was that the foreign policy bureaucracy had a way of smothering initiative by advocating a path of least resistance. The lawyers, businessmen, and former academics who ran the hierarchy generally seemed to place a premium on safety and acceptance rather than on creativity and vision. The result was that any innovative statesmanship tended to expire in the feudal fiefs of the bureaucracy or come to grief on the rocks of organizational inertia.

There was ample basis for Kissinger's impatience. SALT might have been initiated at the Glassboro summit in 1967, between Lyndon Johnson and the Soviet leaders, but there had been no decisive leadership. Nor had there been a clear-cut stand on the possible limitation of strategic arms. Instead, there were endless arguments among the Joint Chiefs of Staff, the Pentagon, the State Department, and academic experts in the field of arms control. Similarly, the Arab-Israeli war of 1967 had presented opportunities for American diplomacy and mediation, but there had been no one with a plan, let alone the courage to place himself between competing claims. Instead, there emerged from the bowels of the bureaucracy countless position papers by learned academic experts. There was no agreement on an overall strategy for mediation in the Middle East, only an almost fatalistic sense of hopelessness and drift.

This was the reason why Kissinger decided, immediately after

January 20, 1969, to establish personal control over the bureaucracy. Those whom he could not dominate, he would manipulate. And those whom he could not manipulate, he would try to bypass. He embarked on this course of action as a result of a rational decision. He simply feared that *unless* he dominated, bypassed, or manipulated, nothing would get done. He, too, would ultimately be submerged in a long twilight struggle of modern feudal baronies. This he was simply not prepared to accept.

In his position as Assistant for National Security Affairs, Kissinger came to dominate the bureaucracy as no other figure before him had done, and as no other is likely to do for a very long time to come. He promptly established his control through the establishment of a few small committees each of which he personally chaired. These were a number of interdepartmental groups: a Review Group, a Verification Panel for SALT, a Vietnam Special Studies Group, the Washington Special Actions Group for Crisis Control, and the Forty Committee which dealt with covert intelligence operations.

It was out of these committees that Kissinger forged the great initiatives that have assured his place in history: SALT I in 1969, the opening to China after his secret trip to Peking in 1971, and the diplomatic mediation in the Middle East after the October war in 1973. It is true, of course, that some of the more dubious decisiↄns also had their genesis in this small elitist structure, particularly in the Forty Committee. The "destabilization" of the Allende government in Chile in 1971, alleged payments to Italian neo-fascists in 1972, and the denouement in Indochina are some of the more disturbing examples. Only history can provide the necessary distance for a balanced assessment of these various initiatives. But what can already be asserted with a fair amount of certainty is that Kissinger was right in his assumption that, in order to put into effect a coherent global policy, he would have to concentrate as much power in his hands as possible.

Kissinger's pursuit of power had a very clear-cut purpose. During two decades of reflection he had evolved a theory of global order which, in his judgment, would bring the world a few steps closer to stability and peace. Nothing was more important to him in 1969 than the chance to test that theory. He believed with the most absolute conviction that he was the one best qualified. On one occasion, in 1968, when Rockefeller's speech writers had made some changes in a Kissinger position paper, the author exclaimed furiously: "If Rockefeller buys a Picasso, he doesn't hire four housepainters to improve on it." In Kissinger's own view, this was not an arrogant statement. It was merely the reflection of an enormous, though quite genuine, intellectual self-confidence. He believed, quite matter-of-factly, that he was the Picasso of modern American foreign policy.

Henry Kissinger believed that, in creating a design for world order, realism was more compassionate than romanticism. The great American moralists, in his judgment, had been failures. In the end, Woodrow Wilson had proved ineffectual and John Foster Dulles had turned foreign policy into a crusade that had led straight into the Indochina quagmire. Kissinger did not make peace or justice the objective of his policy nor was he particularly interested in "making the world safe for democracy." He merely wished to make the world safer and more stable. This was a lesser goal, one that offered no illusions, but also brought fewer disappointments. It was also not quite in the mainstream of American history. But then, Kissinger was a European in America, his thought rooted firmly in the European philosophical tradition.

There has been a great deal of confusion about Kissinger's intellectual debt to Metternich for his vision of stability. Kissinger himself has made it abundantly clear that he never looked to Metternich for guidance on *substantive problems* of statecraft: "Most people associate me with Metternich. And that is childish . . . there can be nothing in common between me and Metternich. He was chancellor and

foreign minister at a time when it took three weeks to travel from
Central Europe to the ends of the Continent, when wars were conducted by professional soldiers and diplomacy was in the hands of the
aristocracy. . . ." What Kissinger admired in Metternich was the
Austrian diplomat's *conceptual insight* in having recognized the revolutionary character of the Napoleonic challenge, the need to neutral-
ize that challenge without humiliating retribution, and, having
achieved that end, his commitment to stability and balance which
ushered in a century without a global war.

If Castlereagh taught Kissinger that a statesman must create a
vision and remain faithful to it even in adversity, Metternich taught
him how to adjust that vision to reality. If Castlereagh taught him
about courage and a grand design, Metternich taught him about
cunning and manipulation. But when all was said and done, the
lessons Kissinger could learn from these two nineteenth century
aristocrats were limited. In the end, Kissinger, too, had to stand
alone.

Henry Kissinger once told me that a statesman, to be successful,
had to have some luck. He knew well that he was no exception to
this rule. His appearance on the world stage coincided most fortui-
tously with a new nadir in the relations between China and the Soviet
Union. By 1969, Mao Tse-tung and Brezhnev feared each other more
than they feared America, and thus had become more concerned
with moderating their relations with the United States than with the
pursuit of revolutionary goals of conquest vis-à-vis the West. Thus,
the timing of Kissinger's arrival as a world statesman could not have
been more fortunate for the particular objective that he had in mind:
a new stability in the relations among the world's three great powers.

The drawing up of any balance sheet on the centerpiece of Kissinger's foreign policy—détente with the Soviet Union—must remain
a highly personal business on which thoughtful people may have
widely differing opinions. Any such analysis must enter in the realm
of competing values, since in creating that centerpiece, choices had

to be made and a price had to be paid. Hence, it is only fair that, as we enter this discussion, I reveal the basis of my judgment and share my values and prejudices with the reader.

I believe that Henry Kissinger was right when he declared that the overriding reason for détente with Russia was the avoidance of a nuclear catastrophe. I believe that if such a world cataclysm has become less likely, this is in no small measure to be credited to Kissinger. I am fully aware that the American relationship with Russia leaves a great deal to be desired. But there is no question in my mind that the danger of nuclear war has substantially receded. It no longer intrudes into our daily lives the way it did when Kissinger and I were students. Mothers worried about radioactive waste and strontium-90 in their children's milk; and a decade later, John F. Kennedy almost went to nuclear war with Khrushchev over missiles in Cuba. Today, we argue with the Soviet Union about strategic arms control, trade, and human rights, but we no longer live in daily terror of a nuclear exchange. The fearful scenarios that were conjured up in Herman Kahn's *Thinking About the Unthinkable* today read almost like horrible anachronisms. In addition to the elements of luck and timing, it was also Kissinger's design and courage that made détente possible at all.

I know the price that Kissinger has paid on behalf of the United States has been enormous. But, to be fair, we must ask ourselves in each case whether the alternatives would have yielded better results. In strategic arms control, Kissinger's accusers have blamed him for his acceptance in SALT I of Soviet superiority in missile numbers. They have also been suspicious of his lack of interest in alleged evidence that the Soviet Union had violated the spirit and perhaps even the letter of SALT I. Critics have also taken umbrage at his reported willingness—during the SALT II negotiations—to exclude the Soviet Backfire bomber from an overall ceiling while including the American cruise missile.

But the critics, in my judgment, have never given a convincing answer to Kissinger's own question: "What in God's name," he asked in 1974, "is strategic superiority? What is the significance of it, politically, militarily, operationally, at these levels of numbers? What do you do with it?" Kissinger simply did not believe that a marginal "overkill" capacity on either side could be translated into a meaningful strategic or political advantage. To my mind, there is no conclusive evidence that such a translation can in fact be made.

The "great grain robbery" of 1972 was not one of Kissinger's proudest moments. The Russian harvest was so poor that the Soviet leadership probably would have paid a better price. As it turned out, however, the American taxpayer helped to underwrite the Soviet purchases and got in return only a few ephemeral benefits: a little Soviet help in Hanoi and Brezhnev's decision to meet with Nixon at the Moscow summit despite the President's decision to place mines in Haiphong harbor.

Kissinger was right, however, in my judgment, in his dispute with Senator Henry Jackson over the linking of most-favored-nations status for the Soviet Union with emigration of Soviet Jews to Israel. It was unreasonable for Jackson to couple an international agreement with Russia to a demand for internal changes within the Soviet state. How would Jackson have responded if the Soviet leadership had linked the conclusion of SALT I to a demand for a lifting of all American immigration quotas? The point I am making is not that the demand was ethically unjustified, but that it was asymmetrical. A *quid pro quo* of Soviet cooperation in the Middle East would have been more sensible and would not have brought up the delicate issue of Soviet internal politics. To those who argued that he was insensitive to the human rights of Jews wishing to emigrate to Israel, Kissinger could point to his record with not inconsiderable pride. Before the Soviets cancelled the 1972 trade agreement in their anger over the Jackson amendment, the annual figure of Jewish emigrants from Russia reached 35,000. After Jackson made his public demands, this figure was cut by more than half. In this instance, without a doubt, private diplomacy tactfully conducted had yielded better results than open covenants stridently demanded.

The great paradox of Kissinger's conception of détente is in his relative tolerance vis-à-vis the Soviet Union, still the fountainhead of communism, and his combativeness toward local Communist movements in peripheral areas. How can Kissinger proclaim détente with the Soviet Union, the supporter of Communist causes everywhere, and yet fight communism to the death in Indochina, warn Western European heads of state against coalition governments with Communists, and demand action against the Communists in Angola?

The key to this riddle is to be found in Kissinger's primary commitment to stability. In the central relationship between the superpowers, there can be no decisive change in the power balance, short of nuclear war. The balance could be changed dramatically, however, if a minor nation shifted its allegiance from one side to the other and thus added appreciably to the strength of one of the two main contenders. The direct jockeying for mutual advantage between Russia and the United States was not likely to affect the global balance. But Communist advances elsewhere could, at least cumulatively, affect the balance of power in the world. Hence, Kissinger's concern with stemming Communist advances in peripheral areas.

This logic, however, runs into serious difficulties. It may stand up in an area such as Angola where thousands of Cuban troops were imported to do battle for the Communist cause. In such a case, there was at least good circumstantial evidence for direct Soviet-sponsored intervention. But there was little, if any evidence that the Soviet Union was very active in helping the Communists in Portugal, Italy, or France. The growth of the Italian Communist movement in Italy under Enrico Berlinguer might be attributable more to that Italian's "historic compromise" with democratic socialism than to subversion by the Soviet Union. Yet, Kissinger accused the Portuguese Foreign Minister of being a "Kerensky," quarantined Portugal from NATO, and had secret payments made to a neo-fascist Italian general. In such cases, a good argument can be made that, by his indiscriminate opposition to all local forms of communism, Kissinger might force breakaway groups back into Moscow's arms and thus bring about the very developments he was so eager to prevent.

On a deeper level, Hans Morgenthau has made the most telling criticism:

> Since the causes and effects of instability persist, a policy committed to stability and identifying instability with communism is compelled by the logic of its interpretation of reality to suppress in the name of anticommunism all manifestations of popular discontent and stifle the aspirations for reform. Thus, in an essentially unstable world, tyranny becomes the last resort of a policy committed to stability as its ultimate standard.

This is how, in Morgenthau's opinion, Kissinger, despite his extraordinary brilliance, often failed. He tended to place his great gifts at the service of lost causes, and thus, in the name of preserving stability and order, aligned the United States on the wrong side of the great historic issues.

Morgenthau may be a little harsh in such a judgment. What if the Italian Communists renounced their "historic compromise", made common cause with Moscow, and other European countries followed suit? The result could well be a catastrophe for the United States. Morgenthau, as critic, does not have to make that awesome choice. But can a statesman dare to take such risks at a moment when he must base his decisions on conjecture rather than on facts? Here the scholar, in my judgment, owes the statesman a measure of empathy and tolerance.

In this entire realm of argument, Kissinger is most vulnerable, in my view, on his Indochina policy. No one, of course, can blame him for the escalation which he regarded as a national disaster. But I have always differed with his judgment that the presence of 500,000 Americans had settled the importance of Vietnam since credibility was now at stake. Rather, it was my impression that American credi-

bility rose rather than fell when that suicidal commitment finally
came to an end. I have also never understood Kissinger's answer to
the argument that a negotiated settlement could have been attained
in 1969 on terms at least as favorable as those that he finally negotiated in 1973. His explanation that, for three years the North Vietnamese had refused to accept his "double track" plan of separating
military from political matters always struck me as rather unconvinc-
ing. Finally, the Cambodian invasion that dragged a neutral nation
into a war that it might have been able to avoid, struck me as the
greatest, and possibly most tragic, blunder. And, in the end, when
Saigon fell in April 1975, Kissinger looked like all the other Americans who had come to Indochina to lose their reputation to Ho Chi
Minh and the Vietcong.

There may be a psychological interpretation of Kissinger's paradox-
ical approach to Communism. It may be found in his profound
suspicion of the revolutionary as the greatest threat to a stable world
order. In theory, as Kissinger had made clear in an essay on Bismarck,
it made little difference to him whether a revolutionary was "red" or
"white". But in practice, he always feared the "red" revolutionary
infinitely more. It is not that he approved of a Greek or Chilean junta,
but he simply did not believe that it posed the kind of threat to
international stability as that presented by a Cunhal, an Allende, a
Castro, or a Ho Chi Minh. These were the types of leaders, rather
than a Brezhnev or a Mao Tse-tung, who were most likely to upset
the global balance. They still retained that messianic revolutionary
quality that had a vast potential for dislocation and contagion. In
relation to the Soviet Union and China, one could afford to take some
chances without risk to equilibrium. But when it came to the smaller
revolutionaries, Kissinger believed that the war-maker still made the
most effective peacemaker.

The opening to China was probably Kissinger's most uncon-
taminated triumph in his tenure as a statesman. It was also his
greatest diplomatic adventure. Once he preceived the depth of the

rift between China and the Soviet Union, he became convinced that rapprochement with China might make the Soviet Union more receptive to a genuine détente. In short, China, in his view, had become the key to Russia. In addition to establishing this triangular linkage, Kissinger's secret trip to Peking in 1971, had made him the first messenger of reconciliation. Furthermore to discover that beyond the Himalayas, there were men who elicited his admiration and respect only added to his elation. One of the few times that I heard Kissinger happily admit that he had been wrong was an occasion when he discussed his change of heart about Mao Tse-tung and Chou En-lai. In 1966, during the "Cultural Revolution", he had perceived the Chinese leaders as the two most dangerous men on earth. Five years later, he had come to regard them as rational statesmen who pursued China's national interest in a manner not altogether inconsistent with the rules of international stability. But then it was Henry Kissinger who had once said about himself that while he had a first-rate mind, he had a third-rate intuition about people. In the case of China, fortunately, the reality turned out to be more pleasant than the fantasy.

As for the charge that Kissinger's relationships with adversaries were often better than his relationships with friends, I would hardly cloak this statement in a mantle of universal application. There is, however, ample evidence for it if one contemplates Kissinger's policies toward the continent where he was born. Europe brought out the darker side of his personal diplomacy and his reluctance to delegate responsibility. His declaration of a "Year of Europe" in 1973 had come almost as an afterthought in response to complaints by Western European statesmen that their capitals had become little more than refueling stops for Kissinger on his way to or back from Moscow. It reminded one European diplomat of an unfaithful husband's decision to declare a "year of the wife." Kissinger's outbursts of exasperation in moments of frustration did little to improve relations. When he exclaimed in a moment of anger that he "didn't care what happened to NATO," this momentary lapse was taken seriously by his NATO partners. And his lectures to the Portuguese aroused their anger and resentment. In many of these instances, Kissinger followed his own judgment and generally ignored the advice of experienced foreign service officers.

The case that combined all the weaknesses of personal diplomacy, of course, was Cyprus. Kissinger made policy decisions with regard to Cyprus almost absentmindedly. Distracted by the final act of Watergate, he paid only the most cursory attention to events on that tormented island. His dislike for Archbishop Markarios prompted him to lean toward the Greek extremist, Nikos Sampson, of whose reputation he knew little. When the Turks, predictably enough, responded by mounting an invasion, Kissinger did little to deter them even though a democratic government in the meantime had assumed control in Athens. Thus, Kissinger managed to alienate *both* Greece and Turkey in an amazingly short period of time. Perhaps even more serious, the failure of his Cyprus policy led directly to the first of many strictures to be imposed upon him by an increasingly suspicious and hostile Congress.

Since Kissinger's main objective has always been the pursuit of international stability, his attention had been focussed on the world's major power wielders. The pawns on the global chessboard seemed quite expendable to him, until quite suddenly and without warning, some of them decided to improve their lowly status. The Arab oil embargo and the demands for a "new international economic order" that swept through the Third World like a hurricane, convinced Kissinger that he finally would have to pay attention to the smaller nations of Africa, Latin America, and Asia. He quickly realized that his vision of stability would have to become bifocal. Unless he did so, his policies might prevent World War III, but they were certain to prepare the ground for World War IV.

When, in the spring of 1976, Kissinger declared his clear support for black majority rule in southern Africa, he reversed a long tradition of American equivocation. While this reversal was triggered primarily by the Soviet victory in Angola, it was also motivated by Kissinger's desire to build détente between the races and the rich and poor. And when he pledged a dedicated effort to "roll back the desert" in famine-stricken African lands, his promise had the ring of truth. This compassion for the world's dispossessed came late, but when it came, it was sincere.

For almost thirty years, the United Nations had existed in the suburbs of Henry Kissinger's consciousness. Its lack of authority and power had convinced him that he could ignore it with impunity. The increase of Third World bloc voting, however, and the rise of a "tyranny of the majority," made him pay attention. When this majority, having driven the United States into the role of opposition, finally passed an Orwellian resolution that equated Zionism with racism, Kissinger's antennae, always sensitive to power, registered an ominous alert.

Somber warnings that the United Nations might become an empty shell, coupled with Ambassador Moynihan's blunt rhetoric, placed the Third World nations on guard that they were not immune to Kissinger's favorite mixture of diplomacy and force. When Moynihan, however, engaged in so much bluntness that it began to resemble "overkill," Kissinger became alarmed. The differences between the two men finally led to the ambassador's resignation. Even a Kissinger weakened by mounting criticism and congressional opposition was still a formidable adversary.

We cannot say with certitude whether the critics of the step-by-step approach to peace in the Middle East were justified in their assertions that Kissinger avoided the heart of the conflict by refusing to address himself to the Palestinian problem. What the record does indicate, however, is that Kissinger has managed to narrow the differences between Israel and the Arabs more successfully than any other mediator in the long history of that tragic conflict.

The essence of Kissinger's Middle East diplomacy has been the avoidance of the appearance of victory. Convinced that only a stalemate could contain the seeds of peace, he steered the October war to an inconclusive end. In doing so, he resisted enormous pressure from each side hungering for military victory. It was in the aftermath of this military stalemate that he succeeded in negotiating the two disengagement accords, first between Israel and Egypt and then, between Israel and Syria. The two agreements were achieved in no small measure because of Kissinger's personal tenacity. The Sinai agreement which followed in September 1975, was the first accord reached by Israel and an Arab state that was not an armistice to end a war. It was a voluntary agreement reached in times of peace. Even when shortly afterward Syria temporarily linked its future to the PLO, Kissinger's approach of "peace by pieces" had already achieved remarkable results.

It is in the Middle East that Kissinger's intellectual courage had to undergo its acid test. It was not easy always to negotiate between a hammer and an anvil. His striving for balance and equilibrium was never popular with either side. As a Jew, he did not find it easy to deny victory to the state of Israel. Personally, he endured considerable suffering. Yet, he remained faithful to his intellectual conviction that a victor's peace would plant the seeds of yet another war. He might be mistaken in this belief though history provides considerable evidence to back him up. But while his judgment may be open to debate, his sincerity is not. Nowhere in his statesmanship has Henry Kissinger shown greater courage than in his quest for a Middle Eastern peace.

If there is any iron law of history, Kissinger once said, it is that no longing is ever completely fulfilled. His own pursuit of a stable world order is no exception to this general rule.

After Nixon's resignation Kissinger remained the only major figure in the government who had been closely associated with the former president. He now had to pay the price exacted by a resurgent Congress in the post-imperial presidency.

Kissinger's autocratic temperament, highly personal style, and persistent secrecy, now made him a natural target. What had been admired in him earlier now was questioned and condemned. Within one year, between 1974 and 1975, the Congress placed severe restrictions on his freedom to maneuver in virtually every single area of foreign policy, from Turkey to Angola. The man who could do nothing wrong now suddenly could do nothing right. As Kissinger himself observed, "I have been praised excessively, so now I am being blamed excessively." Seldom has a man been more exposed to the fickleness of popular acclaim.

While Kissinger was still widely perceived as an asset to the United States as a *nation* in its relationships abroad, many Americans, by 1976, were deeply ambivalent about his impact on America as a *people* at home. Kissinger himself has been consistent. He has never wavered in his striving for a stable world order. But he was fated to experience in practice what he had learned in theory a quarter of a century before: that a statesman who removes himself too much from the experience of his people may doom himself to disappointment and despair. In February 1976, he stated that America was more endangered by her "domestic divisions than by her overseas adversaries." "A great nation that does not shape history," he continued, "eventually becomes its victim." In his frustration with a Congress that had persistently disavowed his policies and had simply refused to heed his counsel on Angola, he sounded a bleak and somber warning:

> Unless the country ends its divisions, our only option is to retreat
> —to become an isolated fortress in a hostile and turbulent global
> sea, awaiting the ultimate confrontation with the only response
> we will not have denied ourselves—massive retaliation.

Once again, Kissinger walked as a loner, with the ghost of Oswald Spengler by his side. His career showed clearly that vision and courage may not be enough to ensure success. As he himself had written, popular support was essential as well. Luck and timing also played a crucial role. Thucydides had realized this long ago in ancient Athens when he had elevated fortune to the rank of goddess.

Perhaps the most haunting questions about Henry Kissinger's foreign policy are of a philosophical nature. What is the role of ethics in Kissinger's world of stability and power? What is the relationship between personal and political morality? What room does Kissinger's pursuit of a stable world order leave for justice? What should be our criterion for success—his intentions or the consequences of his actions? In short, what must concern us, in conclusion, is the problem of statesmanship and moral choice.

There is little doubt that Kissinger, when facing Goethe's dilemma —the choice "between justice and disorder, on the one hand, and injustice and order, on the other," has tended to prefer the latter. In Kantian terms Kissinger made the pursuit of a stable world order the categorical imperative of his foreign policy. If, in the process, the human element had to be sacrificed at times on the altar of stability or of a larger strategic vision, so be it, because without stability, peace could not be born at all and justice, too, would be extinguished. He felt that, in a tragic world, a statesman was not able to choose between good and evil, but only among different forms of evil. Indeed, whatever decision he would make, *some* evil consequences were bound to flow from it. All that a realistic statesman could do in such a world was to choose the lesser evil.

The competing claims of stability and justice permeate the world of Henry Kissinger. A few examples from the record will suffice to demonstrate the pervasiveness of this terrible dilemma.

In the Indochina war, the problem presented itself in its starkest form in the Nixon decision to mine the ports of North Vietnam and to order all-out bombing attacks on Hanoi and Haiphong in 1972. These actions, which were publicly supported by Kissinger, tested the determination of the Soviet Union and China to stand by their North Vietnamese ally. When no action was forthcoming either from Moscow or Peking, Nixon and Kissinger realized that they had managed to isolate North Vietnam. The war was therefore brought to an end for American combat soldiers, but at a price that aroused the moral indignation of many nations and that of many Americans as well. The question that remains is whether this brutal means was justified to attain the desired objective of a "peace with honor," a peace which, in the end, proved to be ephemeral. Could not another, less dreadful, way have been found?

In his relations with the Soviet Union, Kissinger has also been accused of indifference to the human element. As Richard Falk has observed in a thoughtful essay, "Kissinger's effectiveness in dealing with foreign governments arose from his capacity to avoid unpleasant criticisms about their domestic indecencies." Since most powerful states have skeletons hidden in their closets, most statesmen, Falk observed, "found Kissinger's Machiavellian posture a welcome relief." If, in short, a choice had to be made between détente and human rights within the borders of the Soviet Union, there was little doubt how Kissinger would choose.

When India went to war with Pakistan in 1971, Kissinger "tilted" toward Yahya Khan. Not only had the Pakistani president helped in the preparations for the secret trip to China, but an Indian alliance with the Soviet Union threatened to dismember a weakened Pakistan. When Yahya Khan turned on his Bengali fellow-Moslems in a ferocious civil war, and drove ten million of them into exile, Kissinger remained silent. The imperatives of the strategic balance, once again, had overshadowed the human tragedy.

Until the nations of the Third World gained a measure of power through the oil embargo and bloc alignments in the United Nations, Kissinger had little time for the problems of the small and poor. Until famines in the Third World reached catastrophic dimensions, they remained on the periphery of his political awareness. Falk observed of Kissinger's early attitude that "it was inconceivable that afflictions of this magnitude in the Northern Hemisphere would not have been perceived as a catastrophe of historic significance." "Kissinger's outlook," Falk continued, "presupposed that it (was) possible to manage international relations mainly by moderating conflictual relations among governments in the Northern Hemisphere." Once more, Kissinger stood accused of ignoring humanity in the name of order.

It would not be fair to Kissinger to let these judgments stand without giving him a hearing. On Indochina, the question he might ask is this: "What is more merciful and more compassionate, an end with horror or a horror without end? On the problem of ignoring human rights in Russia, he might well respond by asking whether the avoidance of an atomic holocaust was not itself the highest moral imperative of our age. On India and Pakistan, he might query his accuser as to whether Soviet domination of the Indian sub-continent might not have been the greater evil. And on the matter of the world's poor and dispossessed, Kissinger could now respond that his numerous proposals to build bridges between the world's rich and poor more than compensated for his earlier indifference.

When Henry Kissinger entered Harvard as an undergraduate in 1946, another Jewish refugee, almost a generation older, had just published his first book in the United States. Hans Morgenthau's *Scientific Man versus Power Politics* contained a paragraph that foreshadowed Kissinger's dilemma in all its awesome starkness:

> We have no choice between power and the common good. To act successfully, that is, according to the rules of the political art, is political wisdom. To know with despair that the political act is inevitably evil, and to act nevertheless, is moral courage. To choose among several expedient actions the least evil one is moral judgment. In the combination of political wisdom, moral courage and moral judgment, man reconciles his political nature with his moral destiny. That this conciliation is nothing more than a *modus vivendi*, uneasy, precarious, and even paradoxical, can disappoint only those who prefer to gloss over and to distort the tragic contradictions of human existence with the soothing logic of a specious concord.

In such a world, is it not easier to abstain from any decision altogether? Kissinger has never thought so. He knew that abstention from evil did not affect the existence of evil in the world, but only destroyed the faculty of choice. As Albert Camus had said, not to choose, too, was a choice.

When history would make its judgment on the foreign policy of Henry Kissinger, the chronicle would not pay much attention to his personal anguish when forced to choose between competing claims. Its iron pen would merely register the objective consequences of his acts. Nor would history reveal its alternatives had he acted otherwise. He would never know where the road *not* taken might have led. The unending quest for meaningful choices in a tragic world in which the only certainty was risk simply was a statesman's lot. It was, therefore, in action in the present that courage and humanity were born.

When a quarter of a century ago, on that October day in 1950, I first met Henry Kissinger, I had a premonition that one day he might enter history. I think the world is a safer place today because of his courage and his vision. It might even be a little better. No mortal man could ask for more.

Index

ABMs (antiballistic missiles), 87–90, 95
Adenauer, Konrad, 24
Africa, 160–161, 169–173, 220–221
    See also Angola; Third World
Agnew, Spiro, 58
Allende, Salvador, 211, 218
Allon, Yigal, 202
America, Kissinger's attitude toward, 18–19, 41
Amin, Idi, 169
Angola, 96, 102, 108–9, 145, 172, 216, 221, 223
Anti-war movement in U.S., 55–56, 58
Arabs, 100–103, 107–8, 140, 160, 166–67, 169–70, 176–83, 186–92, 194–96, 200–203, 210, 221
    See also Middle East
Arafat, Yasir, 165, 195, 202
Arms race, 82–87, 94
    See also SALT agreement
Assad, Hafez el, 178, 192–93, 200
Austria, 179

Ball, George, 141, 191–92, 199–200
Bangladesh, 101, 105–6, 110, 160–62
Berlinguer, Enrico, 150–51, 153, 216
Brandt, Willy, 84–85
Brezhnev, Leonid, 60–61, 63–64, 73–74, 84, 89, 91, 93–95, 99, 104, 107–9, 117, 127, 135, 152, 178, 187–89, 213, 215, 218
Bruce, David, 132
Bush, George, 125–26
Butz, Earl, 163

Caetano, Marcello, 145
Cambodia, 49, 53–54, 56–59, 75–76, 118, 122, 127, 218
Carlucci, Frank, 147–48
Carrillo, Santiago, 151–52
Castlereagh, Viscount, 3, 11–14, 16–19, 21, 35, 76, 111, 145, 208, 213
Castro, Fidel, 218
Ceausescu, Nicolae, 119
Central Intelligence Agency (CIA), 95, 121, 131
Chi Peng-fei, 128, 131
Chiang Kai-shek, 113, 125–28, 130–31
Chiao Kuan-hua, 128–30
Chile, 171, 211, 218
China, Nationalist (see Taiwan)
China, People's Republic of, 1, 43–46, 56, 63–66, 68, 73–74, 80, 84, 89, 97, 107–8, 111, 113–36, 152, 173, 202, 211, 213, 218–19, 224–25
Chou En-lai, 64, 74, 114, 118–25, 127–29, 132–34, 136, 208, 219
Clements, William, 182–83
Clerides, Glavkos, 143
Cold War, 80, 111–12, 135, 163
    See also Détente; Great Deterrent
Colson, Charles, 73
Common Market, 150
Congress, U.S.:
    and détente, 79
    direct confrontation with Kissinger, 222–23
    and disarmament, 88–89, 94

Congress *(continued)*
  foreign policy, 108–9, 144, 220
  and the Middle East, 181, 183–84,
    188, 198–99
  and trade with the Soviet Union, 99–
    100
  and the Vietnam War, 57–58, 61,
    76
Connally, John, 62
Costa Gomes, Francisco da, 146–47
Council on Foreign Relations, 22–23
Cuba, 102, 104, 109–10, 153, 216
Cuban missile crisis, 79–80, 104, 111,
    214
Cunhal, Alvaro, 145–46, 148–50, 218
Cyprus, 139–44, 149, 195, 220
Czechoslovakia, 84, 117, 148, 151–52

Dayan, Moshe, 187
De Gaulle, Charles, 52, 138, 208
Dean, Gordon, 23
Denktash, Rauf, 143
Détente, 50, 62–64, 79–112, 116, 133–
    34, 138, 148–49, 157, 173, 178–81,
    213–14, 216, 218, 225
  Kissinger's definition of, 82, 111–12
  See also Cold War; Great Deterrent
Developing nations (*see* Third World)
Diem, Ngo Dinh, 55
Dinitz, Simcha, 179–86, 189
Diplomacy, Kissinger's attitude toward,
    12–18, 22, 27, 41, 104, 111, 192–93,
    202, 208–9, 212–13
Disarmament (*see* Arms race; SALT
    agreement)
Dobrynin, Anatoly, 53–54, 85, 103–4,
    119
Downey, John, 131
Dulles, John Foster, 23–24, 40, 114, 152,
    212

Eban, Abba, 195
Ecevit, Bulent, 142–44

Echeverria Alvarez, Luis, 168
Egypt, 98, 102, 107–8, 177–180, 182,
    185, 187–201, 222
Eisenhower, Dwight, 27, 40, 125
Elazar, David, 179
Elliott, William, 2, 4, 22, 35, 39–40
Energy crisis, 158–59, 164, 173
  Kissinger's attitude toward, 158–59,
    173
  See also Oil
Europe, 110, 137–53, 171, 208, 216–17,
    219–20

Fairbank, John K., 115–16
Faisal, King, 178, 188, 192
Federal Bureau of Investigation (FBI),
    53–54
First World War, 17, 161
Food crisis, 160–63, 166, 173, 221
  See also Third World
Ford, Gerald, 75–76, 94–96, 109, 111,
    133, 146–47, 161, 163, 198
Foreign policy, Kissinger's attitude to-
    ward, 39, 45, 50, 212, 224
Forty Committee, 211
France, 92, 115, 137, 148, 150–52, 157,
    196, 216
Fulbright, J. William, 52

Gandhi, Indira, 101, 104–6
Geneva peace conference (Middle East),
    191, 194–95, 198
Germany:
  Berlin, 26, 92
  East, 24, 85, 93
  Nazi, 8, 12, 21, 31–33, 35, 102,
    175–76
  post-war, 24, 137
  West, 24, 84–85, 92–93, 157
Golan Heights, 170, 187, 194, 201
Gonçalvez, Arelino, 145
Grain sales:
  to China, 133

to the Soviet Union, 97–98, 100, 160–61, 215
Great Britain, 92, 140, 157
Great Deterrent, 23–25
    See also Cold War; Détente
Greece, 139–44, 218, 220
Gromyko, Andrei, 90, 92, 200

Haiphong, mining of, 49, 60–63, 106, 131, 215, 224
Hammarskjold, Dag, 122
Hanoi, bombing of, 49, 60–61, 73–74, 106–7, 131, 224
Harvard University, 1–4, 7, 22, 24, 28, 31, 34, 36, 39–40, 46, 55, 73, 115–16, 122, 143, 155, 175, 208, 226
Hegel, G. W. F., 209
Helms, Richard, 57, 62
Helsinki accord (1975), 110
Helsinki talks (SALT), 85, 88–89
    See also SALT agreement
History, Kissinger's attitude toward, 7–9, 15–16
Hitler, Adolf, 12, 33, 42–43, 102, 176, 199
Ho Chi Minh, 54–55, 76, 218
Hua Kuo-feng, 133
Huang Chen, 132
Hungary, 24
Hussein, King, 103, 195–96

ICBMs (intercontinental ballistic missiles), 87, 90, 95
India, 101, 104–6, 129, 160–61, 225–26
Indochina War (*see* Vietnam War)
Israel, 100, 102–3, 107–8, 139, 165, 169–70, 175–204, 210, 221–22
    See also Middle East
Italy, 148, 150–53, 157, 211, 216–17

Jackson, Henry M., 98–100, 215
Japan, 45, 109, 126, 129, 131, 137–38, 151, 156, 170

Jewish emigration from the Soviet Union, 99–101, 215
Johnson, Lyndon, 40–41, 43, 52, 55, 62, 209–10
Joint Chiefs of Staff (*see* Pentagon)
Jordan, 102–103, 110, 194–196

Karamanlis, Constantine, 143–44
Kaunda, Kenneth D., 171–72
Keating, Kenneth, 179
Kennedy, John F., 40, 50, 62, 79, 104, 209–10, 214
Khan, Yahya, 105–6, 119, 121
Khrushchev, Nikita, 99, 104, 214
Kissinger, Henry:
    in the army, 8, 32, 35, 103
    Assistant for National Security Affairs, 46, 50, 96, 211
    campaigning for Rockefeller, 36, 43, 45, 116, 212
    China trip, 120–24
    and Congress, 222–23
    consultant to Johnson, 210
    consultant to Kennedy, 210
    early home life, 31–32
    editor of *Confluence*, 40
    ethics of, 224
    as a Jew, 8, 31–33, 102, 175–76, 192–93, 203, 222, 226
    Nobel Peace Prize winner, 71, 75
    Paris talks (Vietnam war) (*see* Paris talks)
    professor at Harvard, 28, 39–41, 46
    as a refugee in America, 8, 226
    SALT talks (*see* SALT agreement)
    as Secretary of State, 75, 123–24, 156, 162, 177
    "shuttle diplomacy" of, 192–93, 196–97
    student at Harvard, 1–4, 7, 21, 31, 34, 39–40, 115–16, 122, 155, 226
    temperament of, 222–23
    values of, 207–9

Kissinger *(continued)*
  as a youth in Nazi Germany, 8, 31–32,
    36, 175
Kissinger, Henry, attitudes toward:
  America, 18–19, 41
  Détente *(see* Détente)
  diplomacy, 12–18, 22, 27, 41, 104,
    111, 192–93, 202, 208–9, 212–
    13
  energy crisis, 158–59, 164, 173
  foreign policy, 39, 45, 50, 212, 224
  history, 7–9, 15–16
  peace, 3, 9, 11–14, 22, 45, 101, 190,
    212
  power in the nuclear age, 21–29, 36–
    37, 79–80, 103
  revolution, 12–13, 27, 35, 41–43, 58,
    76–77, 116, 128, 173–74, 200,
    218–19
  United Nations, 165–68
  Vietnam *(see* Vietnam war)
Kissinger, Henry, works by:
  American Foreign Policy, 39
  "The Meaning of History" (doctoral
    dissertation), 2, 4, 9, 16, 144–45
  The Necessity for Choice, 28, 40
  Nuclear Weapons and Foreign Policy,
    21, 23, 25–26, 40, 45–46, 86, 116
  The Troubled Partnership, 18, 40, 137
  "The Vietnam Negotiations," 51
  A World Restored, 7, 11, 15, 27,
    128
Kissinger, Nancy, 142
Korea, 129
Korean War, 1, 115, 122, 132
Kraemer, Fritz, 35–36, 123
Kreisky, Bruno, 179

La Malfa, Ugo, 152
Laird, Melvin, 57, 61–62, 70
Lake, Anthony, 57–58
Laos, 59, 120
Latin America, 171, 220
  See also Third World

Le Duc Tho, 56, 59–61, 64–66, 68, 71–
  72, 74–75, 124
Lebanon, 102, 201
Lin Piao, 118–19, 125, 132
Lon Nol, 56, 75–76

MacArthur, Douglas, 115, 120
McCarthy, Joseph, 1, 115
Makarios III, Archbishop, 140–41, 220
Mao Tse-tung, 113, 116, 118–21, 126–
  28, 133, 135, 208, 213, 218–19
Marchais, George, 150–151
Marshall, George C., 139
Meir, Golda, 178–80, 192–93, 196
Metternich, Prince Klemens von, 3, 11–
  14, 16–19, 21, 34–35, 76, 111, 208,
  212–13
Mexico, 168
Middle East, 37, 45, 75, 84, 96, 98–99,
  101–3, 107–8, 110, 139–41, 146,
  155–56, 158, 160, 166, 170, 175–
  204, 211, 215, 221–22
MIRVs (multiple independent re-entry
  vehicles), 87, 91, 93–95
Morgenthau, Hans J., 21–22, 26, 37, 176,
  199, 203, 209, 217, 226
  Politics Among Nations, 21
  Scientific Man versus Power Politics,
    226
Moscow summit talks (1972), 89, 91–92,
  106, 127, 215
Moscow summit talks (1974), 93
Moynihan, Daniel P., 167–70, 201, 221

Napoleon, 3, 11–13, 16, 35, 43
National Council of Reconciliation and
  Concord for
  South Vietnam, 65, 67
National Liberation Front *(see* Viet-
  cong)
National Security Council, 54, 57
Nixon, Richard, 27, 35–36, 45, 104–5,
  139, 208, 222
  and China, 116–21, 123–31, 133

and détente with the Soviet Union, 116

and Middle East, 103, 178, 181, 184–85, 188–89

and SALT talks, 83–84, 86, 89–90

and trade with the Soviet Union, 98

and Vietnam War, 50, 52, 54, 56–59, 61–66, 68, 70–75, 106, 118

See also Watergate

North Atlantic Treaty Organization (NATO), 23, 25, 40, 137–41, 144–52, 157, 208, 216, 220

North Vietnam, 49, 51–56, 58–66, 68–77, 106–7, 120, 127, 215, 218, 224–25

Nuclear power, Kissinger's attitude toward, 21–29, 36–37, 79–80, 103

See also Détente

Organization of African Unity (OAU), 109, 169

Oil, 100, 102, 156–60, 166, 169, 178–79, 183, 185, 188, 190, 220, 225

See also Energy crisis

Oil Producing and Exporting Countries (OPEC), 158–60

Pakistan, 101, 105–6, 120–21, 129, 161, 225–26

Palestine Liberation Organization (PLO), 165, 170, 195–96, 201–2, 222

Palestinians, 108, 169–70, 178–79, 190–91, 195, 201–3, 221

Palma Carlos, Adelino de, 145

Panama Canal, 171

Paris talks (Vietnam war), 52, 54, 56, 59, 61, 64–68, 71–72, 74–75, 106, 131

Pax Americana, 33

Peace, Kissinger's attitude toward, 3, 9, 11–14, 22, 45, 101, 190, 212

Pentagon, 57, 93, 95, 103, 142, 181–82, 184, 210

"Pentagon Papers," 121

Pham Van Dong, 55

Podgorny, Nikolai, 64, 92

Poland, 24

Portugal, 102, 108, 139–40, 145–50, 152–53, 195, 216, 220

Power in the nuclear age, Kissinger's attitude toward, 21–29, 36–37, 79–80, 103

See also Détente

Rabin, Yitzhak, 103, 196–99, 202

Rahman, Mujibar, 105

Reagan, Ronald, 171

Reston, James, 8, 72, 74

Revolution, Kissinger's attitude toward, 12–13, 27, 35, 41–43, 58, 76–77, 116, 128, 173–74, 202, 218–19

Rhodesia, 172

Rockefeller, Nelson, 27, 35–36, 40, 43, 45, 116, 212

Rogers, William, 57, 61–62, 70, 85, 102, 118, 120, 125, 127–28, 131, 192

Roosevelt, Franklin D., 173

Rumania, 119

Russia (*see* Soviet Union)

Sadat, Anwar, 178–79, 188, 191–93, 196–200

Saigon, fall of, 49, 76–77, 218

Sainteny, Jean, 54

Salazar, Antonio, 145, 147

SALT agreement, 60, 62–63, 82, 84–96, 101–2, 104, 108–9, 117, 121, 210–11, 214–15

See also Arms race

Sampson, Nikos, 140–43, 220

Sato, Eisaku, 126, 131

Saudi Arabia, 102, 178, 188, 190

Saunders, Harold, 201

Scali, John A., 167–68

Schlesinger, James R., 93, 96, 180–86

Second World War, 32–33, 82, 97

Sharon, Ariel, 180

"Shuttle diplomacy," 192–93, 196–97

Sihanouk, Norodom, 53, 56
Sinai agreement, 108, 170, 189, 194, 196–201, 222
Sisco, Joseph, 105, 140–41
Smith, Gerard C., 89
Snow, Edgar, 119
Soares, Mario, 145–47
South Africa, 172
South Vietnam, 49–61, 64–77, 107, 120, 124
Soviet Union, 23–26, 43–46
  and China, 126–29, 132–36, 213
  and détente, 79–112, 116, 133–34, 138, 148–49, 157, 173, 178–81, 213–14, 216, 218, 225
  and Europe, 110, 151–53, 216–17
  grain sales from U.S., 97–98, 100, 160–61, 215
  and Middle East, 102–3, 107–8, 110, 160, 177–80, 182, 185–89, 191, 199–200
  and trade, 96–101, 104, 107–9, 160–61
  and Vietnam war, 50, 52, 54, 56, 60–66, 73, 108–9, 127, 224–25
Spain, 151–52
Spengler, Oswald, 2, 7–8, 32, 84, 146, 194, 223
  The Decline of the West, 7, 32, 84
Spinola, Antonio de, 145–146
Stalin, Joseph, 1, 33
Stoessel, Walter J., Jr., 118
Strategic Arms Limitation Talks (*see* SALT agreement)
Suez Canal, 187–88, 194
Syria, 102–3, 107–8, 178–80, 182, 185, 187–88, 190–95, 200–1, 222

Taiwan, 113, 118, 121, 123–26, 129–31, 133
Tanaka, Kakuei, 126
Thieu, Nguyen Van, 53, 59–61, 64–72, 74
Third World, 155–74, 220–21, 225

Trade agreements:
  with China, 128, 131–33
  with the Soviet Union, 96–101, 104, 107–9, 160–61
Turkey, 139–44, 220, 223

Uganda, 169
United Nations, 2, 25, 93, 107, 110, 119, 121–22, 125, 155–58, 160, 162–70, 172, 188–90, 194, 199–201, 221

Vienna talks (SALT), 89
  See also SALT agreement
Vietcong (National Liberation Front), 51, 53, 65, 74–75, 218
Vietnam (*see* North Vietnam; South Vietnam)
Vietnam war, 37, 42–44, 49–77, 80, 83–84, 97, 101–2, 106–8, 110, 115, 117, 120–21, 124, 127–31, 136, 149, 153, 198, 211, 215, 217–18, 224–26
Vietnamization, 54, 56–58, 61
Vladivostok summit talks (1974), 94–95

Waldheim, Kurt, 194
Warsaw talks (Sino-American), 118
Washington summit talks (1973), 93
Watergate, 73, 75, 93, 139–40, 143–44, 146, 149, 184, 195, 220
  See also Nixon, Richard
Wiesel, Elie, 203–4
Wilson, Woodrow, 212
World Food Conference, 162
World War I (*see* First World War)
World War II (*see* Second World War)

Xuan Thuy, 54

Yugoslavia, 152

Zambia, 171–72
Zionism, 168–70, 200–203, 221
Zumwalt, Elmo R., 95